THE CLASSICAL MUSIC MAP OF BRITAIN

RICHARD FAWKES

First published 2010 by Elliott and Thompson Limited
27 John Street, London WC1N 2BX
www.eandtbooks.com

Paperback edition published in 2012
978-1-90764-278-4

Electronic edition published in 2010
978-1-90764-213-5

9 8 7 6 5 4 3 2 1

A CIP catalogue record for this book is available from the British Library.

Typeset by Envy Design Ltd

Printed and bound by CPI Group (UK) Ltd, Croydon, CR0 4YY

ACKNOWLEDGEMENTS

I am indebted to the many librarians around the country who have helped me with my research for this book. In particular I would like to thank Clare Trend, Jodie North, Anne Maskell and Denise Price. I am also extremely grateful for the help provided by Dr Stuart Kinsella (the archivist of Christ Church Cathedral in Dublin), Lionel Carley, Richard Bradbury, Jaap and Ghislaine Buis, Barbara Coombes, Alistair Hinton, Rolf Jordan, Roxanna Panufnik, Lady Panufnik, Laura Ponsonby, Graeme Kay, Rev Sue Tucker and Malcolm Rudland. My apologies to anyone I may have inadvertently omitted.

Information for a project such as this comes from many sources: newspapers, magazines, books, a chance conversation, guide books, brochures, radio programmes, the internet. The internet has proved invaluable for providing a starting point and for cross-checking, although it does have to be approached with a certain degree of circumspection. I would like to acknowledge my gratitude to the various composer societies and composer trusts that maintain such invaluable websites. Among the magazines that have been especially useful have been Classical Music, edited by Keith Clarke, and the BBC Music Magazine.

Books I have consulted frequently are The New Grove Dictionary of Music and Musicians, The Oxford Companion to Music, the Dictionary of National Biography and Who's

Who in Music. The following are books which proved to be particularly helpful and to which I returned regularly: A Musical Gazetteer of Great Britain and Ireland by Gerald Norris (David and Charles 1981), The London Blue Plaque Guide by Nick Rennison (Sutton 1999), Musical Landscapes by John Burke (Webb and Bower 1983), Gilbert and Sullivan's London by Andrew Goodman (Faber 2000), Music Landmarks of London by Edward Lee (Omnibus 1995), Scotland's Music by John Purser (Mainstream 1992) and Who's Buried Where in England by Douglas Greenwood (Constable 2006). I also consulted numerous composer biographies and autobiographies.

I would like to thank Mark Searle for his unquenchable enthusiasm for this project, Darren Henley of Classic FM for setting it in motion and Clive Hebard for all his hard work correcting my mistakes. Any that are left are mine, not his.

Finally my thanks to Cherry, Harry, Leo and Caitlin, just for being there.

AUTHOR BIOGRAPHY

Richard Fawkes is an award-winning author and director. He is the author of nine books, including a history of the Welsh National Opera and *Opera on Film*. His *History of Opera* and *History of Classical Music*, both for Naxos Audiobooks, won Talkie Awards. He has written plays for the stage, television and radio, and series on Edith Piaf and Johnny Halliday.

CONTENTS

FOREWORD

As you might expect, there are a multitude of exciting benefits about working at Classic FM, making radio programmes that reach millions of people each week. We are able to listen to the greatest music ever composed, all day, every day. We meet the finest classical musicians of their generation when they drop into our studios for an interview. And we work closely with the very best of British orchestras, as they develop the next generation of classical music lovers.

But, if there is one word that encapsulates day-to-day life at Classic FM, it would have to be 'discovery'.

Every morning, mountains of freshly minted CDs arrive on our desks. Many contain new recordings of familiar works by the very greatest composers. But, in amongst the big names, there are always one or two hidden gems: either completely new pieces penned recently by living composers, or long forgotten works dating back hundreds of years. There is always a sense of thrill about discovering a great piece of classical music for the first time - that moment when you instinctively know that it is a piece that you will return to again and again.

It is important to remember, though, that Classic FM is not only a radio station for people who already have a passion for classical music. As well as creating radio programmes for existing classical music lovers, we are passionate about taking our music to the widest possible audience. No matter what your age, geography or background, all of us at Classic FM believe that classical music can - and should - play an important part in your life.

In this book, Richard Fawkes has set out on a voyage of discovery of a slightly different kind. Richard is among our most respected classical music writers and when he first told me about the idea for this book, I instantly loved it. As you will read, he has painstakingly plotted a journey around the British Isles, uncovering his own hidden gems about classical music and the people who have composed and performed it. Some of the talent such as Elgar, Vaughan Williams and Parry is home-grown. Other entries cover some of the classical luminaries to whom we have played host over the years, including the likes of Mozart, Mendelssohn and Bruch. All are united in playing a part in Britain's classical music heritage.

This is a book for you whichever particular stage of your own personal journey you happen to be at. If you are just starting out, you will find plenty here to whet your classical appetite. And if you are a seasoned aficionado, then the next 300 or so pages will help to further your journey into classical music.

Wishing you many happy discoveries!

Darren Henley
Managing Director
Classic FM

INTRODUCTION

When I was writing my biography of the Victorian playwright Dion Boucicault, I visited his home town of Dublin. It was walking the streets he had once walked, seeing the sights he had once seen, staying in the only surviving house in the city in which he had lived, that gave me a much greater understanding of the man than any amount of reading had done.

It is hard to say exactly why that should be, but there is something special about standing where an artist once stood. To look at the view which inspired Elgar to write his Serenade for Strings; to listen to an organ on which Handel or Mendelssohn played; to stand outside the house where the eight-year old Mozart wrote his first symphony; to visit the birthplace of Gustav Holst – such experiences help us, in an intangible way, to understand more about a composer and his music.

There has always been a fascination with places linked to great artists. Whether strolling through Monet's gardens at Giverny, standing outside one of Corbusier's residential or civic buildings, or attending a play on the site where Shakespeare's finest works were first performed, we can all gain something from inhabiting, even just for a moment, the same spaces as our icons. This book is a guide to those places in England, Wales, Scotland and Ireland with musical connections that will help you discover for yourself the wealth of stories and secrets to be found within these isles.

When he was on his deathbed, Beethoven was given a picture of Haydn's birthplace. He loved the picture and kept hold of it because it reminded him that such a great man was born in such a humble dwelling place.

It is this bond between us and the musically creative artist that I hope will be nurtured by this book.

One thing the book is not is a *Who's Who* of British composers and musicians. I am aware of composers I have not included, of fine musicians left out. Nor is the book a list of all the places in which a particular composer might have lived or worked. Rather, you will read of those locations that played a significant part in their life or output, as well as numerous obscure locations that were the backdrop to notable, hitherto unknown – or just downright odd – developments in their career, and thus in the evolution of Britain's musical heritage. Some characters, such as Vaughan Williams, changed lodgings and homes as frequently as the calendar changes months, and to have listed them all would have been to turn this project into an address book. I have also deliberately avoided including all the sites of houses in which composers and musicians have stayed, unless the connection to the composer is either very strong or very interesting. This is a guide to places which, generally speaking, can be seen or visited. I have also deliberately not included living composers on the grounds that to give out details of where they live is an invasion of privacy. I have also, with one or two exceptions, not included concert halls and performace venues.

I do hope that by discovering something of the people behind the notes, readers will be sent on a voyage of discovery, that they will be encouraged to listen to music they may never have heard before or may not have heard for a long time. Whether you are a seasoned classical music buff or a curious amateur, everyone will have a corner of the country they'll want to visit to see for themselves how a favourite artist or work played their part in making Britain an important contributor to many of the major movements in classical music.

ENGLAND

THE ORGAN

There can hardly be a church in the City of London which does not claim to possess an organ on which Henry Purcell, John Blow, Handel, or even Mendelssohn, once played. There's no doubt the quartet did play on a great many City instruments, but few have survived. Over the years, pipes have needed replacing and bellows mending, so that although the casing may be original, what's inside certainly isn't.

Organs are thought of today as being largely church instruments. Originally though, they were associated more with Roman gladiators entering the ring than sacred rituals within houses of prayer. It wasn't until the eighth century that organs began to take a prominent part in the liturgy. During the Civil War large numbers of organs were destroyed by Oliver Cromwell's men. Following the Restoration of King Charles II in 1660, Britain saw a boom in organ building and playing. In Germany people such as Dieterich Buxterhude and JS Bach demonstrated just what the organ can do by composing numerous ambitious large-scale works, while in England, Purcell, Blow and, in particular, Handel, produced brilliant pieces for the instrument. Handel not only used the organ for accompaniment, he wrote several organ concertos. To become organist of the Chapel Royal was one of the highest positions in the land to which a musician could aspire. No instrument, other than the piano, has a more varied repertoire. Small wonder Mozart called it the King of Instruments. Every so often there is a revival of interest in the organ as a concert hall instrument, and it still requires a Mighty Wurlitzer to fill a cinema auditorium. A modern organ going flat out is the equivalent of three symphony orchestras' worth of sound.

1. ALDBOURNE, Wiltshire

– Beech Knoll, Aldbourne –

In 1933, the composer Gerald Finzi married the artist Joyce Black (known as Joy), gave up his job at the Royal Academy teaching composition, and moved out of London to the country. Witnesses to the marriage included Vaughan Williams who had conducted the first performance of Finzi's Violin Concerto in 1928. The place the Finzis chose to live initially was Beech Knoll in Aldbourne, a village on the B4192, south east of Swindon. They then decided to have a house built at Ashmansworth, staying at Beech Knoll until it was ready in 1939. Finzi, a slow worker, often took years to complete a composition. Among those he finished or worked on at Beech Knoll were the *Dies Natalis*, *Two Milton Sonnets*, *Earth and Air and Rain*, the *Interlude for oboe and strings*, settings of poems by Robert Bridges and the string trio *Prelude and Fugue*. He also began his vitally important work cataloguing the works of the poet and composer Ivor Gurney. Aldbourne is famous as the place where the brothers Robert and William Cor, who made harnesses for horses, produced the first tuned handbells between 1696 and 1724. The US 101st Airborne Division was based here just before D-Day.

2. ALDEBURGH, Suffolk

The seaside village of Aldeburgh will forever be associated with the composer Benjamin Britten who was born in nearby Lowestoft in 1913 and died at The Red House, in Aldeburgh, in December 1976.

In 1937, Britten's widowed mother died and his relationship with the tenor Peter Pears, which was to last until his own death, was just beginning. With the legacy left by his mother, he bought the Old Mill in Snape, a converted stump of a former windmill overlooking a Victorian industrial complex known as the Maltings. In 1942, after a failed attempt to settle in America, Britten returned to Suffolk to work on his opera *Peter Grimes*. In 1947, the success of *Grimes* allowed him and Pears to move to Crag House at 4 Crabbe Street, Aldeburgh, backing onto the seafront. Here he wrote the *Spring Symphony*, *The Little Sweep*, *Billy Budd*, *The Turn of the Screw* and *The Prince of the Pagodas*. He and Pears moved again in 1957, when Britten was working on *Noye's Fludde*, to The Red House in a straight swap with the painter Mary Potter, whose marriage had broken up. The Red House, at the bottom of a rough track alongside the golf course, was to remain Britten's home until his death.

Britten never composed at the piano and pieces were therefore written in a number of rooms. His work pattern rarely changed: composition from 8am until 1pm, lunch at 1.15pm, followed by a walk across the golf course to the sea to think about what he had done, then back home to score between tea-time and dinner. His major compositions written at the Red House were the *Missa*

Brevis, *Nocturne*, *A Midsummer Night's Dream*, the *War Requiem*, the *Symphony for Cello and Orchestra* and the *Church Parables* (which were also worked on in Venice). In 1970, Britten purchased Chapel House, Horham, to get away from the constant stream of visitors to The Red House (Kodaly, Shostakovitch and Poulenc among them), and it was there that much of his work after *Owen Wingrave* was done.

The Britten-Pears archive is open to scholars by arrangement and is sometimes opened to the public during the Aldeburgh Festival.

A memorial window to Britten, designed by John Piper (who designed sets for his operas), can be seen in the church of St Peter and St Paul. There is a memorial bust nearby of George Crabbe, the poet who was born in Aldeburgh in 1754. It was on Crabbe's best-known poem, 'The Borough', that Britten based his first opera *Peter Grimes*.

The Aldeburgh Festival was established by Britten and Pears in 1948 and most of Britten's major scores were written for the festival. In 1967, at Snape, six miles up the river Alde from Aldeburgh, he and Pears converted one of the Maltings (red-brick Victorian buildings built to process barley) into a concert hall. This burnt down two years later and was restored the following year. Apart from hosting concerts during the annual June Festival, there are activities throughout the year, some centred on the work of the Britten-Pears School for Advanced Musical Studies which is based here. The complex is open all the year round.

A 12ft high sculpture in memory of Benjamin Britten can be seen on the shingle beach between Aldeburgh and Thorpeness. Designed in the shape of a scallop shell by

Maggi Hambling (who lives in nearby Rendham) it was unveiled in November 2003, and is inscribed with a quotation from the libretto of *Peter Grimes*. The idea for the sculpture came from Hambling herself. It was paid for by private subscription with support from charitable trusts, and then donated to the local council. Its position on the beach was controversial with more than 600 people signing a petition to have it removed.

Aldeburgh Festival website: www.aldeburgh.co.uk

3. ASHMANSWORTH, Hampshire

– Church Farm, Ashmansworth –

This is the house composer Gerald Finzi had built for himself and his family in this village off the A343, south of Newbury. It was his home from 1938 until his death in Oxford in 1956 from Hodgkins Disease. Beneath the porch of the house, he buried a copy of the favourite of his own songs, a setting of James Elroy Flecker's *To a poet a thousand years hence*. Finzi was mad about apples and introduced many rare species to his orchard. During World War Two he opened the house to Czech and German refugees. Finzi also founded the Newbury String Players.

Among the works Finzi completed here were the *Clarinet Concerto* (the work by which he is probably best known), the cello concerto, the *Grand Fantasia and Toccata*, many songs and *Intimations of Immortality*, a soberingly ironic title when one considers that he was only seven when his father died, one brother died young from pneumonia, and his other brother committed suicide. Finzi himself was given only ten years to live while still a comparatively young man. He was fifty-five when he died at Church Farm on 27 September, the day after the première of his cello concerto. Finzi is buried in the churchyard of St James' Church, Ashmansworth, close to the church porch where there is an engraved glass window by Laurence Whistler dedicated to English music.

Vaughan Williams was a frequent visitor and in 1956 wrote part of his Ninth Symphony here.

4. ATTLEBOROUGH, Norfolk

– 26 Springfields, Attleborough, Norfolk NR17 2PA –

This is the undistinguished house to which sixty-year old Malcolm Arnold moved in 1984 after he had spent the previous seven years in an alcoholic mist, told by his doctors he only had a short time to live. It was thanks to Anthony Day, who was employed to look after him, that Arnold not only survived but began to write again. The trigger was seeing the Danish recorder player Micala Petri on television: Arnold was so moved by her performance he wrote a recorder concerto especially for her. There then followed a set of *Irish Dances*, the *Attleborough Suite*, the cello concerto commissioned by Julian Lloyd Webber, the final, dark, bleak *Ninth Symphony*, dedicated to Day, and a march for the RAF. He then turned his back on composition, having said all he wanted. Arnold, who was born in Northampton in 1921, died in hospital in Norwich on 23 September 2007, a month short of his eighty-fifth birthday. Out of fashion for long periods in his career,

Arnold is now recognised as being one of Britain's major composers. He was knighted in 1993.

5. BADSEY, Worcestershire

– Vine Cottage, 8 Chapel Street, Badsey –

This was the cottage near Evesham in which the composer Muzio Clementi, mentor of Beethoven and Father of the pianoforte, is supposed to have died, even though he never actually lived in or as far as we know stayed in the village. What allegedly happened is that Clementi, arguably the most famous musician of his day – he is buried in Westminster Abbey – was living in retirement in a cottage on the edge of Evesham, with views across to Bredon Hill, when he died on 10 March 1832. That cottage was later sold to be demolished since it was considered unsightly and a man called Robert Knight bought it. Knight is supposed to have dismantled the building, cleaned up the bricks and taken them to Badsey where he built Vine Cottage and the adjoining Rose Cottage. Local records certainly show that a Robert Knight did own Vine Cottage, and locals have been quoted as being told by parents that Clementi had lived in the village, but otherwise there is no proof that the story is true.

6. BARNARD CASTLE, Co Durham

– The Bowes Museum, Barnard Castle, DL12 8NP –

The museum was built in the nineteenth century by local businessman John Bowes and his French actress wife

Joséphine, to introduce art to local people. Among the staggering collection of silverware, Sèvres porcelain, Canalettos and Goyas are a number of interesting musical instruments collected either because of their decorative aspect or because of local interest. Most of them are between one hundred and three hundred years old and include early pianos, a Kirchman harpsichord dating from about 1785, locally made violins, flutes, a serpent and barrel organs.

www.thebowesmuseum.org.uk

7. BARNSTAPLE, Devon

– St Anne's Chapel, Barnstaple –

The upper part of the chapel, close by the parish church, probably dates from 1456 but the crypt is much older. From the end of the seventeenth century until 1910 the building was used as the Barnstaple grammar school. John Gay, who in 1728 wrote *The Beggar's Opera* (on which the Weill/Brecht *The Threepenny Opera* was based), was a pupil here. The building is opened occasionally but there are plans to turn it into a concert venue.

8. BATH, Somerset

– 13 Gay Street –

The home of the celebrated castrato Venanzio Rauzzini (he also lived for a time at 17 Queen Square). Born in Camerino, Italy, in 1747 he became a member of the Sistine Chapel choir where he had the snip to stop his voice breaking. A strikingly handsome man and a wow with the ladies, he was soon singing in the opera houses of Italy. He then moved to Munich where he was run out of town because of his many affairs with married women (women generally were attracted to castrato singers, probably because they wanted to know whether they could or they couldn't). Arriving in Vienna, he was heard by the young Mozart who promptly offered him the leading role of Cecilio in his new opera, *Lucio Silla*. It was for him that Mozart wrote the motet *Exsultate Jubilate*. When he retired from the stage in 1780, Rauzzini settled in Bath to become a singing teacher and help organise the subscription concerts. He took them over completely the following year. Rauzzini was fabulously wealthy, commanding huge fees – he was paid £2,000 a year, for example, to appear at the King's Theatre in London (that's roughly a quarter of a million pounds in today's money). He was a prolific composer for the voice, which included writing six operas. As well as his town houses in Bath, Rauzzini rented Perrymead Villa overlooking the city. It was here that Haydn visited him in 1794 and wrote a canon about Turk, Rauzzini's dog. Rauzzini died in 1810 and is buried in Bath Abbey where there is a memorial to him.

– Linley House, 1 Pierpont Place, off Pierpont Street, – Bath, BA1 5LA

Linley House was the home of the Linley family from 1764 until 1771 although the blue plaque outside doesn't mention either composer Thomas Linley Senior or Thomas Linley Junior, only Elizabeth Ann Linley who ran away to France with the playwright Richard Brinsley

Sheridan. A singer, she lived in the house from 1767 until 1771. Thomas Linley, her father, was a gifted musician in charge of the Bath orchestra. He also became, with his son-in-law Sheridan, manager of the Theatre Royal, Drury Lane, for which he wrote much incidental music as well as writing songs and madrigals. Thomas Linley Junior, one of Britain's greatest violinists and a friend of Mozart, was born in nearby Abbey Green. He was to die in a tragic boating accident at Bourne when only 22-years-old. Others of Linley's large family also became professional musicians: Ozias was an organist, Samuel sang and played the oboe, Maria was a singer and William a composer of glees and songs. The house was also supposed to have been rented for a while by Emma Hamilton (best remembered as the mistress of Lord Nelson and the muse of George Romney). Nelson certainly lived just around the corner in Pierpont Street.

There are portraits by Gainsborough of both Thomas Linley Senior and Thomas Linley Junior, the Linley Sisters (Elizabeth and Mary) and William in Dulwich Picture Gallery.

~ 19 New King Street, Bath, BA1 2BL ~

For many years, this Grade II listed Georgian building was the home of Sir William Herschel, the King's Astronomer, famous for discovering the planet Uranus in 1781.

Herschel, whose first names were really Friedrich Wilhelm, was born into a family of musicians in Hanover in 1738. As a boy he played in the band of the Hanoverian Guards. At the age of nineteen he came to England, changed his name to William, and became a bandmaster and organist in Yorkshire before moving to Bath to become organist of the Octagon Chapel and a music teacher. He was also a talented composer and conductor, who did not give up composition until he was 40. These include symphonies, chamber works, church music and some military music. Much of it has been lost; what remains rarely gets a performance. Although he was enjoying a successful career as a musician, Herschel began to develop an interest in astronomy, as did his sister Caroline, who had joined him in Bath as a singer, and his brother Alexander. The interest became a passion and it was in this house, to which they moved in 1777, that Herschel, using a telescope of his own design, discovered Uranus. His sister Caroline, who could well have become a professional singer but preferred instead to help her brother with his astronomy, became the first woman scientist and astronomer to be elected to the Royal Society. Herschel's interest in telescopes led him, with the aid of a £4,000 grant from King George III, to build the largest telescope in the world, 40 feet long with a 48 inch reflecting mirror. This was kept at Observatory House in Slough and was destroyed in a gale in 1839, seventeen years after Herschel's death. As well as discovering Uranus, Herschel discovered Saturn's satellites and infra-red radiation. His discoveries helped double the known size of the universe. He died at his home in Slough on 25 August 1822.

According to legend, one very important visitor to Slough, in June 1792, was Haydn. Having finished his concert series in London, Haydn had taken a few days off to go sightseeing (including visits to Windsor Castle and Ascot races). He arrived to see Herschel and was invited to look through the telescope, a moment of such wonder that he apparently said nothing for twenty minutes until he uttered the words 'So high… so far' and decided there and then to write *The Creation*. While there is evidence that Haydn looked through Herschel's telescope (Haydn noted the instrument's measurements in his diary), there is none that it inspired his oratorio. Indeed, another story claims that after hearing a performance of Handel's *Messiah*, he commented that he would like to write something similar but where to start? The leader of the orchestra that had played his symphonies is supposed to have picked up a Bible, handed it to Haydn and said, 'There, take that and begin at the beginning.'

Herschel's Bath house is now the Herschel Museum of Astronomy.

www.bath-preservation-trust.org.uk

– Parade Gardens, Orange Grove, Bath, BA1 1EE –

An attractive formal garden by the side of the River Avon overlooking Pulteney Bridge and the weir, which Bath citizens can enter for free; visitors have to pay an entrance fee. In the gardens is a bronze statue of the young Mozart playing his violin, based by sculptor David Backhouse on the famous statue in Salzburg. Mozart stands, 140cm high, on a raised, pierced and scrolled bronze base adorned with three doves, two squirrels and a mouse. The sculpture was commissioned on her death-bed by Mrs Purnell of the AM Purnell Charitable Trust to commemorate her music-loving son Mark who died in 1985. The opening ceremony in 1991 was attended by Yehudi Menuhin, a trustee of Bath's annual Mozartfest Music Festival, and local MP Chris Patten who went on to become the last Governor of Hong Kong.

On Sundays during summer concerts are given on the Parade Gardens bandstand.

9. BAWDSEY, SUFFOLK

– St Mary's Church, Bawdsey, a village 9 miles from – Woodbridge at the end of the B1083.

The composer Roger Quilter is buried in the impressive Quilter family vault outside the west door. Nearby Bawdsey Manor was built by Quilter's father, Sir Cuthbert, an MP and real ale enthusiast. It was bought by the RAF in 1936 for use as a secret research establishment and it is where radar was developed at the beginning of World War Two. Quilter, who was born in Brighton in 1877 and died in London in 1953, never lived in Bawdsey Manor which is now a residential conference and educational centre. Although he wrote incidental music for plays and even an opera after schooling at Eton, Quilter, who developed mental problems following the death of his nephew in World War Two, is most noted for being one of the finest English songwriters of the twentieth century. He wrote over a hundred songs, the best known of which is probably *Oh Mistress Mine,* one of his many settings of Shakespeare.

10. BIRCHINGTON-ON-SEA, Kent

– All Saints Church, The Square, Birchington, CT7 9AF –

The English composer Rosalind Ellicott, is buried here. In her day she was considered one of Britain's leading female composers, quite the equal of Dame Ethel Smyth, the pioneer of women's suffrage and composer of opera. Ellicott had been born on 14 November 1857 in Cambridge, where her father, Charles Ellicott, a distinguished theologian, was Professor of Divinity. He was indifferent to music but her mother was a singer who helped found the London Handel Society and the Gloucester Philharmonic Society and it was she who encouraged Ellicott's interest in music. By the age of six, when her father became Bishop of Gloucester, she was already composing, and at the age of seventeen she went to the Royal Academy of Music to study the piano. When her teacher heard a piano quartet she had written, he advised her to study composition as well. Her first published piece was *A Sketch* in 1883. Her father may not have cared much for music but it cannot have been a drawback to her getting her first major orchestral piece, an overture, commissioned for the Gloucester Three Choirs Festival, to be the daughter of the Bishop. Many of her other works, including two cantatas, were written for the Three Choirs. Finding it difficult, even with the Bishop connection, to get performances, Ellicott began to work on smaller scale chamber pieces. But then, around the turn of the century, in spite of people such as Parry thinking her better than many male composers, her output dried up and she floated off into a musical backwater. Her father, after thirty-four years in Gloucester, retired to a bungalow named Tresco in Spencer Road, Birchington. Rosalind moved with him and when both parents died, took over the house. She died here on 5 April 1924 and was buried close to her parents in the local churchyard. Most of her music has disappeared with only a handful of songs, some instrumental pieces (including an attractive piano trio), the cantatas *Elysium* and *The Birth of Song*, and *A Reverie* for piano and cello, surviving.

Also in the churchyard is the grave of the pre-Raphaelite painter Dante Gabriel Rossetti.

11. BIRMINGHAM, West Midlands

St Barnabas' Church, Erdington

St Barnabas contains an 1888 Bevington organ built originally for the Church of the Redeemer on Hagley Road. It was moved here in 1976, following that church's demolition. Among those who visited the Church of the Redeemer to play the instrument were the composers Marcel Dupré, Flor Peters, Jeanne Demissieux and Fernando Germani, organist of St Peter's in Rome. The instrument may also have been played by Louis Vierne and Maurice Duruflé. They were all invited to give evening recitals when visiting Birmingham for the traditional organ lunchtime concert in the Town Hall.

– Town Hall –

Birmingham Town Hall merits an inclusion simply because it is one of the oldest purpose-built concert halls in the world. The city had been holding a triennial music festival ever since 1768 using such buildings as St Philip's Church (now Birmingham Cathedral). So successful was the festival that Birmingham decided to build a special venue. A competition was held and won by 27-year-old Joseph Hansom (of Hansom cab fame) with a design based on the Temple of Castor and Pollux in Rome, an ancient edifice in the Forum originally built in gratitude for victory at the battle of Lake Regillus. An organ was commissioned from William Hill, and the hall opened in 1834. Many famous composers have subsequently visited and performed in the building. They include Mendelssohn who wrote *Elijah* for the Birmingham Festival and conducted the first performance, Johann Strauss, who appeared as a guest conductor, Grieg who, in 1897, gave one of his last piano recitals, and Dvořák, who conducted the world premiere of his *Requiem* here in 1891. Gounod's *La Redemption* was first heard in Birmingham in 1881. Standards were high. As Saint-Saëns wrote: 'I wish people who describe the English as unmusical could hear the Birmingham singers. This choir has everything: intonation, perfect timing and rhythm.' The Town Hall also witnessed the first performance of Elgar's *The Dream of Gerontius*. It was not a success. The choir master died not long before the premiere and the parts arrived late, giving conductor Hans Richter only ten days to study the score. 'I always said God was against art,' commented Elgar afterwards. Elgar's other great connection with Birmingham was that he was the University's first Professor of Music.

The Town Hall organ was the largest in England at the time with over 3,000 pipes. Samuel Wesley gave the first recital on it in 1834 and Mendelssohn also played it.

12. BLANDFORD FORUM, DORSET

– Stepleton House, Iwerne Steepleton, Blandford Forum –

A private house on the A350 between Blandford and Shaftesbury, not open to the public, this is where Sir Peter Beckford, who is buried in the churchyard of St Mary's Chapel on the estate, brought the young Muzio Clementi in 1766. Beckford's family money came from sugar and slavery in Jamaica. It was while he was in Rome, on a European Grand Tour, that he first heard thirteen-year-old Clementi, the son of a Roman silversmith, playing the organ in the church of San Lorenzo, in Damaso. Realising the boy's talent, Beckford, a cousin of writer William Beckford and future Member of Parliament, did a deal with Clementi's father to bring the boy to England for tuition. Clementi stayed at Stepleton for seven years, until he was twenty-one, perfecting his keyboard technique and performing for Beckford's guests whenever it was required. He left for London to find fame and fortune. He became not only 'the Father of the Pianoforte' but a composer (one of the first to write for the piano and considered at the time to be second only to Haydn as a symphonist), a conductor, an editor and influential teacher. He even became a piano manufacturer, designing his own instruments. In Vienna, on a European tour, he was entered into a musical duel with Mozart, a duel that the Holy Roman Emperor Joseph declared a draw. Clementi was full of admiration for Mozart, even though Mozart did go on to steal one of his tunes for *The Magic Flute* overture; Mozart dismissed Clementi as a charlatan. Clementi died in Evesham in

1832 and was buried in Westminster Abbey with three of his students, John Field, Johann Baptist Cramer and Ignaz Moschelles, acting as pallbearers.

13. BLICKLING, Norfolk

– Blickling Hall, Blickling, Norwich, Norfolk NR11 6NF –

Built in the early seventeenth century and now owned by the National Trust, Blickling Hall is one of England's finest Jacobean houses. The organist and composer Richard Davy (c1467–c1516) apparently lived here when it was the home of Sir Thomas Boleyn, father of Anne Boleyn, the mother of Queen Elizabeth I. He seems to have been here from about 1506 until the time of his death some ten or so years later, possibly as Sir Thomas's house musician. Very little is known about Davy other than that there are some pieces by him in the Eton Choirbook and he was organist at Magdalen College, Oxford, from 1490 until 1492 when he became the college choirmaster. A Richard Davy who may or may not have been the same person was organist at Exeter Cathedral.

14. BLYTHBURGH, Suffolk

– Lark Rise, Dunwich Road, Blythburgh –

The village of Blythburgh on the A12 near Halesworth was the home for the last fifteen years of his life of composer William Alwyn. Alwyn had been born in Northampton on 7 November 1905. He became a flautist and it was while playing in a cinema orchestra that he got his first compositional break: the man engaged to write the score they were due to play couldn't manage it and Alwyn was asked to take over. It was to be the start of a career as one of Britain's finest film composers. He eventually wrote the scores for more than 200 films including such classics as *Desert Victory*, *Odd Man Out* and *The Crimson Pirate*. He was also Professor of Composition at the Royal Academy of Music, a post he held from 1926 until 1954. As well as film scores, Alwyn wrote a number of concertos, five symphonies, four operas and a considerable amount of chamber music. He was a founder of the Composers Guild of Great Britain and vice-president of the Society for New Music. Although he was respected by the musical establishment (he was championed by Sir Henry Wood and Sir John Barbirolli, to whom he dedicated one of his symphonies), Alwyn had difficulty in getting his more serious works performed: the thinking of the day was that if you were first and foremost a film composer, your other music had to be light and insubstantial.

Alwyn moved to Blythburgh in 1960 having suffered a nervous breakdown due to his turbulent private life – he left his wife for his mistress – and the constant film deadlines. Here he began painting and writing poetry, and although he did cut down on the amount of music he was writing, he continued to compose. Amongst the pieces completed here were his Fifth Symphony, the opera *Miss Julie*, several songs and the *Sinfonietta for Strings*. He died in 1985, two years after suffering a massive stroke.

15. BOREHAM, Essex

~ Shottesbrook, Church Road, Boreham ~

A blue plaque marks the house in which composer Dame Elizabeth Maconchy lived for forty years. She was born in Broxbourne on 19 March 1907 but moved with her family to Ireland where she began playing the piano. Advised to apply to the Royal College, she studied composition. She was just starting to make it following the performance of her orchestral suite *The Land* at the 1930 Proms conducted by Sir Henry Wood, and the piano concerto which received its premiere on her 23rd birthday. However, in 1932 she was diagnosed with tuberculosis and advised to live in Switzerland. Instead, she moved to the Kent countryside and lived outside, allegedly curing herself. When her house in Kent was destroyed by a bomb in 1945, she and her husband, William LeFanu, moved first to Wickham Bishops in Essex (where their composer daughter Nicola LeFanu was born), then in 1954, to Boreham, a village off the A12 three miles northeast of Chelmsford. Her output here included her string quartets numbers 7 to 12, the oboe quartet, clarinet quintet, sinfonietta, *Ariadne*, and *Héloïse and Abelard*. In 1987 Maconchy was made a Dame. She died on 11 November 1994.

16. BOSTON, Lincolnshire

~ St Botolph's Church, Boston ~

John Taverner (c1495-1545), composer and organist, spent the latter part of his life in Boston and died here on 18

October 1545. He composed chiefly church music in Latin, including eight masses which were highly esteemed in his own time and still are, especially *The Western Wynde*. Many think he was the most important composer of his time. Imprisoned for heresy, Taverner apparently abandoned music after his release to become an agent for Thomas Cromwell in the dissolution of the monasteries and the suppression of idolaters. Modern research has cast some doubt on this. We do know he retired to Boston reasonably well off and became a landowner. He is buried in St Botolph's Church beneath the famous bell-tower, 272 feet high and known as the Boston Stump, a landmark for sailors and travelers. The composer Sir John Tavener is apparently a direct descendent.

17. BOURNE, Lincolnshire

– Grimsthorpe Castle and Gardens, Bourne, PE10 OLY –

It was in the lake here that Thomas Linley Junior, known as the English Mozart, died in a boating accident in 1778. Linley was the third child and second son of Thomas Linley Senior and his wife Mary. He was born on 7 May 1756 at the Abbey Green in Wells and baptised in St James's Church, Bath, on 11 June. He studied the violin with John Richards, a prominent soloist and leader of the Bath orchestra during the 1750s and 60s. Linley was a child prodigy and one of the most musically gifted individuals ever to have been seen in England. At the age of ten he appeared at the Covent Garden Opera House playing the part of Puck in the masque *The Fairy Favour* by Thomas Hull. His sister Elizabeth Ann was also in the cast. In April 1770, while studying in Italy, he met Mozart. They were exact contemporaries and quickly became friends, later corresponding with one another regularly. Linley returned to Bath to appear in the new concert season, aged fifteen. From 1772 until 1776 he was regularly the leader of the Bath orchestra or its soloist, and from 1773 until 1778, he appeared at Drury Lane as well as playing concertos between the acts of oratorios. He was also studying composition with William Boyce and was achieving some success with his first large scale work *Let God Arise*, the incidental music for plays and, in 1776, his *Shakespeare Ode*.

In 1778 Linley and his sisters were invited to Grimsthorpe Castle, three miles north-west of Bourne, as guests of the Duke of Ancaster and his family. The castle dates mostly from the reign of Henry VIII. On 5 August, Linley and two friends went boating on the lake, the weather turned bad and the boat overturned. Linley was drowned. He was buried in St Michael's Parish Church, Edenham, a mile west of the castle, on 11 August. He was 22. He was, Mozart said of him, 'a true genius'.

18. BOURNEMOUTH, Dorset

~ 2 Richmond Hill, The Square, Bournemouth ~

A blue plaque marks the house in which Sir Hubert Parry, composer of *Jerusalem* and Master of the King's Musick, was born on 27 February 1848. His father was Thomas Gambier Parry, an artist, collector and benefactor of the

Courtauld Institute; his mother, Isabella. She had been sent to Bournemouth on medical advice, being in the advanced stages of consumption, and died twelve days after her son and third child was born. She was 32 and was buried in St Peter's Churchyard, the church in which Parry was christened. Parry was brought up at Highnam Court, the family home in Gloucestershire.

– St Peter's Church, Hinton Road, Bournemouth, BH1 2EE –

As well as containing the grave of Parry's mother, the churchyard contains the graves of Constantin Silvestri, the charismatic Hungarian conductor of the Bournemouth Symphony Orchestra from 1961–9, and of Dan Godfrey, founder and first conductor of the Bournemouth Municipal Orchestra before it became the BSO. Mary and Percy Bysshe Shelley are also buried here.

– 15 St Winifred's Road, Bournemouth –

This was the retirement home of light music composer Frederic Curzon. Born in London in 1899, he was exceptionally talented, playing the piano in a theatre orchestra by the age of 16. By the time he was twenty, he had his own orchestra. Curzon was a prolific composer with an output that included orchestral suites, overtures and pieces for piano and orchestra, many of them programmed in Bournemouth Symphony Orchestra concerts by Sir Dan Godfrey. He wrote for Tommy Handley in *ITMA*, the popular war-time radio series, he wrote for films, and he wrote the orchestral intermezzo, *The Boulevardier,* one of his most popular compositions. He died in Bournemouth on 6 December 1973.

19. BOWDEN, Cheshire

- 27 The Firs, Bowden -

A blue plaque marks the home of Hans Richter from 1901 until 1911 while he was conductor of the Hallé Orchestra. In addition to being a painter, graphic artist, avant-gardist, film experimenter and producer, Richter was one of the most distinguished conductors in the world having conducted the premieres of such works as Wagner's *Ring Cycle,* Tchaikovsky's *Violin Concerto* (which was played by Adolph Brodsky who lived in Bowden for thirty years), Brahms' *Third Symphony* and Elgar's *First*. Bela Bartok stayed with Richter for a week in February 1904.

- Inglewood, St Margaret's Road, Bowden -

Also marked with a plaque is the birthplace of the composer John Ireland. He was born on 13 August 1879, the youngest of five children. His father, a publisher and newspaper proprietor, was 70 when he was born, his mother 40. Both died when he was a teenager and Ireland was bullied by his siblings. When he ran away from the boarding school he hated and returned home, his sisters locked him up. His only real escape from this living hell was in music and not long after his fourteenth birthday, he entered the Royal College of Music to study the piano and the organ. He became a Fellow of the Royal College of Organists before his sixteenth birthday, the youngest fellow ever. He also taught at the Royal College where Moeran and Britten were among his pupils. When he was 47 he married another of his students, Dorothy Phillips. She was 17. The marriage, which may well never have been consummated, only lasted two years. Carl Hallé, the German-born pianist who became Sir Charles Hallé and in 1857 founded the orchestra that bears his name, was a frequent visitor to the house. There are plaques on two of Hallé's homes in Manchester: Duxbury Square, Moss Side, and 3 Addison Terrace, Victoria Park.

20. BRADFORD, YORKSHIRE

– 6 Claremont, Horton Lane, Bradford –

The house where Frederick Delius was born on 29 January 1862. Fritz Theodore Albert Delius, to give him his correct name (he changed the Fritz to Frederick much later on), was the fourth of fourteen children born to Julius and Elise Delius, a German couple from Bielefeld. They had moved to Bradford because of Julius's wish to become involved with the wool trade and rented a house in Claremont, then an enclave for German immigrants. As his business prospered and the size of his family grew, Julius moved everyone over the road to No 1 Claremont, knocking it through with number 3. Fritz was christened in St Peter's Church, now Bradford Cathedral, and later attended the German Church which his parents helped found and is now the Delius Arts and Cultural Centre. Holidays were spent in rented cottages in the spa town of Ilkley. The Delius children (ten boys, four girls) all had a privileged upbringing in which music played its part. Julius was a regular and generous subscriber to St George's Hall in Bridge Street, where concerts are still held, and before he was a teenager, Delius was a highly proficient player of both the violin and the piano. For four years

Delius was a pupil at Bradford Grammar School on the Keighley Road, before being sent down south to the pioneering International School in Isleworth. His father wanted him to take over the business and Delius did join the firm for a time but he wasn't happy. Going to concerts while on business trips abroad only convinced him he wanted to be a musician. Father was having none of it but did eventually agree to set him up in Florida to run an orange plantation. Solano Grove was several hours up-river from Jacksonville and one of the first things Delius did when he got there was acquire a piano and start studying harmony and composition with a local organist. It was in Florida that his compositional career really began – the sound of slaves singing was to have a profound effect on him. After eighteen months in Florida, Delius moved to Danville, Virginia, where he set himself up as a music teacher. His father finally gave in to his son's desire to become a musician and paid for him to go to the Leipzig Conservatorium where he was befriended by Edvard Greig, who became a lifelong friend. Delius's first major work, *The Florida Suite*, was written in Leipzig.

He later moved to Paris where he anglicised his name to Frederick, and met and eventually married the German artist Jelka Rosen. They lived in Jelka's house in Graz-sur Loing where, apart from a period during World War One when the Germans were advancing on Paris, he stayed for the rest of his life. Although he had problems getting his music performed, Delius was a prolific composer who wrote, despite living in France, some of the most quintessentially English music of all time.

Delius's final years were blighted by blindness and

paralysis, caused by contracting syphilis as a young man. The story of how Eric Fenby, a Yorkshireman who first got to know Delius as the result of a fan letter, became the composer's amanuensis, writing down the music from dictation, was the subject of Ken Russell's 1968 film *Song of Summer* in which the irascible Delius was played by Max Adrian and Fenby by Christopher Gable. Fortunately for us, Delius's poor health did not affect his creative abilities and during this time he composed several major works.

Delius died on 10 June 1934 and is buried in the churchyard at Limpsfield.

21. BRAY, Buckinghamshire

– The Long White Cloud, Bray –

Frank Schuster, a wealthy patron of the arts in Britain and friend of Elgar, owned this house on the bank of the Thames, opposite Monkey Island. It was called, at that time, The Hut. Leo Frank Schuster, known to his friends as Frankie, was of German extraction and had been educated at Eton. His London home, 22 Old Queen Street, became a meeting place for artists, writers and musicians, among them John Singer Sargent, Walter Sickert, Siegfried Sassoon and Edward Elgar. Schuster was a great promoter of Elgar's music and the two became firm friends. It was at Schuster's London home that Elgar first met the young conductor Adrian Boult, and one evening in 1904, both Elgar and Richard Strauss were guests at dinner. The young William Walton was a visitor, as was Gabriel Fauré who used to stay with Schuster on his trips to London.

Elgar was a frequent visitor to The Hut, especially during the summer months, and wrote part of his violin concerto in the summerhouse-cum-studio on the lawn. Fauré also worked on some songs here. When Schuster died in 1927, he left Elgar £7,000 in his will. The name of the house was later changed to The Long White Cloud when it was bought by a couple from New Zealand. A blue plaque commemorates the Elgar connection.

22. BREDON HILL, Worcestershire

A 961ft outcrop of the Cotswolds overlooking the River Avon midway between Tewkesbury and Evesham. On the summit is an Iron Age fort with an eighteenth-century tower called Parson's Folly. The hill has been the inspiration of many songs and pieces of music inspired by the poetry of AE Housman. George Butterworth used five poems for his song cycle *Bredon Hill*. The summit can be approached from any of the attractive villages that encircle the hill.

23. BRENTFORD, Middlesex

– 368 High Street, Brentford –

For more than forty years the National Musical Museum, founded by the late Frank Holland as the Piano Museum, was in a temporary home, a leaky, disused church. In 2003 the museum won a lottery grant to relocate to a new purpose-built building also on Brentford High Street. The museum contains a fine collection of more than 300 pianos and organs, including a tiny clockwork musical box and a self-playing 'Mighty Wurlitzer', and over 30,000 piano rolls, some made by the composers themselves.

www.musicalmuseum.co.uk

24. BRIDGE, Kent

~ Bourne Park House, Bourne Park, Bridge ~

A house owned by Sir Horace Mann where Mozart stayed for five nights (from 25 to 30 July 1765) with his father, mother and sister on their way to Dover to catch the ferry to Calais following their recital tour to London. They went to the races on nearby Barham Downs and eventually crossed the channel on 1 August. The voyage took them three and a half hours.

The house has been in disrepair and was, for a time, taken over by squatters. It is being restored.

25. BRIGHTLING, Sussex

~ St Thomas à Becket Church, Brightling ~

John 'Mad Jack' Fuller was a wealthy eccentric patron of the arts and Member of Parliament, being elected when he was only 22. Born in 1757, he succeed to the family fortune and property (including sugar plantations in Jamaica) when he was twenty, and became the squire of Brightling, a hamlet six miles north-west of Battle. Fuller was a good friend of William Shield, the Master of the Musick. Shield was a frequent guest at Fuller's musical evenings held either in Brightling or at his London home in Devonshire Place. This friendship partly explains why there is a memorial tablet to Shield in Brightling Church despite the fact that Shield did not live in the area and is not buried here. After Shield's death at his home in Berners Street in 1829, he was buried in Westminster Abbey. Fuller had a memorial plaque made to mark the grave but the Dean of Westminster Abbey rejected it because Shield was described as a gentleman: in death, commented the Dean, all men were equal in the sight of God. So, in a huff, Fuller took his memorial off to his local church in Sussex, where it remains. As the squire – his house was next door to the church – Fuller commissioned a barrel organ for the church in 1820. This is the largest of its kind in Britain still working and replaced an earlier barrel organ which is now in the Wanganui Museum in New Zealand. Fuller also donated nine bassoons to the church to accompany the singing. He is buried in the churchyard beneath the Pyramid.

26. BRIGHTON, Sussex

– 7 North Street, Brighton –

The composer Frank Bridge, best known today for having taught Benjamin Britten, was born here on 26 February 1879. He was the tenth of twelve children and music ran in the family. His father, who had been a printer, had become a violin teacher and conductor of a music hall orchestra, his brother William, a professional cellist. Bridge learnt the violin from his father and gained experience playing in his orchestras. After attending college, he earned his living as a performer and conductor (he was the man they sent for if an orchestra needed a last-minute stand-in). He also played in the British premiere of Debussy's string quartet, an event that inspired him to write his first string quartet.

– The Old Ship Hotel, King's Road, Brighton –

In 1831 Niccolò Paganini arrived at the Chain Pier in a ship named after him and strolled to the hotel with no baggage other than his violin. He gave two concerts at the Theatre Royal on 7 and 8 December before embarking on a tour of Britain which took in almost every town and city with a concert hall. He gave another concert in the hotel on 27 August 1832. The ballroom is named after him. Other famous musical visitors who have stayed here include the conductor Sir Henry Wood. It was in this hotel, the earliest parts of which date back to 1559, that the celebratory banquet was held in 1841 to mark the opening of the London to Brighton railway.

– The Royal Pavilion, Brighton –

On 29 December 1823, Rossini visited the Duke of Clarence (later William IV) at the Pavilion and sang to his own accompaniment. He and the Duke got on well and several times during his London visit, Rossini and the Duke sang duets together.

– 130 Hillside, Moulsecoomb, Brighton –

Following financial difficulties which he was too proud to let become common knowledge, Havergal Brian moved council house in 1922 having lived for a year in St

Anne's Crescent in Lewes and, from October 1920 to 1922, at 14a Marine Square in Brighton. In Lewes he had written his *Third English Suite* and begun work on a new symphony. The first of his symphonies to be given a public performance, it was heard on Brighton's West Pier in April 1921, but is no longer known as his first. That number has been given to the *Gothic Symphony*, the longest symphony ever written, involving an orchestra 200 strong, four brass bands, five hundred singers, four soloists and an organ. He began work on the piece in 1917 in Lewes and completed it in Moulsecoomb in 1927 with the bulk of it being written in 1922. It did not receive its premiere until 1961. Brian wrote thirty-two symphonies in all, eight of them after he had reached 90.

27. BRISTOL, Avon

– Bristol Cathedral –

Sir Henry Walford Davies, Master of the King's Music, is buried in the cathedral's grounds. He died on 11 March 1941 at his home in the village of Wrington, near Axbridge, Somerset, to which he had moved following the transfer of the BBC music department from London to Bristol to escape the expected German bombing of London.

– 7 Brooklyn Terrace, Easton, Bristol –

A plaque marks the house where Ruby Helder, known as 'the girl tenor', was born on 3 March 1890. Her father was a dairyman who took over the nearby Glasshouse pub and it was there that Emma Jane Holder, to give her her real name, began entertaining. From childhood, Helder had a deep and powerful singing voice which attracted attention. An aunt, who was Sir Harry Lauder's housekeeper, arranged for her to go to the Guildhall School of Music in London to study singing and piano. She later studied with Charles Santley, the foremost British baritone of his day. Santley wrote of her: 'Miss Ruby Helder possesses a natural, pure tenor voice of great beauty and power. She also possesses what few can boast, a thoroughly artistic temperament. In my opinion she has no rivals among the artists of the day.' Thanks to records (she made her first in 1908) Helder became known around the world and received many invitations to visit Russia, the United States and other countries. In America in 1915 the great Enrico Caruso heard her and recommended her to the Metropolitan Opera in New York to sing tenor roles but the management backed off, worried she might be regarded simply as a freak. Instead she joined John Philip Sousa's band and toured with them throughout the United States and Canada. In 1920 she returned to England with the American architect and artist Chesley Bonestall. They were married the same year at the Marylebone Register Office. After her marriage, Ruby slowly drifted out of the public eye but when she returned to live in the United States, she did make some radio broadcasts in New York. She retired officially in 1935 and concentrated on throwing lavish parties for her musical friends. She died at the Highland Hotel in Hollywood after a long battle against alcoholism on 21 November 1938. She was 48.

28. BURY ST EDMUNDS, Suffolk

– Hengrave Hall, Bury St Edmunds, Suffolk, IP28 6LZ –

The present hall was built between 1525 and 1538 by Sir Thomas Kytson, a wealthy wool merchant, adventurer and former Sheriff of London. His son, also Thomas, became owner of the hall in December 1561. An intimate friend of the Duke of Norfolk and a recusant (a Catholic who refused to go to a Protestant service), Kytson was viewed with some suspicion by the Court. But whatever the feelings about him, he was obviously trusted enough for Queen Elizabeth I to stay at Hengrave Hall for three days in August 1578 as part of her Suffolk Progress to Norwich. In return, the Queen knighted Kytson who had to promise her to attend Protestant services. The promise didn't last long. Soon afterwards, Kytson's wife was imprisoned for refusing to go to church and both are on a list of recusants drawn up in March 1588. In about 1594, a young man, possibly still in his teens, was taken on by Sir Thomas as one of his house musicians. John Wilbye (1574–1638), who had been born in Diss, was to become Kytson's Chief of the Minstrels and the house contains a fine minstrels' gallery from which Wilbye and his musicians must have serenaded Kytson and his guests many times. Sir Thomas also owned a town house in Austin Friars in the City of London, to which Wilbye would have accompanied the family on their London visits. It was from there that he issued his First Set of Madrigals in 1598. A second volume appeared in 1609. Wilbye was a master of various styles. In spite of his reputation and the attempts of others to lure him to London, Wilbye stayed with the Kytson family for thirty years working for Lady Kytson for twenty years after Sir Thomas's death. In 1613, as a reward for his loyalty, she gave him a lease on what was considered to be the best sheep farm in the area. Working the farm certainly cut down on composition time for although he continued to supervise music at Hengrave Hall, he produced little new work. After Lady Kytson's death, Wilbye worked for her youngest daughter, moving with her to Colchester. In 1952 Hengrave Hall became the property of the Religious of the Assumption who converted it into a boarding school for girls. It is now run as a wedding venue.

www.hengravehall.co.uk

– Langham Hall, nr Ixworth, Bury St Edmunds –

A Georgian house built in about 1756, set in rolling parkland with large gardens, and the home of Sir Patrick Blake, who succeeded to the baronetcy in 1784. In November 1791, Haydn was his guest here for three days. Langham Hall is a private residence but does occasionally open to the public.

– St Mary's Church, Bury St Edmunds –

The composer George Kirbye, who died in 1634, is buried here. Little is known about Kirbye except that he was in service as the house musician at Rushbrooke Hall, a few miles south-east of Bury. This was the home of Sir Robert Jermyn, a member of the family that built London's Jermyn Street. The finest and largest moated Tudor mansion in Suffolk, it caught fire and was demolished without permission in 1961. Although no trace of the hall remains, it is possible to see where the building stood. Kirbye wrote a considerable number of fine madrigals, dedicating his 1597 set of English Madrigals to Sir Robert's two daughters, and some church music. He has been credited with writing the tune of the carol *While Shepherds Watched their Flocks by Night*. After his retirement, Kirbye lived in Whiting Street, Bury St Edmunds, until his death.

29. CAMBERLEY, Surrey

– 489/497 London Road, Yorktown, Camberley –

The McDonalds Drive Thru in Yorktown on the A30 has a plaque on the wall noting: 'Arthur Sullivan lived here'. This was the site of a small terrace of two-up two-down Georgian houses called Albany Place which were demolished for redevelopment. In 1845, Sir Arthur Sullivan's father, Thomas, became bandmaster at the Royal Military College, Sandhurst, and moved with his family into number 4 Albany Place, almost directly opposite the College gates. Arthur, who had been born on 13 May 1842, was three. He went to Yorktown National School (run by the local church) and because of his father's job learnt to play every wind instrument from a very early age. Years later he recalled that he wrote the anthem *By the Waters of Babylon* in Camberley when he was about eight. His father lived in this house for twelve years, until appointed Professor of Brass Instruments at Kneller Hall. Meanwhile, Arthur had been sent to boarding school in London and become a chorister of the Chapel Royal. In the summer of 1886, Sullivan rented the house next door to the one in which he had spent his childhood and wrote much of his cantata *The Golden Legend* there.

See the entry for Frimley for Ethel Smyth's Camberley connection.

30. CAMBRIDGE, Cambridgeshire

Numerous famous musicians have lived in, worked in or visited Cambridge. Professors of Music at the University have included Maurice Greene, Thomas Walmisley, William Sterndale Bennett, Sir George Macfarren, Charles Stanford and Charles Wood. Eduard Grieg received an honorary degree in 1894, Federico Busoni one in 1913. Saint-Saëns, Tchaikovsky, Max Bruch and Arrigo Boito were similarly honoured. The University Library contains some important musical manuscripts including the earliest known English songbook dating from around 1200.

– 17 Cranmer Road, Cambridge –

The home of composer Charles Wood from 1898 until his death on 12 July 1926. Wood is one of those composers known to everyone who has ever sung in a church choir. Born in Armagh, he became one of the first intake of students into the Royal College of Music, then moved to Cambridge to become a college organist and teacher before succeeding Stanford as Professor of Music in 1924. Although he wrote an opera and eight string quartets, it is for his church settings and his songs that Wood is remembered today. He died in 1926 and is buried in St Giles's Cemetery, Huntingdon Road.

– Fitzwilliam Museum, Trumpington Street, CB1 1RB –

The museum contains an important collection of manuscripts and a small but very important collection of instruments including a seventeenth-century Italian harpsichord and an Erard square piano. The manuscripts include the Fitzwilliam Virginal book, an important source of music in Elizabethan England.

– Girton Gate, opposite Girton College –

The home of the Rev Hugh Stewart, Alban Berg stayed here in 1931 when he was a juror for the International Society of Contemporary Music. Zoltan Kodaly also stayed here when he conducted the first English performance of his *Psalmus Hungaricus* on 30 November 1927. Another visitor was Swiss composer Arthur Honegger who conducted a performance of *Le Roi David* in Cambridge in 1929.

– 10 Harvey Road –

A blue plaque marks the Cambridge home of the composer Charles Villiers Stanford when Professor of Music. Antonín Dvorák and his wife stayed with him here in June 1891 when Dvorák was given an honorary doctorate by the University. Dvorák conducted the first British performance of his *Eighth Symphony* and a performance of his *Stabat Mater* in Cambridge Town Hall.

– King's College Chapel –

The college chapel, one of the greatest medieval buildings in Britain with its superb acoustics, is famous around the world for its choir, founded in the fifteenth century, and for the Christmas Festival of Nine Lessons and Carols which has taken place here every year since 1918. Orlando Gibbons (who is sometimes said to have been born in Cambridge – he wasn't; he was born in Oxford in 1583) was a choir-boy here. The ceiling, the largest fan vaulted ceiling in the world, has been described as the noblest ceiling in existence. When Haydn visited in 1791, he could scarcely believe it was four hundred years old and carved in stone.

www.kings.cam.ac.uk

– 14 Madingley Road –

This was the home of the composer Roberto Gerhard (1896–1970). Born in Valls near Tarragona, Spain, on 25 September 1896, he studied with Granados, Pedrell and then, in Vienna and Berlin, with Schoenberg. Gerhard became the leading composer of the Spanish avant-garde, heavily influenced by Catalan music and culture but writing serially. He was on the side of the Republicans during the Spanish Civil War and fled Spain in 1939 when they were defeated. Franco retaliated by banning his music. He settled in Cambridge, where he continued composing using mainly serial techniques. In 1955, he became the first composer to write an electronic score for the theatre with his incidental music for the RSC's production of *King Lear*. Towards the end of his life his music began to achieve some popularity, especially his opera *The Duenna*, based on the play by Sheridan. Gerhard died in 1970 and is buried in the Parish of the Ascension Burial Ground, All Souls Lane, Huntingdon Road, Cambridge.

31. CANTERBURY, Kent

– The Cathedral –

In the nave is a memorial to the composer Orlando Gibbons who is buried in the cathedral. Gibbons, one of the greatest names in early seventeenth-century music, died in Canterbury in 1625 at the age of forty-one from an apoplectic fit on his way to Dover with the Chapel Royal musicians to welcome Queen Henrietta Maria. Gibbons was the leading composer of his time, as skilled writing for instruments as he was for voices, writing music both sacred and secular. His sudden death came as an enormous shock and it was rumoured he had died from the plague. An autopsy was carried out, the results of which are in the National Archive (he didn't have the plague).

One of the organists at Canterbury was George Marson who was born locally in about 1570 and died here in 1632. A lively madrigal written by him is in *The Triumphs of Oriana*, an important collection of twenty-nine madrigals composed for Queen Elizabeth I by twenty-six composers under the editorship of Thomas Morley.

32. CASTLE HOWARD, North Yorkshire

– York, North Yorkshire, YO60 7DA –

The Orleans room houses paintings from the collection of the Duke of Orléans and includes one by Marco Ricci (1680–1730) entitled *The Opera Rehearsal*. This depicts Dr Pepusch (the man who assembled the music for John Gay's *The Beggar's Opera*) at the harpsichord, with the singers

Nicolini and Margaretta and the instrumentalists Festini and Corporali. There is also a portrait by Domenico Feti (1589–1624) entitled *The Music Master,* which is thought to be of Monteverdi. In the Music Room there is a very early Broadwood piano dating from 1796. Beethoven owned a similar model.

33. CHELTENHAM, Gloucestershire

– 4 Clarence Road, Cheltenham –

This modest Regency terraced house, in what was formerly known as Pittville Terrace, was the birthplace on 21 September 1874 of Gustav Holst, composer of *The Planets*. Holst was of Swedish descent and came from a family of musicians. His father was a music teacher and organist at All Saint's Church, his mother a pianist, and it was always intended he should enter the music profession in some capacity. He studied at the Royal College of Music (where he met and became good friends with Ralph Vaughan Williams) disliked his piano course and switched to composition under Stanford. He then took up the trombone and after graduation, played for the Carl Rosa Opera Company and the Scottish Orchestra, before becoming a music teacher at Dulwich Girls School (from 1903 until 1920), Director of Music at St Paul's Girls School (from 1906 until his death in 1934), Morley College (1907–24), and in 1919, professor of music at Reading University, all in order to earn enough money to compose. Although *The Planets* is Holst's best-known work, he was a prolific and very distinctive composer, inspired by Sanskrit writings as much as English folk-song. He wrote in most genres from solo songs and chamber pieces to huge orchestral works and operas.

Holst lived in Clarence Road until he was eight and first tried his hand at composition here. He left following the death of his mother. The house was bought in 1974, the centenary of the composer's birth, with funds raised by public appeal and from the local council, and is now the Gustav Holst Birthplace Museum. The ground floor music room contains the piano on which Holst composed *The Planets*, the portrait of Mozart he liked to have near him while composing, a 1920s oil portrait and various other pieces of Holst memorabilia, much of it donated by his daughter Imogen. The rest of the house, including the bedroom in which Holst was almost certainly born, has been recreated to show what life was like upstairs and downstairs in Regency and Victorian times.

www.holstmuseum.org.uk

– Montpellier Gardens, Cheltenham –

The bandstand in Montpellier Gardens was cast at Coalbrookedale in Telford, Shropshire, and erected in 1864, making it the oldest surviving iron bandstand in Britain, if not the world. There is a stone bandstand which predates it by seventeen years in Birkenhead Park, designed by Joseph Paxton, the architect of the Crystal Palace. The iron bandstand in London's Hyde Park was originally erected in Kensington Gardens in 1869.

– Imperial Gardens, Cheltenham –

The gardens, close to the Town Hall, contain a statue of Holst by sculptor Anthony Stones. It was unveiled by the conductor Sir Mark Elder on 4 April 2008. The octagonal plinth beneath the statue contains plaques depicting the planets in recognition of his most famous work.

The composer John Barnett (1802–90) lived in Cheltenham and is buried in the churchyard at Leckhampton on the southern outskirts of the town.

34. CHESTER, Cheshire

Did Chester hear the first performance of Handel's *Messiah* when Handel stopped off in the city on his way to Dublin for the official first performance? He was stranded here waiting for a favourable wind to catch the ferry to Ireland and apparently got together some local choristers to bash through the choruses in his lodgings. He was not pleased with the result. After many attempts, the lead chorus was still unable to sing *And with his stripes we are healed*. Handel lost his temper, swore in four or five languages and cried out in broken English: 'You scoundrel! Did you not tell me you could sing at sight?' to which the chorister replied 'Yes, sir, and so I can, but not at first sight.'

William Lawes, the prominent court composer, was killed fighting for King Charles I at the siege of Chester on 24 September 1645.

35. CHICHESTER, Sussex

~ The Cathedral ~

The present Cathedral dates from the twelfth century and thanks to the tomb of St Richard of Chichester became an important centre of pilgrimage until the tomb was destroyed during the reign of Henry VIII.

Thomas Weelkes (c1576–1623), one of the most gifted madrigal composers, was organist here from 1603 to 1622. He was so highly esteemed by his peers that Thomas Morley invited him in 1601 to contribute to *The Triumphs of Oriana*, an anthology issued in honour of the aging Queen Elizabeth. Marrying well (at All Saints' Church, Chichester) Weelkes's future seemed assured. However, he appears to have taken to the bottle (along with many other members of the cathedral staff: in 1610 a decree was issued enjoyning church officials not to frequent tippling houses). As a result of his heavy drinking, he became involved in a lawsuit with his own wife and mother-in-law, was admonished by his Bishop for drunkenness, and in 1617, when he began to play for a service while smashed out of his mind, dismissed from his post. No suitable successor seems to have been found, for Weelkes returned to the cathedral, despite continuing with his old habits. Notwithstanding his transgressions, there is a memorial to him in the north transept. Fortunately Weelkes did not live to see the destruction caused to the cathedral by the Puritans who 'brake down the organ in the cathedral, and dashed the pipes with their pole-axes, crying in scoff, "Harke how the organ goes!"' The present organ has been rebuilt twice since being installed in 1678, although some of the original decoration does remain. Weelkes died in London having been on an almighty bender with the inappropriately named Henry Drinkwater.

Beneath Weelkes's memorial tablet, an inscription on the floor marks the spot where the ashes of Gustav Holst are buried. Their close proximity is highly appropriate since Weelkes was Holst's favourite Tudor composer. Towards the end of his life, Holst, who had never been particularly strong even as a child, fell ill and discovered he was suffering from a duodenal ulcer. He was given the choice of having a minor operation and leading a restricted existence, or major surgery which would allow him to continue life as normal. He chose the major surgery which took place on 23 May, 1934. The operation was a success but two days later, Holst's heart gave out. 1934 was the same year that claimed the lives of Elgar and Delius.

Thomas Kelway (1695–1744) was a choirboy here and later organist from 1720 until his death in 1744 (not 1749 as it says on his tombstone due to a careless repair). Kelway, who was probably born locally, wrote some church music still in use today and is buried in St Clement's Chapel off the south aisle.

The composer Eric Coates, well-known for his marches, died in Chichester's Royal West Sussex Hospital on 21 December 1957 at the age of 71.

36. CHINGFORD, Essex

– 6 Buxton Road, Chingford –

Kaikhosru Shapurji Sorabji, composer, pianist and critic, was born here on 14 August 1892. Christened Leon Dudley

Sorabji, he was the only son of a Parsi civil engineer from Bombay and, it was always said, a Spanish-Sicilian opera singer who now turns out to be boringly English. Sorabji was a very private man, always at pains to hide both the date and the place of his birth. A late developer, he was largely self-taught, and became widely known for his formidable technique as a pianist. He disliked playing for people he didn't know and so gave up the concert platform in 1936 and moved to Corfe Castle in order to concentrate on composition.

37. CLIVEDEN, Bucks

– Cliveden House, Taplow, Berkshire SL6 0JF –

Once the home of the Astor family, now a luxury hotel, this Buckinghamshire mansion is famous as the setting for the meeting between Minister of War John Profumo and call-girl Christine Keeler which led to the downfall of the Macmillan government. Its musical claim to fame is that it was on the parterre or formal gardens at Cliveden (the present house is not the original) that Thomas Arne's *Rule Britannia* was first heard in public on the night of 1 August 1740. Anxious to gain favour with the British aristocracy, Frederick, Prince of Wales, eldest son of George II and then resident at Cliveden, decided to commission an evening of British magnificence, ostensibly to celebrate his daughter's third birthday. Two Scottish poets came up with the words for a masque called *Alfred*. Dr Arne, the English nightingale (whose harmony for *God Save the Queen* is still standard) was invited to write the score. The moment it was heard, the tune of *Rule Britannia* was a hit. Its first eight bars, said Wagner later, embody the character of the British people while Beethoven wrote a set of variations on it. In 1746 Handel borrowed the tune for his *Occasional Oratorio*.

38. COLCHESTER, Essex

– Holy Trinity Church, Trinity Street, Colchester –

The composer John Wilbye, who was born in the Norfolk town of Diss in 1574, lived in Colchester from 1628 until his death in September 1638. He is buried here. From about the age of twenty-one, Wilbye worked as the house musician of Sir Thomas Kytson at Hengrave Hall near Bury St Edmunds. Following the deaths of Lord and Lady Kytson, Wilbye was taken into the household of Kytson's youngest daughter, coming eventually to live in the imposing brick mansion near the west end of the church (an event marked by a plaque). Wilbye is considered to be one of the best madrigal composers. Few of his other works have survived. Among those that have are some church music (in Latin and in English) and some pieces for viols. He was a contributor to *The Triumphs of Oriana*. When he died he left his best viol to the Prince of Wales, who was to become King Charles II. There is a memorial tablet to Wilbye in Holy Trinity which is now used as an arts centre.

39. CORFE CASTLE, Dorset

– The Eye, Higher Filbank, Corfe Castle, Wareham –

The eccentric composer Kaikhosru Shapurji Sorabji, having given up performing as a pianist, moved from London to the Dorset village of Corfe Castle, giving rise to rumours that he lived in a castle. As a writer he championed the cause of such composers as Medtner, Szymanowski and Busoni. As for his own compositions, he ploughed a very individual furrow, not least in terms of length. His *First Organ Symphony* lasts some two hours; the later organ symphonies are even longer. His *Symphonic Variations* requires eight hours. His *Opus Clavicembalisticum* of 1930, for solo piano, lasts four and a half hours and was in the *Guinness Book of Records* as the longest piano work ever. As the result of hearing a poor performance of this piece, Sorabji banned his music from being performed without his express permission, which meant for forty years it rarely got an airing. That didn't stop Sorabji writing at a furious pace, unconcerned whether his music would be heard or not. Most of his music is technically very difficult and obscure, making enormous demands on both performers and listeners. His recluse-like existence led to him being labeled the Howard Hughes of music. Any casual visitors to his house, which he nicknamed The Eye, were sent packing; a notice on the gate warned 'Visitors Unwelcome'. He died in Winfrith Newburgh on 15 January 1988.

40. CORSHAM, Wiltshire

– Parkside, 36 High Street, Corsham –

A plaque marks the house where Sir Michael Tippett lived for ten years from 1960 to 1970, and was resident in 1966 when knighted. His music room was on the first floor and he only left the town when his peace was threatened by a proposed car park next door. Works written here include his opera *King Priam*, *Songs for Ariel*, *Concerto for Orchestra*, *The Vision of St Augustine*, *Songs for Dov* and a large part of *The Knot Garden.* He also began work on his *Third Symphony*.

41. COVENTRY, West Midlands

– St Bartholomew's Church, Binley, Coventry –

Capel Bond, composer, organist and administrator, is buried here. He was born in Gloucester, where his father was a bookseller, in 1730, and apprenticed to the Gloucester Cathedral organist at the age of twelve. He became organist of St Michael and All Angels in Coventry when he was nineteen. The second largest parish church in England, this was to become Coventry Cathedral. Bond also took on the post of organist at Holy Trinity, Coventry, keeping both positions until his death.

He founded music festivals in the Midlands, including one in Birmingham, staged subscription concerts and was a leading light in Midlands' music. Although little of his own music has survived, what has shows a composer of considerable talent. He wrote a particularly fine trumpet concerto on a par with Handel. Bond died on 14 February 1790.

42. CROYDON, Surrey

~ 30 Dagnell Park, South Norwood, Croydon ~

A blue plaque marks the married home for two years of Samuel Coleridge-Taylor, composer of the incredibly popular cantata *Hiawatha's Wedding Feast*. His marriage to Jessie, a fellow student at the Royal College of Music, had created a stir in Jessie's home since her parents were steadfastly against a mixed race husband for their daughter. But the marriage eventually took place and the couple moved here in 1900. Coleridge-Taylor (the hyphen was allegedly kept after a printer's mistake) had been born illegitimately in Holborn, London, in 1875. His father, who never knew of his son's existence, was from Sierra Leone, his mother English. He was brought up in Croydon by his mother and her father, a blacksmith, and spent almost all of his short life in and around the area. Until he was nineteen, his home was at 67 Waddon New Road. He then moved to Holmesdale Road, to Fernham Road, to Saxon Road, Selhurst, and to several other addresses before his final home at Aldwick, St Leonard's Road, Waddon. As a young boy, Coleridge, as he was known to his family, showed an immediate talent for music. His grandfather, whose own son was a professional musician, taught him the violin while Colonel Herbert Walters, choirmaster of St George's Church where Coleridge-Taylor sang in the choir, was sufficiently impressed to arrange for him to attend the

Royal College of Music in 1890 when he was fifteen, and guarantee the fees. He started as a violinist before switching to composition. In 1898, when he was 23, his talents were publicly revealed with the performance of his *Ballade in A Minor*, a commission for the Three Choirs Festival for which he had been recommended by Elgar. This was followed the same year by his most famous composition, *Hiawatha's Wedding Feast*. First performed at the Royal College with Stanford conducting, it became a popular success when heard at the Royal Albert Hall two years later. In 1904 Coleridge-Taylor paid the first of three visits to the United States where he became a hero to African-Americans and was nicknamed the Black Mahler. In 1912, while on West Croydon Station waiting for a train, he collapsed and died shortly afterwards, aged only 37, from pneumonia. His death was reported globally. He was buried in Bandon Hill Cemetery, Wallington.

43. DANBURY, Essex

– St John the Baptist Church, Church Green, – Main Road, Danbury

Cecil Armstrong Gibbs is buried here. Armstrong Gibbs (he hated the name Cecil and refused to use it) was a gifted songwriter and stalwart of musical festivals which he did much to promote. He was born in Great Baddow, not far from Danbury, on 10 August 1889, read history at Trinity College, Cambridge, and stayed on to study music with EJ Dent and Charles Wood. Realising he would never be able to earn a living as a composer, he became a school master.

He was asked to write the incidental music for a play being staged to mark the headmaster's retirement; a young man named Adrian Boult was brought in to conduct. Boult was so impressed by Gibbs's score he offered to pay for him to study at the Royal College for a year as a mature student. Gibbs subsequently studied conducting with Boult and composition with Vaughan Williams. He later joined the Royal College staff himself, teaching composition. He moved to Danbury in 1919, living in a house called The Crossings. When this was requisitioned during World War Two to become a hospital, Gibbs moved to Windermere in the Lake District. The death of his son in action in Italy, led to his *Third Symphony*, 'The Westmorland'. Gibbs also wrote an opera, an operetta, incidental stage music, music for choirs, chamber music (including five string quartets), concertos and three symphonies. He considered the Second, a choral symphony, to be among his finest work. He died on 12 May 1960.

Vaughan Williams and his wife stayed in a cottage in Danbury in 1923 while he was working on his oratorio *Sancta civitas* (*The Holy City*).

44. DINTON, Wiltshire

– Lawes Cottage, Dinton –

This five bedroom, seventeenth-century detached farmhouse in a village eight miles west of Salisbury, gets its name from the fact that the composer Henry Lawes is supposed to have been born in what might have been, for a short time, the family home. There is no direct evidence that the Lawes family did live in the house, although their mother, Lucris Shepherde, certainly came from the village. In 1594 she had married Thomas Lawes, a bass choir singer from Somerset. Their first son, Henry, born in 1595, was baptised in the local church of St Mary the Virgin, Dinton, on 5 January 1596. Their next son, William, was baptised in Salisbury on 1 May 1602, the family having moved there shortly before his birth following Thomas's appointment as a lay vicar at the cathedral. The family then lived in The Close. As well as Henry and William, two other brothers became musicians: Thomas Junior who stayed in the choir at Salisbury, and John who became a well-known 'singing man' at Westminster Abbey.

Both Henry and William studied with Giovanni Coprario (real name John Cooper), then worked at court, Henry as a gentleman of the Chapel Royal and composer, William as a composer and musician to the King. William, noted in particular for his viol consort suites, joined the King's army and was shot and killed during the siege of Chester on 24 September 1645. There is a portrait of him dressed as a cavalier in the Faculty of Music at Oxford. Henry, after the Restoration in 1660, returned to the Chapel Royal and wrote an anthem for Charles II's coronation. He is probably best known for setting Milton's masque *Comus*. He died in 1662 and was buried in Westminster Abbey.

Lawes Cottage, which is on a 27-acre estate, has been owned by the National Trust since it was bequeathed to them in 1940 by Mary Engleheart, the widow of George Engleheart. The property is available to rent.

www.nationaltrust.org.uk

45. DORKING, Surrey

– Dorking Halls, Reigate Road, Dorking RH4 1SG –

A statue of Ralph Vaughan Williams stands outside the Halls, while a plaque on the wall commemorates the fact that the Dorking Halls were built originally as the home of the Leith Hill Music Festival. This had been founded in 1905 by Margaret Vaughan Williams, the composer's sister, and local resident Evangeline Farrer, as a choral competition between Surrey choirs and neighbouring choirs. Vaughan Williams conducted the opening concert and was festival conductor every subsequent year until his resignation in 1957. The Halls, financed by the local gentry, had opened their doors in 1931 and allowed Vaughan Williams to do something he had always wanted to do: perform Bach's St Matthew Passion with all the competition's competitors taking part. Even after his official retirement from the Festival, he would return from London every year to conduct the piece.

– Leith Hill Place, Leith Hill Lane, Dorking RH5 6LY –

This was the house, five miles south of Dorking, in which Ralph Vaughan Williams grew up. Following the death of his father, the vicar of Down Ampney, in 1875 (when Vaughan Williams was three) his mother decided to return to her family home, Leith Hill Place. She was a Wedgewood of pottery fame. It was here that Vaughan Williams was brought up and spent his holidays from school in Rottingdean and at Charterhouse. His aunt, who gave him his first musical tuition, installed an organ for him, and he wrote his first piece of music here when he was six: a piano piece, four bars long. In 1890 Vaughan Williams left to go to the Royal College of Music, and although he came back frequently, it was not to live. When in 1944 he inherited the house, he promptly gave it to the National Trust. He never lost his affection for the area and in 1929, bought The White Gates, a bungalow in Westcott Road acquired because his wife Adeline was crippled with arthritis and having difficulty going up and down stairs. It became his home for twenty-four years, and he was visited there by friends such as Arnold Bax, Gustav Holst, Gerald Finzi, Arthur Bliss and Elizabeth Maconchy. He wrote four of his symphonies there, plus the opera *The Pilgrim's Progress* and a large number of major works. The White Gates has since been demolished. The grounds of Leith Hill Place are open to the public.

www.nationaltrust.org.uk

46. DOWN AMPNEY, Gloucestershire

– The Old Vicarage, Down Ampney Road, – Down Ampney, Cirencester

The composer Ralph Vaughan Williams was born in All Saints' vicarage on 12 October 1872; his father was the local vicar. Vaughan Williams, the youngest of three children, was baptised in the church. His father died at the early age of 40 when Vaughan Williams was only three and the family moved to Leith Hill Place near Dorking in Surrey. There is a memorial in All Saints to Vaughan Williams' father, who is buried in the churchyard, and the organ was restored and extended as a result of an appeal in memory of the composer himself. There is a small exhibition in the bell tower of the life and times of Vaughan Williams.

47. DURHAM, County Durham

– Durham Cathedral –

One of the great churches of Christendom and burial place of the Venerable Bede whose tomb is in the Galilee Chapel. In the centre of the chapel's floor is the gravestone of John Brimley, the last Cantor of the Monastery and the first Master of the Choristers after the Reformation. Among the cathedral's organists was James Heseltine, who held the position from 1711 until his death in 1763. He wrote a number of anthems still performed today, although he destroyed much of his work following a row with the Dean and Chapter. Heseltine was succeeded by Thomas Ebdon, a local boy, born in 1738, whose name has been found carved with a pocket knife on the choir screen so it is assumed he was a choirboy here. He is particularly known for his *Service in C*. John Dykes Bower (1905–81) held the post for three years from 1933. He had previously been organist at Truro Cathedral and New College Oxford. He left Durham in 1936 for St Paul's Cathedral in London. During the Blitz, the St Paul's choir was evacuated to Truro where they sang in Truro Cathedral, leaving the lay clerks to sing services in St Paul's. Dykes Bower was a formidable choir trainer, known to the choir as Dickie-Boo. His beat when conducting was, according to one chorister, like that of God: no beginning and no end. He was knighted in 1968 shortly after his retirement and died in Orpington in 1981.

48. EASTBOURNE, Sussex

– The Grand Hotel, King Edward's Parade –

The French composer Claude Debussy (1865–1918) stayed here from 24 July 1905 until the end of September, in search of peace and quiet following the break-up of his first marriage. His wife Lily had tried to commit suicide after he left her to live with Emma Bardac, a singer and wife of a businessman. That summer Emma was six months pregnant (they eventually married), most of his friends had deserted him and he was trying unsuccessfully to complete his three orchestral sketches, *La Mer*. He and Emma decided to leave France and booked into rooms 227–9 at the Grand (now the Debussy Suite). At first he found Eastbourne 'a pleasant, even charming spot... a lovely place to cultivate one's egotism.' There were also no musicians discussing painting and no painters discussing music. But after a month, its delights began to pall. 'It's a little English seaside place,' he wrote to a friend, 'silly as these places sometimes are. I shall have to go because there are too many draughts and too much music.' However, his attempt to get-away-from-it-all obviously worked for while at the Grand he managed to complete *La Mer*, and also wrote his first set of *Images*. Other musical visitors to the hotel include Elgar, Dame Nellie Melba (several times), Paderewski, Sir Henry Wood, Sir Thomas Beecham and Eugene Ysaye, the violinist, composer and conductor.

49. EAST CLANDON, SURREY

– Hatchlands Park, East Clandon, Guildford, Surrey –

Hatchlands Park, four miles east of Guildford on the A246, was built in the eighteenth century, using money he had taken from the French, by Admiral Edward Boscawen, one of the heroes of the Battle of Louisburg in Nova Scotia shortly after the outbreak of the Seven Year War. The interiors are by Robert Adam, the garden by Humphrey Repton. Since 1988, the property has housed the collection of old master paintings and historic keyboard instruments assembled by Alec Cobbe. There are some thirty-eight instruments in the collection, twelve of which were owned or played on by such composers as Purcell, JC Bach, Mozart, Beethoven, Chopin, Liszt, Mahler and Elgar, making it the largest group of composer-related instruments in one place in the world. Among the highlights of the collection are the 1664 virginals by Johannes Player, once owned by Charles II and played by Purcell; a 1636 harpsichord built in Antwerp by Andreas Ruckers; a 1777/9 square fortepiano owned by Johann Christian Bach; a 1787 Erard square piano owned by Marie Antoinette, and an Erard grand once owned by Jane Stirling and played by Chopin. There is the Broadwood grand on which Chopin gave his last recital and an 1844 Broadwood owned and signed by Elgar. There is also an 1836/7 Conrad Graf grand piano owned by Mahler. Regular recitals are held in the house using the instruments. There is also a programme of concerts out of doors. Hatchlands is now a National Trust property.

www.cobbecollection.co.uk

50. EAST MOLSEY, Surrey

– East Molsey Cemetery –

The singer, actor and composer John Orlando Parry is buried here. Born in London in 1810, Parry was the son of the Welsh harpist John Parry. He, naturally, had to learn the harp, but when his voice broke was discovered to have a fine baritone voice. He studied in Italy and became a popular stage singer, particularly of comic songs many of which were written for him, most he wrote himself. He was an excellent pianist, who accompanied Liszt on a concert tour in England, and a talented artist. He died at his daughter's house, Pembroke Lodge, East Molsey, on 20 February 1879.

51. ELSTED, WEST SUSSEX

– St Paul's Church, Elsted –

The church dates from the time of Edward the Confessor, and the rectory, which no longer exists, is the most likely birthplace of Thomas Weelkes (c1576–1623), the most original and daring of the English madrigal composers. Several other places claim to be his birthplace but without any real evidence. What we do know is that Weelkes's father was rector here until his death in 1597 and was the incumbent at the time of Weelkes's birth. Weelkes was baptised in the church on 25 October. He began his working life in service with Edward Darcye, a courtier. All the time he was writing madrigals. In 1598, the year after his father's death, when he was about 22, he was appointed organist at Winchester College at a salary of 13s 4d a quarter plus board and lodging. In 1602 he graduated from New College, Oxford, and took up a post at Chichester Cathedral. Weelkes wrote more Anglican services than any other major composer of the time.

52. ELY, Cambridgeshire

– Ely Cathedral –

St Ethelreda founded an abbey on the site of the present cathedral in 673. The current building, known as the Ship of the Fens, was started in 1083 on what was then an island.

It would appear that from early times the cathedral possessed an organ although nothing of any antiquity survives; the present instrument has been much modified and rebuilt, and the present case was built in 1850 by Sir Gilbert Scott. Among the organists and choirmasters who have held office in Ely, possibly the most significant was John Anmer, a local boy, born in Ely in 1579. He received music degrees from both Oxford and Cambridge before returning to Ely to take up his position as organist. He was later ordained. As a composer, he produced some highly individual music. In 1615 he published a collection of *Sacred Hymns of 3, 4, 5 and 6 parts for the Voyces and Vyols*, a collection which includes most of his known works. Other pieces he wrote include *Preces* for five voices, arrangements of the daily canticles, and several four- and five part anthems. Anmer died in 1641 and is buried in the cathedral.

Other notable organists include Christopher Tye who

held the office from 1542 until 1561 when, having been ordained a priest, he accepted the living of nearby Doddington-cum-Marche where he died in 1573.Tye wrote music for both sides of the religious dispute then plaguing England: elaborate settings of Latin texts alongside simpler, shorter works for the Anglicans.

From 1566 to 1570, John Farrant senior held the post. Farrant was notable for being the only cathedral organist ever to attempt to murder his Dean.The attempt took place after Farrant had become the organist at Salisbury Cathedral.

53. EVESHAM, Worcestershire

– Northwick Arms Hotel, Waterside, Evesham, – Worcestershire, WR11 1BT

During World War Two, Eric Coates moved to Evesham and wrote two of the four movements of his symphonic suite *The Three Elizabeths* in this hotel. Every morning he would work in the hotel lounge and then, until opening time, in the bar. *The Three Elizabeths* was given a first performance by the BBC Symphony Orchestra on Christmas Eve 1944.

The Italian pianist, composer, teacher and piano manufacturer, Muzio Clementi died in Evesham in 1832. See the entry under Badsey.

54. EXETER, Devon

– The Cathedral Church of St Peter, Exeter –

The precociously talented cathedral organist Matthew

Godwin (1569–86) is buried here under the north tower. His memorial, featuring musical instruments, is on the north wall of the nave. Godwin came to Exeter from Canterbury Cathedral but within a year he was dead. He was seventeen-and-a-half, and was, according to his epitaph, 'a gentle, pious and clever youth, the most skilful chief musician of the Cathedrals of Canterbury and Exeter'.

Among others to hold the post was Samuel Sebastian Wesley (1810–76), the son of Samuel Wesley and the finest organist of his day. He was organist from 1835 until 1842. Young Samuel inherited his father's genius. He was a choirboy of the Chapel Royal and organist of three London churches before beginning to move around the country's cathedrals. At the time of his death he was organist of Gloucester Cathedral. Wesley fought long and hard to raise the standard of church music and was a more than competent composer. He was offered, on Gladstone's recommendation, either a knighthood or an annual pension of one hundred pounds. He chose the pension but lived for only a further three years. He is buried in Old Cemetery, Exe Street.

www.exeter-cathedral.org.uk

– Killerton House, Broadcylst, Exeter, Devon, EX5 3LE –

Killerton House, seven miles north-east of Exeter off the B3181, was the ancestral home of the Acland family. The library houses fair copies of the songs in *Songs of the West*, Sabine Baring-Gould's collection of Devon and Cornish folk songs, together with other musical papers belonging to Baring-Gould who lived at Lewtrenchard. The music room contains a chamber organ and sheet music by Samuel Sebastian Wesley dedicated to the wife of the 10th Baron who took lessons with him when he was organist at Exeter Cathedral. The house and estate were given to the National Trust in 1942.

www.nationaltrust.org.uk

55. EYNSFORD, Kent

– The Cottage, High Street, Eynsford –

A blue plaque marks the cottage in which Peter Warlock and EJ Moeran lived from 1925 to 1928, surrounded by a large entourage of cats. It was a pretty wild time. Warlock would ride his motorbike around the village with no clothes on, they would play the piano in the nude and Moeran would sing loud songs to drown out the sound of hymns coming from the next-door Baptist Chapel. They held wild parties and not for nothing were they living opposite The Five Bells pub. Surprisingly they were three productive years for Warlock in which he wrote (with Cecil Gray) a study of Gesualdo, songs such as *The Birds*, *Cradle Song* and *Robin Goodfellow*, and choral settings of Webster and others. Moeran, on the other hand, having lost faith in his ability to write anything, composed virtually nothing and sowed the seeds for his later alcoholism. He even considered giving up music to become a garage proprietor. They were visited here by Bax, Walton, Lord Berners and Constant Lambert amongst others.

56. FAIRLIGHT, East Sussex

– St Andrew's Church, Coastguard Lane, – Fairlight, TN35 4AB

The cluster of coastguard and holiday cottages that make up Fairlight, three miles east of Hastings, can scarcely be called a village, but in the graveyard of St Andrew's Church, up on the hill, are two interesting graves. The first is that of Richard D'Oyly Carte, the founder of the opera company, builder of the Savoy Hotel and Theatre, and friend and patron of Gilbert and Sullivan. He was buried here close to his parents.

The second is that of Thomas Attwood Walmisley (1814-56) who had become Professor of Music at Cambridge when aged only 22. Walmisley, who was a friend of Mendelssohn and edited some of his scores, came from a musical family. His father, another Thomas, was a well-known organist and composer of glees; his godfather and early teacher, Thomas Attwood, had been a pupil of Mozart. At 16, Walmisley became the organist of Croydon Parish Church and then, at 19, organist of Trinity College, Cambridge. Three years later he was appointed professor. He was an inspired organist, choirmaster and teacher, one of the first, apparently, to use live musical examples in his lectures, and together with Samuel Sebastian Wesley, did much to revive English cathedral music. He wrote anthems, odes for installations, symphonic works, overtures and chamber pieces but it is for his church music that he is remembered today, in particular, his evening *Service in D Minor*. He owned a house in Hastings where he died on 17 January 1856 in his early forties.

57. **FAREHAM, Hampshire**

~ 21 High Street, Fareham ~

A blue plaque marks the house in which composer, teacher and organist Sir John Goss was brought up. His father was the organist at Fareham Parish Church. Goss became a chorister of the Chapel Royal when he was eleven and after his voice broke, began to study composition with Thomas Attwood, organist of St Paul's Cathedral. In 1824 he became organist of St Luke's, Chelsea, and in 1838, succeeded Attwood at St Paul's Cathedral. Goss wrote most of his music for church services including the popular carol *See Amid the Winter's Snow*, and the hymn *Praise my Soul, the King of Heaven*. He retired in 1872 and was knighted by Queen Victoria. Among his students was Arthur Sullivan. He is buried in St Paul's Cathedral.

58. **FARINGDON, Oxfordshire**

~ Faringdon House, Faringdon ~

Faringdon House was the home of Lord Berners from 1931 until his death in 1950. The present house, built on the site of a previous Faringdon House which had been badly damaged during the Civil War, was started in 1780. Berners, born in 1883, gave up his job with the Foreign Office upon succeeding to the title in 1918, in order to devote himself to music and the arts. Though he took his music, writing and painting very seriously, Berners was an eccentric. He used to dye his pigeons different colours, built the Faringdon Folly in 1935 in order to give local people work and kept a giraffe as a pet. While working as a diplomat, he had been composing under his family name of Gerald Tyrwhitt. He was for a short period a pupil of Stravinsky, who stayed at Faringdon House several times in the Thirties, and Alfredo Casella. Berners' musical works included *Trois morceaux*, *Fantasie espagnole*, *Fugue in C minor*, and several ballets including *The Triumph of Neptune*, which was based on a story by Sacheverell Sitwell, and *Luna Park*. He composed songs and film scores, most notably for the 1947 film of *Nicholas Nickleby*. He wrote an opera, *Le Carosse du Saint Sacrement*. Among other guests who stayed at Faringdon House, were Constant Lambert, Salvador Dalí and William Walton who wrote his *Three Songs* here and later dedicated *Belshazzar's Feast* to Berners. The house is not open to the public but the orangery and park are occasionally. Lord Berners' ghost is said to still walk the grounds.

www.faringdonfolly.org.uk

59. FITTLEWORTH, Sussex

– Brinkwells, Fittleworth –

With World War One interrupting his composition, and wanting to escape the constant stream of visitors to his house in London (42 Netherhall Gardens), Elgar began to look for a country retreat. He found it in Brinkwells, a thatched cottage in the middle of woodlands just north of Fittleworth. The lease was held by the artist Rex Vicat Cole, who was away at war. Elgar, his wife Alice and daughter Carice, moved in in May 1917. Shortly afterwards Elgar sent to London for his spare Steinway piano, taking over Vicat Cole's studio as his music room. He quickly began composing a violin sonata, string quartet and piano quintet. He also conceived and wrote most of the cello concerto. The idyll was broken, however, when a neighbour in London started building a garage close to his music room and the London house was burgled. Elgar put it on the market. He tried to buy Brinkwells but the owner wouldn't sell. And then in 1920, the increasingly frail Alice died. Elgar went down to Brinkwells to get over his grief, but he had lost the urge to compose. He returned for the last time in 1921 and heralded the end of his creative life in a letter to a friend: 'I feel like these woods – all aglow – a spark wd. start a flame – but no human spark comes.'

60. FLEET, Hampshire

– Stanton Lodge, Crookham Road, Fleet, Hampshire –

It was known as Booth Lodge or Farmhouse when Sir Arthur Sullivan rented this house in the summer of 1888 and wrote practically all of *The Yeomen of the Guard* here. It was Sullivan's practice to rent somewhere, or stay in the homes of friends, just outside London, in order to have the quiet needed to complete his scores. He had been brought up in nearby Camberley but the lure of Fleet may have had something to do with the village's proximity to Farnborough Abbey where Sullivan's friend, the Empress Eugenie, lived. More likely, however, was its proximity to the racecourses at Ascot, Epsom, Windsor and Kempton Park. Between 1894 and 1896 Sullivan owned two racehorses, Cranmer and Mark Blue, both of which he sold at a loss. He frequently lost huge sums of money betting on horses. That summer he also went rowing along the Basingstoke canal to Odiham.

61. FRIMLEY, Surrey

– Frimhurst, Frimley Green, Camberley, Surrey, GU16 6NU –
This Victorian house off the B3012 Guildford Road was the home of Dame Ethel Smyth from the age of nine. She had been born in Sidcup House, on the corner of St John's Road and Sidcup High Street, on 22 April 1858 (her memoirs say 23 April but her birth certificate has the 22nd). The house was demolished in 1929 to make way for Market Parade. Smyth's father was a General in the Royal Artillery who had rented Sidcup House when posted from India to command the Woolwich Artillery depot. In 1867 he was again promoted this time to the Artillery depot in Aldershot and the family moved to Frimhurst. It was to be her home until 1894 when her father died. It was also where she became interested in music. When she was 12, her German governess, who had studied music in Leipzig, played Beethoven to her on the piano and she was hooked. She was determined to become a composer. Her passion for music did not, however, meet with her father's approval. He posted the officer neighbour who was teaching her piano to Northern England so that her lessons might end, but Smyth fought back. She refused to attend family meals, go to social functions or go to church. After two years her father gave in and agreed she could study in Leipzig. There she met Brahms, Greig, Mahler and Tchaikovsky among others. Tchaikovsky wrote of her: 'Miss Smyth is one of the

few women composers whom one can seriously consider to be achieving something in the field of music creation... she has the potential to become a very serious and gifted composer.' He wrote this having heard a performance of her violin sonata. As a woman in a man's world, Smyth had to struggle harder than most for recognition. That recognition eventually came with her 1893 *Mass in D*. Her opera *The Wreckers*, her most popular work, also gained widespread approval. A formidable lady and the most successful woman composer Britain has so far had, she became a suffragette and was jailed for two months for throwing a rock through a minister's window. She wrote the suffragette hymn, *The March of the Women*, and when other suffragettes jailed in Holloway courtyard began to sing it, Smyth conducted them through the bars of her window with a toothbrush. Following her father's death, Frimhurst was sold and Smyth moved into a house on the Portsmouth Road, Camberley, called One Oak. One Oak is now a carvery. In 1910, she moved to her final home, a house on the outskirts of Woking. Frimhurst itself is now Frimhurst Family Centre, a home which disadvantaged families can visit for short breaks.

62. FRISTON, Sussex

– Friston Field, Old Willingdon Road, Friston, – East Dean, Sussex

The composer Frank Bridge had this house built and lived here from 1923 until his death in 1941. Bridge had been born in Brighton in 1879, and was a student at the Royal

College of Music with Vaughan Williams, Gustav Holst and John Ireland. After leaving college, he was in great demand as a viola player and conductor, frequently being called upon to deputise for Sir Henry Wood. He made his first impact as a composer in 1912 with the orchestral suite *The Sea*, a piece which, together with his 1927 orchestral work *Enter Spring*, was to have a profound effect upon Benjamin Britten, who became his pupil and was a frequent visitor to Friston. Britten acknowledged his debt to Bridge with his *Variations upon a theme of Frank Bridge*. *Enter Spring* was written here and was originally entitled *On Friston Down*. Other works written here include the 3rd and 4th String Quartets, the 2nd Piano Trio, *Oration* for cello and orchestra, *Phantasm* for piano and orchestra, the overture *Rebus* and *Divertimenti* for woodwing quartet. Bridge was taken ill while repairing his car at Friston Field and died in hospital in Eastbourne on 10 January, 1941. His ashes are interred in St Mary's Church in Friston where there is a memorial door, with a framed remembrance beside it, inside the south porch.

63. GARSINGTON, Oxfordshire

– Garsington Manor –

Garsington Manor was once owned by Lady Ottoline Morell and among the many visitors here were Peter Warlock, DH Lawrence, William Walton, Aldous Huxley, Lytton Strachey, Siegfried Sassoon, Rupert Brooke and TS Eliot. A Tudor building in a village near Oxford, the Manor was being used as a farmhouse when the Morells bought and restored it. They sold it in 1928. Banker Leonard Ingrams bought the house in 1982, and in 1989 he and his wife Rosalind founded an annual open air opera season in the garden. The Garsington Opera Festival quickly established itself as one of the most vibrant in Britain. Following the death of Leonard Ingrams, the 2010 season was announced as being the last to be held at the Manor House, which is not open to the public.

64. GATESHEAD, Tyne and Wear

~ St Mary the Virgin Church, Church Chare, ~ Whickham, Gateshead

There's a memorial cross in the churchyard in memory of the composer William Shield, one of Gateshead's most illustrious sons. Shield was born in the village of Swalwell on 5 March 1748 and baptised in this church. The house in which he was born, opposite the Three Tuns pub, was demolished in 1936. Apprenticed to a boat-builder, Shield studied music with Charles Avison, was heard playing the violin by Giardini and encouraged to take up music professionally. On Giardini's invitation, he became a member of the Italian Opera orchestra in London and one of London's leading viola players. He was also a friend of Haydn. He wrote many successful theatrical pieces and songs, and in 1817 was appointed Master of the King's Musick. Shield's main claim to fame, however, is that it has now been proved he wrote the tune for *Auld Lang Syne*. It was always supposed that Robert Burns, who wrote the words, had also written the music, basing it on a folk song.

Indeed Burns claimed to have written it in 1788, inspired by hearing a man singing in a pub. Recent research shows, however, that the tune comes from the overture to *Rosina*, a music drama written by Shield five years earlier. The original score for *Rosina* is in Gateshead Public Library. He also provided the music for another Burns song: *Coming through the Rye*. Shield died at his London home in Berners Street on 25 January 1829 at the age of eighty and is buried in Westminster Abbey.

65. GERRARDS CROSS, Buckinghamshire

– Lindens, Bull Lane –

This was the home from 1961 until his death on 14 February 1986 of the composer Edmund Rubbra. Although officially retired as a teacher from both Oxford University and the Guildhall School of Music, he continued to compose. In 1980 he suffered a stroke brought on, he claimed, by the completion of his eleventh symphony. His final composition was the *Sinfonietta* for large string orchestra, and he was working on a twelfth symphony at the time of his death.

66. GLOUCESTER, Gloucestershire

– The Cathedral –

Gloucester Cathedral, one of the most beautiful cathedrals in the world, was built in the twelfth century. Nine-year-old Henry III was crowned here in 1216, and the cathedral contains the tomb of King Edward II who was murdered at nearby Berkeley Castle in 1327. The stunning cloisters were used as a location for the corridors of Hogwarts School of Witchcraft and Wizardry in the Harry Potter films. As one of the homes of the Three Choirs Festival it has seen many first performances. There is a memorial tablet to the composer Sir Hubert Parry, erected in 1922, with lines on it by Robert Bridges, Poet Laureate.

Among organists of the Cathedral was Samuel Sebastian Wesley, the son of Samuel, the founder of Methodism. SS Wesley was born in London in 1810, became a choirboy of the Chapel Royal and organist at several London churches. He then moved to the cathedrals of Hereford (1832), Exeter (1835), Leeds Parish Church (1842), Winchester (1849) and Gloucester (1865 until his death in 1876). Considered to be the finest organist of his time, he was noted particularly for his extemporising. He was a fervent advocate of raising the standard of church music and many of his church compositions are still in use. Herbert Brewer became organist in 1897, remaining in the post until his death in 1928. Born in Gloucester in 1865, Brewer was a chorister at the Cathedral before going to Oxford and the Royal College of Music. A prominent conductor of the Three Choirs Festival and organ recitalist, as well as composer, Brewer did much to help popularise music for which he was knighted in 1926. Among those who studied with him was the poet and songwriter Ivor Gurney. A blue plaque on the wall of Boots in Eastgate Street commemorates the fact that Gurney was born in 3 Queen Street (the building no longer survives) in August 1890. For six years he was a chorister at the Cathedral. He studied at the Royal College with

Stanford who said of him that he was potentially the best composer of all those Stanford had taught but that he was impossible to teach. At the outbreak of the First World War, Gurney enlisted and fought at the battle of the Somme where he was gassed. He already suffered from depression and never really recovered his health. He spent the last fifteen years of his life in mental institutions and died in 1937. He is buried in St Matthew's Churchyard, Twigworth, on the outskirts of Gloucester.

– St Mary de Lode Church, Gloucester –

Contains a stained glass window in memory of Gurney, installed on 22 October 2000. The oldest parish church in Gloucester, it is, according to legend, the burial place of Lucius, a king of Britain who converted to Christianity and established a bishopric in Gloucester during the second century AD. The church contains an historic organ. The original single manual instrument appears to have been used in the Roman Catholic chapel of St Mary, Moorfields, in London and for performances of oratorio in London theatres, which gave rise to another legend that it had been played by Handel. In fact Handel died long before the organ was built in around 1800. A second manual was added later together with an extremely rare 'nag's head' swell mechanism involving a counterweighted lever arm and piece of rope. The organ was installed in St Nicholas Church in Westgate Street in 1831 and moved to St Mary's when the church closed in 1971.

67. GOUDHURST, Kent

– Finchcocks Living Museum of Music, Goudhurst, – Kent TN17 1HH

This Georgian manor house, built in 1725, was acquired by the pianist Richard Burnett in 1970 to house his collection of a hundred historic keyboard instruments, thirty-five of which have been fully restored. There are open days, concerts, musical tours, courses and educational programmes together with (by prior arrangement) the opportunity to play some of the instruments. A piano festival is held in September.

www.finchcocks.co.uk

68. GREAT PACKINGTON, Warwickshire

– St James's Church, Great Packington –

The composer Richard Mudge, who was born in Bideford, Devon, in 1718, was the vicar of St James's Church on the edge of Packington Park. The church was rebuilt in 1789 to celebrate the recovery of King George III from madness, so this is not the building Mudge knew. He was chaplain to Lord Aylesford before becoming rector, and an accomplished composer, particularly of concertos, although so far only six, including a fine trumpet concerto, have been discovered. Mudge was also the vicar at nearby Little Packington. He died in April 1763 but there is no trace of his grave in either place. The church has another important musical connection: the organ was designed by Handel who built it in 1749 for his friends the Jennens family at Gopsall Hall.

69. GREAT WITLEY, Worcestershire

– St Michael and All Angels Church, Great Witley –

This quite remarkable Baroque church, formally part of the Witley Court estate, now Great Witley and Little Witley parish church, has a connection to Handel. The original house on the site was owned by the Foley family. In 1747, Lord Foley decided to rebuild the plain brick country church that was linked to the main house by an underground passage but before work could begin, he died. However, his widow and son decided to go ahead with the rebuilding in his memory. At that time the Duke of Chandos (whose country estate was at Cannons in Edgware, Middlesex, a house described by Daniel Defoe as 'the most magnificent palace in England') had lost the family fortune and was being forced to sell up. Cannons included a marvellous Baroque chapel in which Handel, the Duke's house composer, had played the organ and first performed several important works. Lady Foley and her son, the new Lord Foley, acquired many of the chapel's fittings at auction including the elaborate gilded plasterwork, ten painted glass windows depicting scenes from the New Testament, ceiling paintings by the Italian artist Antonio Bellucci, and the organ. These were taken from Edgware to Great Witley on the back of a cart. The present organ case is the case of the instrument on which Handel played and some of the pipes may also be from the original organ. The building, considered by many to be the finest Baroque church in Britain, has superb acoustics and a regular concert programme. Sir Walter Parratt, Master of the Queen's and King's Musick, was organist here from

1861 until 1868. The main house, converted into one of the finest Victorian palaces in England by the Earl of Dudley, who bought the estate in 1837, was gutted by fire in 1937. The ruined house and its grounds, in which the Jerwood Foundation Sculpture Park of modern British sculpture has been opened, are now the responsibility of English Heritage.

www.greatwitleychurch.org.uk

70. HAMPTON COURT, Middlesex

– Hampton Court Palace –

One of the jewels of English architecture with its extraordinary mix of periods and styles from Tudor to Wren to Georgian. Built by Thomas Wolsey, the palace was purloined by King Henry VIII and so contains one of the King's Chapel Royals. The choir of the Chapel Royal was a fixed body of men who sang the services wherever the King was staying. They did not belong to one building. It was in the Chapel Royal here that Archbishop Cranmer handed King Henry VIII a letter outlining accusations of unchaste behavior against the new Queen, Catherine Howard. She was executed not long afterwards. In the Great Hall there is a minstrels' gallery which is one of the few of its kind still in use in Britain. The sort of music King Henry would have heard performed here can be found in the Royal Appendix at the British Library, a collection of music performed at court, usually by the King's singing men as they were known, and probably put together by one of his courtiers. The collection includes some thirty pieces thought to be by the king himself although how much Henry really had to do with their composition is debatable. Among the rest of the 120 pieces are compositions by court composers such as William Cornyish (c1468-1523) and Thomas Farthing, both of whom must have played at Hampton Court many times. Cornysh was not just a musician, although he did take ten choirboys to the Field of the Cloth of Gold for which he was allowed two pence a day for their food. He was a noted composer, playwright, actor and pageant master who also, on occasions, provided the king with guttering, paving and sanitary conveniences.

www.hrp.org.uk/hamptoncourtpalace

71. HAREFIELD, MIDDLESEX

– Breakspear House –

This large Georgian mansion, set in extensive grounds, allegedly takes its name from the fact that Nicholas Breakspear, the only English Pope, is supposed to have lived in a house on the site. This is probably just fanciful. Its musical connection is that WS Gilbert rented the house as a summer retreat every year between 1883 and 1890, paying an annual rent of £900. He started writing *Princess Ida* in the house and wrote much of the libretto for *The Gondoliers* here. He also played a lot of tennis on the court he had installed. If he had to go for a meeting in London, he would catch the train from nearby Uxbridge to Paddington. It was on one of these trips that he missed the train and had to wait an hour for the next one, a wait which gave him plenty of time to study the advertisements. One in particular caught his eye: a picture of a Beefeater at the Tower of London in an advertisement for the Tower Furnishing Company. This gave him the idea for *The Yeomen of the Guard*. His annual children's parties and firework displays, held in Breakspear House and the gardens, were eagerly anticipated.

The house was acquired by the local council in 1942 and in 1956 was turned into a residential home for the elderly. That closed in 1987 and the house was allowed to fall into disrepair. It has subsequently been converted into flats.

72. HARROGATE, NORTH YORKSHIRE

– Christ Church, The Stray, High Harrogate, HG1 4SW –

The composer Ernest Bristow Farrar was organist here from 1912 until 1916 when he enlisted and went off to war. Farrar, the son of a clergyman, had been born in Lewisham on 7 July 1885 and was brought up in the vicarage of St Mary the Virgin in Micklefield, near Leeds. He won a scholarship to the Royal College of Music to study with Stanford among others. While at the Royal College, he wrote a *Fantasy Prelude for Organ*. Other early works include *The Blessed Damozel* (which was given its first performance in Leeds conducted by Stanford), *The Orchestral Rhapsody No 1*, *The Open Road*, an orchestral suite *Out of Doors*, together with part songs and choral music. Just before he was due to finish at the Royal College, he was offered the post of organist at All Saints, the English church in Dresden, for six months. Farrar then returned to

Yorkshire to become organist and director of music at St Hilda's Church, South Shields, where he wrote the song cycle *Vagabond Songs*. Moving to Christ Church in 1912, he and his new wife Olive, set up home at 15 Hollins Road where Farrar did his private teaching. Among his pupils was the thirteen-year-old Gerald Finzi, for whom Farrar became something of a father figure. Among the works Farrar composed in Hollins Road were the tone poem *The Forsaken Merman* and the symphonic suite *English Pastoral Impressions*. At the outbreak of World War One, Farrar enlisted. Posted eventually to the Somme, he was granted leave in the summer of 1918 to return home to conduct the first performance of *Heroic Elegy*, a piece dedicated to his fallen comrades. Within a few days of his return to the front, he was killed at the battle of Epéhy Ronssoy. Finzi was distraught and wrote a Requiem for him (never published) while Frank Bridge dedicated his piano sonata to Farrar's memory. His widow, his father and her parents gave the Farrar Prize to the Royal College in his memory (won twice by Benjamin Britten).

– Birkholt, 22 Duchy Road, Harrogate –

In 1914, at the outbreak of World War One, thirteen-year-old Gerald Finzi and his mother left London, where he had been born on 14 July 1901, to live in Harrogate. He immediately began his studies with Ernest Farrar and then, when Farrar left for the war, with Sir Edward Bristow at York Minster, attending many of Sir Edward's rehearsals. He left Harrogate in 1922 to settle in the country at Painswick in Gloucestershire, hoping that a quiet life in the country would be conducive to composition.

– Valley Gardens, Harrogate, HG2 0QB –

This seventeen-acre public park in the centre of the town contains Elgar Walk, so called because it was the composer's favourite walk when staying here on holiday. Band concerts are held in the park every Sunday during the summer. The park is open all year round.

73. HARROW, MIDDLESEX

– All Saint's Church, Uxbridge Road, –
Harrow Weald, Middlesex

Lucy Gilbert, widow of WS Gilbert, erected a memorial to her husband in the transept of the church which she attended regularly and where their adopted daughter Nancy often sang. The bas-relief portrait of Gilbert, showing his left profile, is by Sir Bertram Mackennal RA. On either side are marble statuettes of Justice and Comedy while above are the symbolic masks of Tragedy and Comedy. The words beneath the profile were chosen from Proverbs by Gilbert's close friend, the barrister and entomologist Henry Rowland Brown: 'The tongue of the Just is as Choice Silver.'

– Grim's Dyke Hotel, Old Redding, Harrow –
Weald, Middlesex HA3 6SH

Grim's Dyke was built originally in 1870 for the painter Frederick Goodall by well-known London architect Norman Shaw, the man responsible for New Scotland Yard. It was finished in 1872 and takes its name from the ancient defensive earthwork which runs from Pinner Hill to Bentley Priory. In 1890 the house was bought by the writer William Schwenck Gilbert. Here he wrote the librettos for *Utopia Limited*, his satire of the Victorian world, and *The Grand Duke*, his final collaboration with Sullivan. Already enormously successful as a result of his partnership with Sullivan, Gilbert was surrounded at Grim's Dyke by the trappings of success: 110 acres of farmland, tennis courts, greenhouses filled with peaches and melons, forty servants and a lake which he created himself and of which he was extremely proud. On 29 May 1911, Gilbert drowned in the lake, having a heart attack while attempting to save one of two local girls he had invited for a swim. Lady Gilbert stayed in the house until her own death in 1936. It would appear that, such was the estrangement between Sullivan and Gilbert at this time, that Sullivan only visited Grim's Dyke once, in May 1893, in company with his nephew Herbert. They stayed three days while Sullivan and Gilbert discussed *Utopia Limited*.

In 1970, the house, a listed building, was opened as a hotel. The music room, with its minstrel's gallery and impressive floor-to-ceiling Cornish alabaster chimney-piece, is now used for concerts and receptions, while the library in which Gilbert wrote is the hotel bar. There is the inevitable Gilbert Suite, complete with four-poster, and the G&S connection is celebrated with regular musical evenings and soirees, including G&S dinners.

www.grimsdyke.com

– 25 Southway, North Harrow, Middlesex –

The composer Havergal Brian, who had been born in the Potteries in 1876, moved here in October 1940 and stayed for eighteen years. His work, once championed by Elgar, Beecham and Henry Wood, was then out of favour and rarely performed. That didn't stop him working, though. While here he wrote seven symphonies, four operas, his fifth *English Suite*, plus various other orchestral works. In 1958 he left for Shoreham, where his daughter and her husband had a house, only because the lease here had run out and he could not afford any other properties in the area.

74. HEREFORD

– The Cathedral, Hereford –

Hereford is one of the three cathedral settings for the Three Choirs Festival, the oldest continuous music festival in Europe (the others are Gloucester and Worcester). The festival was founded in 1720 and is held annually during the middle of August. Edward Elgar first visited the Three Choirs Festival in Hereford in 1878 as a violinist and made his last appearance here in 1933, the year before he died, conducting the young Yehudi Menuhin as soloist in his violin concerto. He had written the concerto when he lived in the city. According to some, the cathedral was the workplace of the composer, mathematician and astrologer John Dunstable, who is supposed to have been based at Hereford when not travelling abroad in the service of the Duke of Bedford or working as a spy. The evidence is flimsy to say the least and is based almost entirely on the fact that, at the time Dunstable was alive, there was a canon at the cathedral with the name of John Dunstayville.

Among musicians who have definitely worked here are Samuel Sebastian Wesley and John Bull. Wesley was appointed organist in 1832 at the age of twenty-two and stayed until 1835 when he moved to Exeter. Bull was born in England around 1562 and died in Antwerp in 1628. At about the age of twenty, he became the cathedral organist, before being appointed organist of the Chapel Royal, where he had been a chorister. He had a high reputation as a keyboard player and when he had to leave London in a hurry following trouble at court, he was welcomed in the Low Countries. His writing for the virginals in particular marks him out as one of the pioneers of keyboard composition.

– 20 Church Street, Hereford –

This was the home of George Robertson Sinclair, organist at the Cathedral from 1889 until his death in 1917. Sinclair was a great friend of Elgar and it was his dog, Dan, who fell into the River Avon while he and Elgar were going for a walk. The incident is immortalised in the eleventh *Enigma Variation*. Dan was buried under the big apple tree. The tree no longer stands and the stone which marks Dan's grave is alongside a telegraph pole in the grounds of 102 East Street, backing on to 20 Church Street.

– Plas Gwyn, 27 Hampton Park Road, Hereford –

Edward Elgar moved to Plas Gwyn in 1904, the year he was knighted. It is a large house with a large garden and an orchard overlooking the river, a fitting home for Britain's leading composer. That same year Elgar was offered a chair of music created especially for him by Birmingham

University. Plas Gwyn became the centre for a dangerous hobby. Elgar took a keen interest in chemistry (he patented the Elgar Sulpheretted Hydrogen Apparatus) and converted an outhouse in the garden, which he named The Ark, into a laboratory. Strange smells frequently emanated from the Ark, together with the sound of the occasional explosion. Elgar left Plas Gwyn in 1911. While here he played the organs at the Cathedral, St Francis Xavier's Church in Broad Street and St Andrew's Church in Hampton Bishop. He is supposed to have been inspired to write the *Elegy for Strings* by the view from nearby Mordiford Bridge where he would often go fishing. His connection with Hereford was commemorated in 2005 by the unveiling on 25 September in the Cathedral Close of a life-size bronze statue by Jemma Pearson. The bronze, which shows the composer with his beloved Sunbeam bicycle, was unveiled by the mezzo Dame Janet Baker.

75. HIGHNAM, GLOUCESTERSHIRE

~ Highnam Court, Highnam ~

This is the house in which the composer Hubert Parry, best known for his setting of *Jerusalem*, spent his childhood. There had been a manor house on the site for many centuries but the present house dates from about 1660 when the then owner, William Cooke, rebuilt it following the restoration of the monarchy. Further significant alterations were made in the mid-eighteenth century but the house then went into decline and was very run down when bought in 1838 by Thomas Gambier Parry, the composer's father, who set about restoring the house and its 27 acres of parkland.

Hubert Parry inherited the house in 1896 and stayed here intermittently throughout the rest of his life, dividing his time, when not teaching at the Royal College of Music, between Highnam and Rustington. Whenever Parry was staying here during the spring, he would go out into the gardens with a tuning fork and make a note of the pitch and interval of the cuckoo. If he couldn't be there, he would ask members of the staff to listen on his behalf, pick out the notes on a piano and keep a record of the dates.

An attempt was made in the 1980s by several musicians to turn the house into an arts centre but it came to nothing and the house is once again in private hands. It does open occasionally to the public.

www.highnamcourt.co.uk

76. HIGH WYCOMBE, BUCKINGHAMSHIRE

– Strawberry Patch, The Greenway, High Wycombe –

The composer and poet Ivor Gurney stayed here between 1913 and 1915 when he came to High Wycombe every weekend to play the organ of Christ Church, Crendon Street (now demolished). The house was then known as St Michael's, the road Castle Hill. Gurney became such a close member of the Chapman family, who owned the house, that he asked Kitty, one of the daughters, to marry him. She refused. It was a productive time for the 24-year-old. He worked on a symphony, a war elegy, violin sonata, string quartet and, of course, songs. Gurney wrote some 250 songs during his short career, at least half of them as good as almost anything written by a British composer. He returned to the area for a short time after World War One. As a result of being gassed, shell-shocked and wounded at Paschendale, Gurney had begun the slow disintegration that was to end with him being committed to an asylum. After his discharge from the army he had tried studying with Vaughan Williams, living in digs in London's Earl's Court, and then moved out to High Wycombe in 1919 in an attempt to supplement his meagre army pension playing the organ at Christ Church. He lived this time at 51 Queen's Road but only stayed a year.

77. HORHAM, Suffolk

– Chapel House, Horham –

In the 1960s, Britten's home in Aldeburgh was becoming overrun with visitors, particularly at Festival time, while the noise of planes from the nearby USAF base was never far away (even though Britten had managed to negotiate a reduction in flying while the Festival was actually on). He began, therefore, to look for somewhere else where he could write in peace. He tried France first and then Ireland but then found Chapel House, a cottage in a village about 20 miles from Aldeburgh. He built a music studio in the garden where he worked on *Owen Wingrave* and *Death in Venice*. He gave up the house in 1976 and it now belongs to Donald Mitchell, Britten's publisher, who has kept the studio intact. The house is not open to the public.

78. HORBURY, West Yorkshire

– 11 Shepstye Road, Horbury, Nr Wakefield, Yorkshire –

William Baines is one of the 'what might have he become's of English music. He was born here on 26 March 1899, a blue plaque commemorating the event. His father ran the local music shop, was organist at the Horbury Primitive Methodist Chapel and pianist at the local cinema. Baines, a gifted pianist, would sometimes deputise for him. Called up at the start of World War One, Baines was soon back home having been invalided out. He moved to York to earn his living as a composer, staying in Albemarle Road. In 1922, he died from TB, leaving behind some 150 compositions, mostly for piano. He was 22 and already demonstrating a talent that could have seen him become a leading member of his profession. He is buried in Horbury. A plaque to Baines was removed from the Primitive Methodist Chapel when it was demolished and is now in the Methodist Church (itself scheduled for demolition).

79. HUCKNELL, Notts

– Tenter Hill, Watnall Road, Hucknell –

The composer Eric Coates was born here on 27 August 1886. Coates (whose name was actually Frank Harrison Coates, although no one ever seems to have called him anything but Eric) was the son of a surgeon. He did not go to school but was taught by a governess. Hearing a friend play the violin made Coates determined to become a musician. He, too, began violin lessons but soon switched to the viola. He lived in this house until 1906 when he went to the Royal Academy of Music to study with Lionel Tertis. Coates was in great demand as a player especially of chamber music, but he was also busy composing. From the outset he was fascinated by what was known as 'light music' and was one of the first composers to make a living from radio and recording royalties.

80. HUDDERSFIELD, Yorkshire

– St Peter's Church, Byram Street, Huddersfield, HD1 1BU –

Sir Walter Parratt, Master of the Queen's Musick, was born in Huddersfield on 10 February 1841. His father was the organist of St Peter's, the Huddersfield Parish church, and one of Parratt's earliest appointments was as organist of St Paul's Church, Armitage Bridge, 3 miles south of Huddersfield. He was organist at Magdalen College, Oxford, for ten years and became the first Professor of Organ at the Royal College. His influence upon British organ playing was immense. Parratt died on 27 March 1924 in Windsor where he was organist of St George's Chapel for the last thirty-one years of his life. Although being Master of the Queen's Musick (and subsequently King's Musick for Edward VII and George V) meant writing the occasional piece, there is no evidence that Parratt wrote any royal music. Indeed, his compositions generally are few and undistinguished. There is a memorial to him in the grounds of St Peter's which contains the line 'by example and precept the outstanding organist of his time'.

81. INGATESTONE, Essex

– Ingatestone Hall, Ingatestone –

The Hall, on the outskirts of Ingatestone (a town just off the A12 north east of Brentwood) was built for Sir William Petre, Secretary of State for Henry VIII, in about 1540. Queen Elizabeth I was a guest here on more than one occasion. When the composer William Byrd left London and settled at nearby Stondon, he became a frequent visitor to Ingatestone Hall and many of his works were first performed here. Like his patron Sir John Petre, Byrd was a closet Catholic and the works he wrote here, some of them among his best known, included settings of the Latin Mass, an action for which he could have been put to death had he been caught. Although no one knows definitely how Byrd's motets were originally performed, recent research into performing practice suggests they were sung by a handful of people (possibly including servants) seated around a table. The Chapel has been pulled down but the Long Gallery and other rooms are as Byrd must have known them. Ingatestone Hall is open to the public.

www.ingatestonehall.com

82. INGRAVE, Essex

– The Old Rectory, Middle Road, Ingrave –

It was to the Old Rectory, now renamed Heatley's after the building's last incumbent, that two of the Rev Henry Heatley's daughters invited Vaughan Williams in December 1903 to tea to hear local people singing folk songs. Inspired by a lecture on folk song she had heard Vaughan Williams deliver, Georgiana Heatley had assembled some local singers for the composer to hear. But on the day they refused to cooperate. The next day, Vaughan Williams went to the home of Charles Potiphar, a labourer, and heard him sing *Bushes and Briars*. He then spent a fortnight here in the spring of 1904 making a collection of folk songs. He noted that 'they had no idea that the folk song still survived there until I suggested the possibility to them.' He noted down over fifty genuine songs. 'Most of the songs had beautiful and interesting tunes. As to the words, some were old ballads such as *Robin Hood and The Pedlar* or *The Green Glove*, some came off the ballad sheets, as for instance *The Lost Lady*, and others were regular country songs such as *The Painful Plough.*' Over a ten-year period Vaughan Williams collected some 810 folk songs, a labour that was to have a profound effect upon the English Hymnal, and upon English music of the twentieth century generally.

83. IPSWICH, Suffolk

– 11 Constitution Hill, Ipswich –

This was the home of EJ Moeran from 1929 until 1931. He had spent the previous three years living riotously in Eynsford with Peter Warlock. During that time he concluded he did not want to carry on as a composer. However, following the move to East Anglia, he and Warlock collected and arranged folk songs, and when a motoring accident confined him to a long convalescence in bed, he decided to reconsider his future. While Warlock helped nurse him back to health, he began composing again, this time straight from his head rather than from the piano. During this period, he wrote his *Canticles*, *Six Suffolk Folksongs* and the important *Sonata for Two Violins*. Following Warlock's suicide in December 1930, Moeran decided to go to Lingwood where his father had become the vicar.

– St Lawrence's Church, Dial Lane –

A fifteenth-century church in the middle of the town, possessing the oldest five-bell peal in Christendom. Four of the bells were cast in about 1450, the fifth in 1480. The bells are known as Wolsey's Bells after Henry VIII's Lord Chancellor who was born and raised in the town and must have heard them. It is reputed that Wolsey's uncle paid for one of them to be cast. In the 1970s, with no parishioners, the church was declared redundant and closed. It fell into disrepair but after twenty-five years as a ruin, was restored as a community centre and the bells, still undamaged, unmodified, and with their original clappers, replaced. Their opening peal rang out on 9 September 2009.

84. ISLE OF WIGHT

– Osborne House, East Cowes –

Queen Victoria had visited the Isle of Wight as a child and loved it, so when she and Prince Albert decided they needed a holiday home this was where they looked. They found a suitable house and estate on the island in 1845 and promptly knocked it down, rebuilding both the house and the gardens. It became their favourite home and was where Queen Victoria died in 1901. Among the visitors to the house was Felix Mendelssohn, the Queen's favourite composer. As well as playing for her at Buckingham Palace, he dedicated his Third Symphony, *The Scottish*, to her. The piano on which Mendelssohn played at Osborne is still on show. The house is looked after by English Heritage and is open to the public.

www.english-heritage.org.uk

– Ocean Hotel, Sandown –

In the summer of 1902, Richard Strauss was in London to conduct the Queen's Hall Orchestra in a concert of his music. Once the concert was over, he and his family headed for the Isle of Wight for a traditional seaside family holiday. They enjoyed it so much they returned the following year after Strauss had attended a three-day festival of his music in London. Strauss later recalled his son 'Bubi' (real name Franz) 'running all day in the hot sand, and going in and out of the sea'. Such was the domestic bliss of these two breaks that Strauss began work there and then on his *Symphonia Domestica*, an orchestral tone poem in one movement depicting a day in the life of his family. It also seems he helped entertain fellow guests at the hotel by taking part in a performance of *Enoch Arden*, a melodrama for speaker and piano he had composed in 1897 to a text by Alfred, Lord Tennyson (who was himself an Isle of Wight resident).

– Bermuda House, 3 Alexandra Gardens, Ventnor, – Isle of Wight

A plaque commemorates the stay in this house of Edward and Alice Elgar on their honeymoon in May 1889. They had been married at the Brompton Oratory in London on 8 May. Following Alice's decision to marry an impecunious Roman Catholic music teacher, her family stopped her allowance. The house is now available for self-catering holiday lets.

www.ventnorselfcatering.co.uk

– Holy Trinity Church, Trinity Road, Ventnor, – Isle of Wight PO38 1NS

The organist and composer Edwin Lemare, who became the highest paid organist in the world, learnt to play on Holy Trinity's 1865 Forster and Andrews pipe organ and was a member of the church choir. His father, the local music seller, was the church organist and choirmaster. Lemare was born at a house called The Mount, Ventnor, on 9 September 1865 and at the age of 21 went to the Royal Academy. He was a phenomenal organist and made his name with daily appearances at the 1884 Inventions Exhibition. This led to appointments in Cardiff, Sheffield and at St Margaret's, Westminster, among others. Accused of treating his church services as recitals, he left for a tour of the United States, where he quickly became incredibly popular, playing regularly to audiences of 10,000. He was also responsible for designing the organs in Auckland and Melbourne Town Halls. Few of Lemare's compositions, most of them designed to show off the organ, are performed today. The exceptions are his transcriptions of Elgar and Wagner, and the Andantino in D Flat better known as *Moonlight and Roses*. Lemare died in penury in Los Angeles on 24 September 1834.

85. ISLES OF SCILLY

– St Mary's, Isles of Scilly –

In the graveyard of the Old Town Church on St Mary's is buried Ann Cargill, the most scandalous singer and actress of her age, if not any age. She was born Ann Brown in 1760, the daughter of a coal merchant. At eleven she appeared at Covent Garden singing the role of Titania in Thomas Arne's *The Fairy Prince*. Four years later and a big star, she was appearing in Sheridan's *The Duenna* when she fell in love with a gunpowder maker. The affair became front-page news, forcing her father to obtain an injunction to prevent her leaving the house, so she ran away. A few months later she was due to appear as Polly in *The Beggar's Opera*. Outside the stage door her father attempted to grab her but the public refused to let him. She was, after all, earning £10 a week, making her the highest paid singer in the world (in today's money roughly £628 a week). Next she eloped to Edinburgh with a man called Cargill who was calling himself Doyle to escape his creditors. They actually married but it was not long before Ann was back in London appearing as Macheath in a gender-bending production of *The Beggar's Opera* (all male parts played by girls and vice versa). Enter Captain John Haldane of the British East India Company. They ran away together to India where Ann sang opera to packed, enthusiastic houses in Calcutta and Bombay. She was showered with jewels. But the condemnation of her presence in India by Prime Minister William Pitt, made her leave aboard a ship called *The Nancy*. In February 1784, within sight of the Isles of Scilly, *The Nancy* sank and everyone on board was drowned. A week later, Ann's body was found, dressed in a chemise and clutching what was rumoured to be her illegitimate child. They were buried on Rosevear, then transferred to the graveyard on St Mary's. Her jewels, estimated at the time to be worth £200,000, have never been recovered, although in 2008 two local men claimed to have located the wreck. Ann was 24 when she died.

86. ISLEWORTH, Middlesex

– St Mary's Vicarage, Osterley Road, – Spring Grove, Isleworth

The composer E(rnest) J(ohn) Moeran, known to his friends as Jack, was born here in 1894. He was the younger son of the Rev Joseph Moeran, vicar of St Mary's, Spring Grove. His father was of Irish descent, his mother Esther from Norfolk. The family moved to Bacton not long after Moeran, nicknamed Raspberry as a child because of his ruddy complexion, was born. He always had Irish sympathies combined with a love of East Anglia. An avid collector of Irish and English folk tunes, much of his orchestral writing and smaller scale work was based on folk motifs. He also wrote several large scale works. He died in Kenmare, Co Kerry, when he fell into the sea during a violent storm in December 1950.

– Lancaster House, Borough Road, – Spring Grove, Isleworth

This is all that remains of the London International College, one of the earliest attempts to provide an international education in the belief it would help stop wars and promote free trade. The full name of the school was the London International College of the International Education Society. Work on the building began in 1866 and was completed in 1867. Frederick Delius (1862–1934) was a pupil at the school from 1876 until 1879. Hit on the head with a cricket stump, he was recovering in the school sanitarium when he wrote his first piece of music: a song entitled *When Other Lips*. The school closed in 1889 and the buildings were sold. They later became the Osterley campus of Brunel University and are now part of a luxury housing development.

87. KENDAL, Cumbria

– St Thomas's Church, Shyreakes Lane, Crosscrake, – Kendal, Cumbria LA8 0AB

Mary Wakefield, the founder of competitive singing festivals in Britain, is buried here. The daughter of a local banker, she was born on 19 August 1853 at the Wakefield

Bank House, Stricklandgate, Kendal, later moving to Sedgwick House, four miles outside the town. She was a talented singer who gave many charity concerts and sang at the Gloucester Festival. Barred by the conventions of the day from pursuing a career as a professional singer, she poured her love of music into a desire to make it more available to rural communities. She founded and trained a number of choirs in the villages around Kendal and together with her sister Agnes, brought them together for the first time in 1885 to take part in a 'Singing Competition' held at Sedgwick House to raise money for Crosscrake Church. From this modest beginning, she went on to form the Mary Wakefield Music Festival which still happens today. Several of the choirs she founded still take part in the Festival. Mary Wakefield died in 1910. A plaque in Kendal Town Hall records her achievements.

88. KILCOT, nr Newent, Gloucestershire

– Beavans Hill, Kilcot –

This was the home, from 1927 until his death in 1960, of the composer Rutland Boughton. Now largely forgotten, Boughton was, in his day, more highly regarded than even Vaughan Williams, who visited him here. There is a blue plaque on the wall to commemorate his tenure.

Boughton was born on 23 January 1878 in Aylesbury where his father was a grocer. Offered a place at the Royal College to study with Stanford and Walford Davies, he only lasted a year because his money ran out. Invited onto the staff of the Birmingham Institute of Music by Granville

Bantock, he proved to be an inspirational teacher and choral conductor. As a composer he was heavily influenced by Wagner, and, inspired by what Wagner had done in Bayreuth, set out to create a new form of what he called 'choral drama' in England, based on a projected Arthurian opera cycle. He also began to look for a suitable venue to hold a festival and eventually alighted on Glastonbury. The first Glastonbury Festival took place in 1914. It had been Boughton's intention to build a theatre in the Bayreuth manner but that proved impossible, so he hired the Assembly Rooms. He had also intended the festival to focus on his Arthurian operas but instead it opened with his opera *The Immortal Hour*, accompanied not by an orchestra but by a piano. *The Immortal Hour* was to become Boughton's only unqualified success, running for 216 performances in London, still the record number of consecutive performances for an opera. In spite of the success of the Glastonbury Festival, which put on more than 300 stage productions and over 100 concerts, Boughton staged his last in 1926 and moved to Kilcot. Here he wrote the last two of his Arthurian operas, his second and third symphonies and two oboe concertos, as well as much chamber music. He died at his daughter Joy's house in London in 1960.

89. KIMBERLEY, Norfolk

– St Peter's Church, Wymondham Road, Kimberley –

The composer John Jenkins, who died on 27 October 1678 at nearby Kimberley House, is buried in the church nave. He was born in Maidstone, Kent, in 1592, the son of a carpenter who occasionally made instruments. Next to nothing is known about his early life and he first surfaces as one of the musicians performing the masque *The Triumph of Peace* at court in 1634. He was a virtuoso player of the lute and the lyra viol and when the Civil War broke out, he did what most musicians did, got a job in the country – working first for the Derhams at West Derham, then for Harmon L'Estrange at Hunstanton. At some time in the 1660s he became the house musician of Lord Dudley North. North's son Roger, a keen amateur musician and historian to whom we owe accounts of Baroque performing practice in England at this time, wrote his biography. After the Restoration, Jenkins returned to court, retiring eventually under the patronage of Sir Philip Wodehouse (ancestor of PG Wodehouse) to Kimberley House (which no longer exists as he knew it, having been torn down and totally rebuilt in the eighteenth century).

Jenkins was a prolific composer, writing more than seventy suites for amateur players as well as fancies for viol consorts, settings of George Herbert's poetry and, according to North, dances 'by the cart-load'. His well-crafted music possesses a sensuous lyricism.

90. KING'S LYNN, Norfolk

– St Margaret's Church, King's Lynn –

Charles Burney was organist here from 1751 to 1755. Born in Shrewsbury in 1726, where he attended Shrewsbury

School, he was sent to London to study with Dr Arne of *Rule Britannia* fame, later becoming involved in London's musical life. In 1751, he moved to King's Lynn, hometown of his second wife, for the sake of his health and was immediately made organist of St Margaret's. It was while in King's Lynn that he conceived the idea of writing a history of Western classical music, a book of immense historical importance for which he travelled Europe to research. In 1760, having recovered from his ailments, he returned to London to become organist at the Chelsea Hospital where he stayed until his death in 1814. He was the father of the novelist Fanny.

91. KIRKBY STEPHEN, Cumbria

– Wharton Hall, Kirkby Stephen –

A fifteenth-century fortified manor house, now a farmhouse, this was the family home of the Wharton family. Thomas, Lord Wharton (1648–1715), is attributed with writing the words to the marching song *Lilliburlero* in 1687. He later boasted that it had sung James II out of three kingdoms. The music may have been by Purcell who published the song in a 1689 compilation of his work describing it as a new Irish tune. Indeed its origin could well have been Irish. Located at the end of a private drive some three miles long, the hall is not open to the public.

92. KNEBWORTH, Hertfordshire

– Knebworth House, Knebworth, Hertfordshire, SG3 6PY –

James Oswald (1710–69), Scotland's most prolific and successful eighteenth-century composer, lived here. He had been born in Crail, a small town in the north-east corner of Fife where his father was the local drummer, and was precociously talented. He was able to make up new traditional tunes until the cows came home and played the new-fangled Italian cello like an angel. He moved to Dunfermline and earned his living teaching the latest dance steps to the aristocracy and giving cello recitals, leaving when he was 25 to spend six years in Edinburgh where his patron was James, Duke of Perth, later to become Bonnie Prince Charlie's infantry commander. In 1741, at the age of 31, Oswald moved to London where he became an important music publisher and popular composer of songs, theatre music, chamber works and anything else which involved a fee. He taught music to the royal children and some people credit him with having composed *God Save the King*. He certainly held a court position from which he retired at the age of 53, before marrying his second wife in secret, the widowed Leonora Robinson-Lytton who had been left the run of Knebworth House by her first husband. Oswald became the honorary Lord of the Manor, and among his compositions there were the *Knebworth Jig* and *Norea Themes*. He was a member of the Temple of Apollo, a secret society of musicians in London. Oswald died at Knebworth early in 1769 at the age of 58.

www.knebworthhouse.com

93. LECKHAMPTON, Gloucestershire

~ St Peter's Church, Church Road, Leckhampton, ~ Cheltenham, Glos GL53 0QJ

John Barnett, considered by some to be the first composer of modern English opera, is buried here. Born in Bedford on 15 July 1802, he was supposedly a second cousin of Giacomo Meyerbeer. His father, a Prussian Jew named Bernhard Beer, changed his name to Barnett when he settled in England as a jeweller. Barnett showed such musical talent that by the age of eleven he was singing at the Lyceum in London. He also started writing songs and light theatrical pieces. In 1834, his first opera, *The Mountain Sylph*, was produced at the Lyceum. Unusually for the time, this was completely sung, without any dialogue. It was extremely successful and influenced Gilbert and Sullivan's *Iolanthe*. Barnett followed it up with *Fair Rosamund* and *Farinelli*, neither of which was well received, causing Barnett to give up the stage and move to Cheltenham to become a singing teacher. His compositions also included three string quartets and a violin sonata. It was in Cheltenham that his daughter Clara Kathleen Barnett (1844–1931) was born. She was to become the youngest person to enter the conservatoire in Leipzig. At that time women were not permitted to enroll on the composition course but she began composing, helped with her orchestration by fellow-student Arthur Sullivan. She eventually became an opera singer, settling in the United States where she taught singing and continued composing. Among her output were some hundred songs, two string quartets and a sonata for violin and piano.

Barnett's nephew, John Francis Barnett (1837–1916) was also a composer.

94. LEEDS, West Yorkshire

– St Peter-at-Leeds, Kirkgate, Leeds LS2 7DJ –

Leeds Parish Church is a Victorian construction which replaced a dilapidated medieval church. It was consecrated on 2 September 1841 when the organist, playing on the instrument which had been taken out of the medieval building, was Samuel Sebastian Wesley. Wesley was invited to become the church's organist and choirmaster, and held both posts from 1842 until 1849. He reformed the choir and helped establish the musical life of the church. The organ, on which regular recitals are given, is one of the most famous in Britain, certainly one of the most broadcast.

95. LEICESTER, Leicestershire

– Welford Road Cemetery, Welford Road, Leicester –

William Gardiner, a minor composer but very important promoter of Beethoven, is buried here. As well as his grave, there is a memorial plaque to him. Gardiner, a manufacturer of hosiery, was born in Leicester in 1770. He was gifted musically, singing at his father's friend's wedding when he was six and learning both piano and viola. He was also involved in the first English performance of music by Beethoven, an event which took place in Leicester. In 1793, as French troops approached Bonn, Mrs

Frances Bowater, daughter of the Earl of Faversham, and Abbé Dobler, the Elector of Cologne's chaplain, fled first to Hamburg then to Leicester, where Mrs Bowater lived. The Abbé was soon introduced to Gardiner. Among the music the Abbé had in his luggage was a copy of Beethoven's Violin Trio in E flat. He, Gardiner and a friend played this one evening in Mrs Bowater's house, three years before it was published in London. This was not just the first time a Beethoven work had been heard in England, it was among the first occasions his music had been heard outside Bonn. Gardiner became a fanatical promoter of Beethoven. He also loved Haydn's music and in 1804 sent Haydn six pairs of cotton stockings into which were worked quotations from his music. Sadly, the package never reached its destination. Gardiner also compiled *Sacred Melodies*, setting words of the Psalms to tunes from such German composers as Mozart, Haydn and Beethoven, and wrote the books *Music of Nature* and *Music and Friends*. He died in Leicester on 16 November 1853.

96. LEWTRENCHARD, Nr Oakhampton, Devon

– St Peter's Church/Lewtrenchard Manor –

Sabine Baring-Gould (1834–1924), who is best remembered for writing the stirring hymn *Onward Christian Soldiers*, was both squire and parson here and is buried in the churchyard. He lived in Lewtrenchard Manor, the family home, for the last forty-three years of his long life, and, although the house remains in the family, it is now leased as a country house hotel. Much of the present furnishing is as he would remember it. As well as being a hymn-writer, Baring-Gould was a historian, theologian and author of some 159 books, both fiction and non-fiction. He was, at one time, England's tenth most popular novelist and it was supposedly Baring-Gould who suggested the idea of Pygmalion to his friend George Bernard Shaw (Baring-Gould having met a mill girl while a curate in Yorkshire and sent her away to be educated before marrying her). He was also an eccentric. When teaching at Hurstpierpoint he would take classes with a pet bat on his shoulder. In 1881, he moved to St Peter's Church, to become the rector as well as the local squire. It was then that he became an avid collector of the folk songs of Devon and Cornwall. He visited old singers in their homes and in the fields. He would stay with friends and invite singers to join them. Baring-Gould was not a particularly good musician himself and asked two friends, Dr Frederick Bussell and the Rev HW Fleetwood Sheppard, to help him. One or other would join him on his travels to take down the music while Baring-Gould wrote down the words. Many of the songs were too robust for publication in Victorian times and Baring-Gould chose to modify the words, something for which he has occasionally been criticised. *Songs of the West* took him twelve years to compile and was published in four parts beginning in 1881. The book helped set the pattern for the first folk revival at the beginning of the twentieth century and put Baring-Gould in touch with Cecil Sharp. The two men collaborated closely with Sharp being a frequent visitor to Lewtrenchard Manor. Baring-Gould rated *Songs of the West* as the greatest achievement of his long and very varied life. He donated the manuscript copies of some 202 songs and his original notebooks to the Plymouth Library, while in 1992, his personal handwritten copy was discovered among some of his papers in Killerton House, near Exeter, to where they had been moved in the 1970s.

www.lewtrenchard.co.uk

97. LICHFIELD, Staffordshire

– Lichfield Cathedral, The Close, Lichfield –

Michael East, born in London c1580, was organist and choirmaster here from 1618 until his death in 1648. East had more of his work published than any other of his contemporaries, which may have helped fuel the rumour that he was the son of music publisher Thomas East, a rumour since dispelled. They may have been distantly related; we're not sure. East was a noted writer of madrigals in particular, being a contributor to Thomas Morley's *The Triumphs of Oriana* in 1601. He moved to Ely in 1609 to become a lay clerk in the cathedral choir, and by 1618 was in Lichfield. He held his posts as organist and choirmaster for twenty years.

98. LIMPSFIELD, Surrey

– St Peter's Church, Limpsfield –

The Yorkshire-born composer Frederick Delius (1862–1934) is buried in the churchyard here. Although Delius, who died on 10 June 1934, was buried originally in the French village of Grez-sur-Loing near Fontainebleau, where he had spent much of his life, he had expressed a wish not long before he died to be buried in 'a quiet country churchyard in a south of England village.' St Peter's was chosen, even though Delius had no connection whatsoever with the church, by his friends Beatrice and May Harrison who lived in nearby Oxted and whose mother had been buried here.

Delius had originally been interred in France without a priest present at a very low-key event attended by Delius's amanuensis, Eric Fenby, the conductor Otto Klemperer and a handful of mourners. Almost a year later in Limpsfield, on 24 May 1935, a huge crowd of mourners including Vaughan Williams and many other prominent musicians, gathered for the re-burial. Members of the London Philharmonic Orchestra performed afterwards with Beatrice Harrison playing her cello; the oration was delivered by Sir Thomas Beecham. Jelka, Delius's widow, had caught pneumonia on the Channel crossing with her husband's remains, and was too ill to attend. She died four days later and was buried in the same grave.

There are other important musical graves in Limpsfield. As well as their mother, Beatrice and May Harrison are buried here. There were four Harrison sisters, all of whom learnt a different instrument so that they could play ensemble pieces together. Two of the sisters went on to have very distinguished careers. May (1891–1959) was a violinist, much admired by Kreisler. She gave the first performance of Delius's *Third violin sonata* in 1930, accompanied by Sir Arnold Bax. It was for her and her sister Beatrice (1892–1965) that Delius wrote his *Double Concerto*. Beatrice also gave the first performances of Delius's cello sonata and cello concerto as well as the first performance of Elgar's *Cello Concerto* outside London (at the Three Choirs Festival in Hereford). She became Elgar's favourite interpreter of the work.

The ashes of the phenomenal Australian pianist Eileen Joyce (1908-91), considered by many to be among the greatest pianists of the last century, are buried here next to the grave of the conductor and great Delius champion, Sir Thomas Beecham. When Beecham died in 1961, he was buried in Brookwood Cemetery.Thirty years later, his remains were exhumed and reinterred here, some 10 metres from Delius.There are also the graves of the conductor Norman del Mar (1919-94) and clarinetist Jack Brymer (1915-2003).

– Whitegates Cottage, Grant's Lane –

The composer Michael Tippett first came to the Limpsfield area in 1929, shortly after leaving the Royal College of Music, to take up a job teaching French at Hazelwood Preparatory School. He had learnt the language when his father retired, bought a hotel in Cannes and had taken the family there. When the hotel failed and his parents decided to go travelling, Tippett was sent to boarding school in Edinburgh. He hated it, which may have had something to do with his emerging homosexuality. In any case he was taken away from the school and sent instead to Stamford Grammar School in Lincolnshire. While there he had taken piano lessons and decided, without really knowing what it entailed, that he wanted to be a composer. Someone suggested that if he was serious, he ought to go to the Royal College and so, at the age of 18, he enrolled. Five years later he emerged in desperate need of a job and gratefully accepted the offer from Hazelwood.

Another famous staff member had been the playwright Christopher Fry. Tippett lived initially in Chestnut Cottage in the school's grounds. Three years later in 1932 he moved to Whitegates Cottage and then in 1938 to Whitegates, a house he had had built for himself. This became his home until 1951. As well as teaching, Tippett became heavily involved in local amateur music-making. He was a slow worker but among the works he wrote while living here were *The Concerto for Double String Orchestra*, *A Child of Our Time*, the work which made his name, the *First Symphony* and much of the opera *The Midsummer Marriage*.

99. LINCHMERE, West Sussex

– Shulbrede Priory, Linchmere, nr Haslemere, – Surrey GU27 3NQ

Shulbrede Priory, two miles west of Fernhurst on the Linchmere road, belonged to Sir Hubert Parry's daughter Dorothea (known as Dolly) and her husband Arthur Ponsonby. Still the Ponsonby family home, it was originally an Augustinian priory founded in about 1190. All that remains of the original building is a vaulted hall (or slype) and buttery (part of the refectory) downstairs, and upstairs the prior's chamber. At the Dissolution, the Priory became a farmhouse and the prior's chamber was decorated with Tudor murals. One of them is unique in illustrating the medieval legend that on Christmas Day animals herald Christ's birth in words corresponding to their calls. The cock crows 'Christus Natus Est' ('Christ is born'), the duck quacks 'Quando, quando' ('When? When?'), the raven caws 'In hac nocte' ('In this night'), the bull bellows 'Ubi? Ubi?' ('Where? Where?') and the lamb bleats 'In Bethlem'.

Parry's suite of piano pieces, *Shulbrede Tunes*, was inspired by his daughter's family (especially his two grandchildren), the house and its surroundings. The Priory contains a small exhibition of Parry memorabilia. The house can be visited by special arrangement and is also open to the public on the Sunday and Monday of the May and August Bank Holidays.

Tel: 01428 653 049

100. LINCOLN, Lincolnshire

– The Cathedral –

William Byrd (1539/40–1623), one of the finest of Elizabethan madrigal composers and a leading figure in the musical development of Renaissance Britain, may have been born in Lincoln, although latest research believes it to have been in London where he became a choirboy at the Chapel Royal and studied under Thomas Tallis. In 1563, at the age of 23, he got his first job: as organist and choirmaster in Lincoln, remaining in the post for nine years. It was here that his compositional career really began to flourish. It wasn't all plain sailing, however. He had his pay docked in 1569 for 'certain matters alleged against him'. What those matters might have been we do not know but the guess is that the music he was providing for the Protestant services in the cathedral was considered too ornate, too Catholic. Complaints were certainly made about his over-elaborate use of the organ. But it wasn't all church music Byrd wrote in Lincoln. He also produced a number of important pavans and galliards. He left Lincoln in 1572 to become a Gentleman of the Chapel Royal in London following the death of Robert Parsons who drowned in the River Trent near Newark. Being close to court and to the centre of artistic activity, it was not long before Byrd had become acknowledged as the leading composer of his generation.

John Reading, who later went on to become organist at Winchester Cathedral and at Winchester College (for which he composed the famous school song, *Dulce Domum*) was Master of the Choristers in 1670, and Reginald Goodall, the eminent Wagnerian conductor who was born in Lincoln in 1901, was a choirboy here.

101. LINGWOOD, Norfolk

– Lingwood Lodge, Lingwood, Norwich –

This is where EJ Moeran came following the suicide of his friend Peter Warlock in December 1930, his father having been appointed vicar of St Peter's Church, Lingwood. Freed from the influence of Warlock, Moeran really began composing again. Here he completed *Songs of Springtime*, the *Farrago Suite* and *Four English Lyrics*. He also rewrote *Whythorne's Shadow*, having lost the original manuscript when he was drunk in Brussels on a trip with Warlock to meet Delius. They failed to meet up. It was from here that he started what were to become regular trips to Kenmure in Ireland.

102. LISCARD, Merseyside

– Holly Mount, 19 Holland Road, Liscard –

Granville Bantock moved here in 1898, following his appointment as conductor of the New Brighton Tower concerts. Bantock, the son of a doctor, had been born in London in 1868 and was one of that group of English composers who, in the first half of the twentieth century were popular, prolific and obsessed with Celtic mythology, culture and landscape but whose work is these days hardly ever performed. His father intended him to join the Indian Civil Service but Bantock had other ideas. One of his first jobs after leaving music college was conducting a musical theatre troupe on a world tour; it launched his career as a conductor. In New Brighton (across the Mersey from Liverpool) he performed contemporary music as well as the dances he was booked to provide. Among the composers he promoted were Joseph Holbrooke, Edward German, Hubert Parry and Stanford. He conducted the first performance of Elgar's *Minuet* and was a champion of Havergal Brian. Sibelius dedicated his Third Symphony to him and Elgar, *Pomp and Circumstance No 2*. He went on to become principal of the Birmingham Institute School of Music and succeeded Elgar as Professor of Music at Birmingham University. He helped found the City of Birmingham Orchestra which began its existence playing his overture *Saul*. He wrote a large number of tone poems, four operas, five cello concertos, four symphonies and many choral works. He was knighted in 1930 and is due a revival. Upon his death, his children took his ashes and scattered them on Moelyn Mawr in Snowdonia.

103. LOWESTOFT, Suffolk

– 21 Kirkley Cliff Road, Lowestoft –

A plaque on the wall outside marks the birthplace, on 22 November 1913, of Benjamin Britten. The house is still as it was when Britten's father started the practice, a dental surgery. Britten was the youngest of four children and this was his home until he was twenty-one.

104. LUDLOW, Shropshire

– Ludlow Castle –

There has been a castle in Ludlow for 900 years. Built originally by Marcher lord, Roger De Lacy, it has been enlarged and altered over the years and for a time was a royal palace. The Princes in the Tower were sent here by their father Edward IV; Prince Arthur (brother of Henry VIII) lived here with his bride, Catherine of Aragon; and Queen Mary Tudor and her court spent three winters here between 1525 and 1528. In September 1634, Milton's masque *Comus*, with music by Henry Lawes (1596–1662), a Gentleman of the Chapel Royal of Charles I and teacher of the Bridgewater children, was first performed in the Great Hall as part of the celebrations marking the Earl of Bridgewater becoming President of Wales and the Marches. Lawes took part in *Comus* as the Attendant Spirit. He also wrote the Christmas songs for Herrick's *Hesperides*.

– St Laurence's Church –

St Laurence's is one of the largest parish churches in England, a size which leads many people to think, erroneously, that it is a cathedral. In the north transept is a Snetzler Organ dating from 1764, in its original case. The ashes of the poet AE Housman were scattered outside the north door of the church and a plaque on the wall nearby commemorates him. Although not from Shropshire, Housman loved the countryside around Ludlow and his collection *A Shropshire Lad* inspired many settings, in particular by George Butterworth, Arthur Somervell, Ralph Vaughan Williams, Ivor Gurney and John Ireland. Housman was a dour professor of Latin at Cambridge University, and at a Trinity College dinner, vociferously attacked the settings of Vaughan Williams and Butterworth. He demanded that Herbert Howells, his neighbour, should never attempt to set any of his poems. Howells, who had actually been in the process of setting them, was so terrified he promptly destroyed what he had written. Butterworth also wrote a *Shropshire Lad Rhapsody* using material from his first song cycle.

105. LYDNEY, Gloucestershire

– High Street –

The composer Herbert Howells was born in a house on the High Street 'near to the Baptist Chapel' on 17 October 1892. His father was a painter and decorator who went bankrupt, something which was to have a deep effect on Howells. He won a scholarship to Lydney Grammar School where he soon showed promise as a musician and began composing. One of his first pieces, performed at the school, was a march which, according to family legend, his mother had discovered him composing at the piano in his nightclothes when he should have been in bed. At the age of 13 he became a pupil of Herbert Brewer at Gloucester Cathedral, studying with him for two years and then winning a scholarship to the Royal College of Music. There he studied with Charles Villiers Stanford and his *Mass in the Dorian Mode* was given its first London performance at Westminster Cathedral. A year later a piano concerto was performed in the Queen's Hall. But just as it looked as though he was about to make a name for himself, Howells, who was always physically frail, suffered a breakdown in his health. He spent much of his twenties either in St Thomas's Hospital, London, or in Lydney. His ashes were buried in Westminster Abbey.

106. LOWER BROADHEATH, Hereford and Worcester

− Elgar Birthplace Museum (formerly The Firs), − Crown East Lane, Lower Broadheath, Worcester WR2 6RH

Edward Elgar was born in The Firs on 2 June 1857. His father, William, was a pianist, violinist and piano-tuner; his mother a farmer's daughter. The house was rented and Elgar only lived here for two years but when created a baronet he took the title Sir Edward Elgar of Broadheath. The cottage, three miles east of Worcester, was purchased by the

Worcester City Corporation shortly after Elgar's death in the local hospital in 1934, and converted into a museum in 1973. A visitor and reception centre has been built close by. Among the collection of scores, photographs and other documents is the manuscript of the 2nd Symphony. The notice on the gate – Please Boult the Gate – is a dig at expense of the conductor Sir Adrian Boult, one of Elgar's most fervent champions.

www.elgarfoundation.org

107. MALVERN, Worcestershire

Malvern is a collection of villages along the eastern side of the nine-mile range of the Malvern Hills. The hills were a constant source of inspiration to Elgar who lived here and is buried in Little Malvern. It was in Malvern that he met Caroline Alice Roberts, daughter of Major General Sir Henry Roberts, when she came to him for lessons in piano accompaniment. They were married at Brompton Oratory on 8 May 1889, despite the opposition of her family who didn't think Elgar good enough for someone of her social position. Alice was not just a wife; she became Elgar's companion, inspiration and protector. Her loyalty, and conviction that Elgar was a great composer, never wavered. Immediately after their marriage they lived in Malvern at 7 The Lees, the house Alice was renting. They then moved to London but it was not a success and after two years they returned to Malvern, renting 4 The Lees while they searched for a suitable property in which to settle.

– Forli, 37 Alexandra Road, Malvern Link –

This is the house they moved into with their new daughter Carice in June 1891, and where Elgar wrote the work that finally made his name: *The Enigma Variations*. Elgar was 42 and generally considered to be little more than a competent provincial composer. He was still having to supplement his income by teaching and could only compose as the opportunity presented, so a semi-detached house in Malvern seemed a much better bet financially than staying in London. It was Alice who suggested the *Variations*. After dinner one evening in October 1898, Elgar sat down at the piano and played a theme. To amuse Alice he played it again in different guises asking her to guess which of their friends it might be. Alice recognised that what he was doing might have potential. Written during October and November 1898, *The Enigma Variations* was given its first performance the following June at St James' Hall, London, under the baton of Hans Richter. It was an immediate success. Other compositions written while living here were *The Spanish Serenade*, *The Serenade for Strings*, the *Chanson de Matin* and *Chanson de Nuit*, the cantatas *The Black Knight* and *King Olaf*, *Sursum Corda*, most of *Caractacus*, and the oratorio *The Light of Life*. The Elgars left in 1899 to go to Craeg Lea.

– Craeg Lea, 86 Wells Road, Malvern –

The home of the Elgar family from March 1899 until 1904, this was much more an Elgar house than Forli had ever been. It was detached and from his music room on the first floor he could see out across the Severn Valley. The name of the house is sometimes taken to be of Welsh origin. In fact it's an anagram of the initials of Edward, Alice and their daughter Carice, with their surname Elgar. It was here that Elgar completed *The Dream of Gerontius*, scoring it in his cottage retreat at Storridge. The first performance of *Gerontius* at the 1900 Birmingham Festival was not auspicious. Although conducted by Richter, whose championing of Elgar's music had made Elgar respected in Germany, the orchestra had not learnt the parts sufficiently well and *Gerontius* was deemed a flop. Other works written here include the overture *Cockaigne*, *Pomp and Circumstance Marches 1* and *2*, the *Coronation Ode, In the South*, and part of *The Apostles*. They left in 1904 to go to Hereford.

— St Wulstan's Roman Catholic Church, Ledbury Road, — Little Malvern

Elgar died on 23 February 1934, and is buried here alongside Alice who had died fourteen years earlier in 1920. Their daughter Carice, who died in 1970, is also buried here. Their graves are at the far end of the graveyard. Elgar had wanted to be cremated and have his ashes scattered on the River Severn but Carice persuaded him to be buried alongside Alice. Elgar's funeral was deliberately a very low key affair, attended only by ten or so friends. There was no music and as the service came to an end, flakes of snow began to fall upon the coffin.

— Wynd's Point, near the Herefordshire Beacon —

The summer retreat of the singer Jenny Lind, known as the Swedish Nightingale, and her husband, pianist Otto

Goldschmidt, founder of the Bach Choir. Lind was a close friend of Mendelssohn, Meyerbeer and Hans Anderson, and spent her last years in Malvern. She died on 2 November 1887 and is buried in Great Malvern cemetery in Wilton Road.

108. MARTIN HUSSINGTREE, Hereford and Worcester

– St Michael and All Angels –

Thomas Tomkins, one of the finest of seventeenth-century madrigalists, pupil of William Byrd, and arguably the culmination of the musical Renaissance in England, spent the last two years of his life at the Manor House next to St Michael's Church with his son Nathaniel and his daughter-in-law (who owned the house, now a farm).

Tomkins had been born in St David's, Pembrokeshire. When the family moved to Gloucester, Tomkins is thought to have gone to London to become a Chapel Royal chorister and study with William Byrd. By 1596 he had become organist and Master of the Choristers at Worcester Cathedral and also a Gentleman of the Chapel Royal. For years he commuted between Worcester and London fulfilling his duties to both institutions. In 1625 he took charge of arranging the music for King James' funeral and for the coronation of King Charles I. He lost his job at Worcester in 1642 when the city was captured by Cromwell's forces in the Civil War. The Dallam organ, the installation of which he had overseen in 1612, was destroyed and the choir disbanded. His wife died that same year. He did, however, continue to compose for the keyboard including possibly his best known piece *A Sad Pavan for these distracted Times*. With no job and no income, Tomkins and his new wife Martha, the mother of one of his choristers, moved to Martin Hussingtree to live with Nathanial in 1654. Tomkins died two years later in June 1656 and is buried in the churchyard. The exact site of his grave is not known.

109. MAYFIELD, Derbyshire

– Calwich Abbey, Mayfield, Ellastone –

The abbey which gave its name to the house on this site has long since vanished, as have most of the houses subsequently built here. One of the owners, who built himself a new house, was Bernard Granville (1700–75), an intimate friend of Handel. Handel was a frequent visitor here, helping Granville in 1736 select an organ for the Abbey. Granville was also bequeathed two pictures in Handel's will. In 1912, Granville's collection of original Handel scores was sold. This included fifteen operas. The current house, completed in 1850, is an overgrown wreck, abandoned during the depression between the two world wars. In the grounds is a lake fed by the River Dove. Handel is reputed to have composed his Water Music in the copper-roofed temple on the lake's edge. The temple is still there.

110. MICKLEFIELD, West Yorkshire

– St Mary the Virgin, Old Micklefield, Leeds –

The first occupants of the new vicarage built in 1887 during the restoration of St Mary the Virgin, were the Rev Charles Farrar and his family. Farrar's son, Ernest, was two-years-old. He had been born in Lewisham in July 1885 and was later to go to Leeds Grammar School, whose musical alumni also include the composer John Ireland, and, in later years, Philip Wilby, as well as Ricky Wilson, lead singer of rock band Kaiser Chiefs. There Farrar learnt the organ, becoming organist at St Mary's in 1903 after he had become an associate of the Royal College of Organists. He left Micklefield in 1905 when, at the age of 19, he won a scholarship to the Royal College of Music to study composition with Stanford and organ with Sir Walter Parratt. After graduation, he returned to the north and took up several posts as organist while continuing to compose. He taught the young Gerald Finzi. Farrar was killed on the Western Front in France in 1918.

111. NEWCASTLE UPON TYNE

– The Cathedral Church of St Nicholas, – Newcastle upon Tyne

The composer Charles Avison (1709–70) was organist here for more than thirty years. Born in Newcastle in February 1709, he was baptised at St John's Church in Grainger Street, the fifth child of Richard and Anne Avison who lived in the house alongside St Bartholomew's Nunnery in Nolt

Market. They were both musicians, his father being 'one of ye Waits', the official town band, licensed to teach music in his spare time, his mother a church organist.

Avison's first published composition (*Six Sonatas for Two Violins and Continuo*) was dedicated to Ralph Jenison (1696–1758), MP for Northumberland, member of an old Newcastle family, and patron of the arts, who presumably helped him in some way. Jenison was also the dedicatee of Johann Pepusch's edition of Corelli concertos. Avison was also helped early on by Colonel John Blaithwaite, a retired director of the Royal Academy of Music. Avison may have studied in London, or even in Italy, since according to the music historian Charles Burney, he studied with the Italian composer Francesco Geminiani (1687–1762).

Returning to Newcastle, he was appointed organist at St John's Church in October 1736. A year later he took up a similar post at St Nicholas's Church, now the cathedral, on a salary of £20 a year. Avison became a major figure in the musical life of the city, and not just through his work at the cathedral. He became musical director of the Newcastle Musical Society subscription concerts, a series of fourteen concerts held fortnightly out of doors in the summer, indoors in the winter. He put on similar events in Durham, and was responsible for introducing many new works and composers to the area including Handel and Geminiani. He performed his own compositions which included an adaptation of Scarlatti keyboard pieces for string orchestra and some fifty violin concertos. He also wrote quartets, trios, sonatas for violin and harpsichord and the first part of the oratorio *Ruth* (the other two parts were composed by the Italian virtuoso violinist and opera conductor Feliuce de Giardini). Haydn heard a performance of the oratorio in London and didn't like it. Giardini, he wrote, had 'played the violin like a pig'. Avison was a prominent teacher of the harpsichord, flute and violin. He helped form a Marcello society in Newcastle devoted to performing the choral music of Benedetto Marcello, was involved in local theatre activities, supplying music for the play intervals, and organised benefit concerts and musical events at the Newcastle Pleasure Gardens. In spite of being offered many prestigious positions elsewhere including organist at York Minster in 1734 (accepted by James Nares), posts in Dublin between 1733 and 1740, a teaching position in Edinburgh and successor to Pepusch as organist at the Charterhouse in London, Avison stayed in Newcastle. He died on 10 May 1770, and is buried in the churchyard of St Andrew's, Newgate Street. Charles Burney described him as 'an ingenious and polished man, esteemed and respected by all that knew him; and an elegant writer upon his art'. He was succeeded as cathedral organist by his son, Edward (1747-76) who also became director of the Newcastle Music Society. His younger son Charles (1751-95) also became organist at St. Nicholas and composed several works including a hymn collection.

112. NEWPORT, Essex

~ St Mary the Virgin Church, Newport ~

Zechariah Buck (1798-1879), organist and choirmaster of Norwich Cathedral, spent his last years in retirement at his son's home of Belmont House in Newport, a village 3 miles from Saffron Walden. He is buried in the churchyard of St Mary the Virgin. Buck's teaching methods were slightly unusual. In order to get his choristers to open their mouths properly, he would fill their mouths with beans, marbles, nuts, acorns or coffee berries. The nuts proved a decided failure, as the boys were always cracking them. Jamie Oliver attended Newport Free Grammar School, while seventeenth-century author of books on cookery and household management, Hannah Woolley, was the wife of the local school master in around 1646.

113. NORTHAMPTON, Northamptonshire

– 57 Cambridge Street, Northampton –

The composer Edmund Rubbra was born here on 23 May 1901. He was the elder son of a journeyman shoe-last maker, and clock and watch repairer. According to family legend the family came originally from Bologna in Italy. Although his mother sang in the local church choir, there was little music in the house until Rubbra's aunt married the owner of a Northampton music and piano shop: a demonstration model piano was housed in the Rubbra home and Rubbra learnt to play well enough to demonstrate the piano's capabilities to prospective customers. In 1912, the family moved to Balfour Street, then moved again four years later. By then the young Rubbra had become a more than competent pianist, playing for the Sunday School at their local Congregational church. He had also become interested in composition, one of his first pieces being a school hymn. He left school at the age of fourteen, worked briefly as an errand boy then became a railway clerk, all the time continuing his music. He particularly loved the music of Cyril Scott and Debussy. When, at the age of seventeen, he put on a concert devoted entirely to Scott's piano music, someone sent the programme to Scott who asked to meet the boy and ended up giving him lessons. It was Scott who suggested he should apply for a scholarship to study music at Reading University, a move which brought him into the orbit of Gustav Holst. On Holst's advice he moved to the Royal College of Music to continue his composition lessons with Holst. After leaving the Royal College in 1925, he worked as a freelance pianist, teacher and music journalist, while slowly gaining a reputation for his own pieces. In 1933 he married the French violinist Antoinette Chaplin, and moved from London to a cottage in Speen, Buckinghamshire, where his compositional life really began. He was eventually to compose more than 160 works, including eleven symphonies, a viola concerto, a piano concerto, a violin concerto, masses and considerable chamber music.

– 54 Kettering Road, Northampton –

The birthplace of the composer William Alwyn on 7 November 1905. Alwyn's father was a grocer and at the age of 14, Alwyn left school to help in the shop. There was no music at all in the house, but he had decided to learn the piccolo and became proficient enough at the age of fifteen to get a place at the Royal Academy to study flute and composition. He had to leave the Academy when his father died and there was no money to keep him there. He began work as an orchestral player, eventually becoming principal flautist of the London Symphony Orchestra, and all the time he was busy composing. He made his name as the composer of more than seventy film scores, although his output was much more varied than that. His concerto for harp and string orchestra, *Lyra Angelica*, was chosen by the figure skater Michelle Kwan for her routine in the 1998 Winter Olympics.

– Craigmore, St George's Avenue, Northampton –

Birthplace of composer Sir Malcolm Arnold on 21 October 1921. Arnold was the youngest of five children. His father was a comfortably-off Methodist shoe manufacturer, amateur pianist and organist. His mother, an even more accomplished pianist, was a descendent of William Hawes, master of the choristers of the Chapel Royal and of St Paul's Cathedral, and a composer of stage music and glees. At the age of four, Arnold began to learn the violin, followed a year later by the piano and then, influenced by records he heard of Louis Armstrong and other jazz musicians, the trumpet. This was the instrument he took up professionally, becoming a member of the London Philharmonic Orchestra. He started composing in this house and, like Alwyn, gained a reputation for his film scores. He won an Oscar for his score for *Bridge On the River Kwai*.

114. NORTH STOKE, Oxfordshire

– Brook Lodge, North Stoke –

The Thames-side home of Dame Clara Butt, the singer famous for her appearances at the Last Night of the Proms.

She added the music room to the house. Butt was born at Southwick, Sussex, on 1 February 1872 and became acknowledged as the finest contralto of her generation. She was adored by Queen Victoria. It was said that the best place to hear her practicing was standing on Wallingford Bridge. The house, which contains some memorabilia, is a private home and not open to the public. Butt, who died from cancer of the spine on 23 January 1936, is buried in the local churchyard of St Mary the Virgin.

115. NORWICH, Norfolk

– The Cathedral –

Zechariah Buck was cathedral organist and Master of the Choristers from 1817 until 1877, making him one of the longest serving cathedral organists anywhere in Britain. He had been born locally in 1798, the son of a tradesman, and as a young boy was heard singing in the street by the then cathedral organist, Thomas Garland. Garland promptly whisked him off to join the choir where he became head chorister for seven years. He was also given a thorough grounding in the organ. Garland died not long after Buck had joined the choir and his musical tuition was taken over by Garland's successor, John Christmas Beckwith, from St Peter Mancroft. Dr Beckwith didn't last much longer, dying after only a year in the post. His son, another John, succeeded him. But John Junior then suffered a heart attack which prevented him carrying out his duties. Buck deputised for him, then, when Beckwith died (he is buried at the church of St Peter Mancroft), Buck was offered the post. He was nineteen. During his sixty years at the cathedral, he built up a formidable reputation both for his prowess as an organist and also as a choir trainer. When, in 1877, he finally decided to retire because his arthritic hands could no longer play the organ, he was in tears at his farewell service as the choir sang his own setting of Evensong. He died in 1879 at Newport in Essex.

Another local musician who became the cathedral organist was William Cobbold, a composer of madrigals who held the post from 1598 until 1608.

~ St Peter Mancroft Church, Market Place ~

One of the finest medieval parish churches in England, St Peter Mancroft has played an important role in the musical and cultural life of Norwich and the county of Norfolk. It stands opposite the city's Theatre Royal (where Paganini gave five recitals in 1831) and is known as the actor's church. Several great church musicians have been numbered among its organists. They include John Christmas Beckwith (1750–1809), who was given his middle name because he was born on Christmas Day. A brilliant organist, Beckwith became organist at Norwich Cathedral in the last year of his life. He was noted for his ability to extemporise and composed much church music. Edward Bunnett (1834–1923) was organist here from 1877 until 1908. An assistant to Zechariah Buck in the cathedral, he composed the highly popular service, *Bunnett in F*. Buried in the church is Alfred Pettet (1790–1837) who held the post of organist from 1810 until his death and composed sacred music including *Domine Probasti* and *Hic Breve Vivitur*.

Among those who trained on the St Peter Manroft organ was William Crotch (1775–1847) who was born locally in Green's Lane, St George's Colgate, the son of a carpenter. At the age of two, Crotch taught himself to play *God Save the King* on an instrument his father had built. By four he was giving daily organ recitals in London. His first oratorio was performed in Cambridge when he was fourteen and a year later he was appointed organist at Christ Church Cathedral, Oxford. He was Professor of Music at Oxford by the time he was twenty-two and went on to become the first principal of the Royal Academy of Music. Crotch was also a talented painter and ambidextrous: when composing he would often write on two staves simultaneously. Although he wrote extensively and his music was popular in its day, apart from *Westminster Chimes*, it is hardly remembered today (and there's some doubt whether he actually wrote that). Zechariah Buck (1798–1879) also started on the St Peter Mancroft organ before being allowed to play in the cathedral.

The bells of St Peter Mancroft are famous. There are fourteen of them, eleven dating from 1775, and it was here, on 2 May 1715, that the first church bell peal with more than 5,000 changes was recorded, rung by the Norwich Scholars (as the ringers were then known). Over the centuries the bells have been used to celebrate major events in the life of the city and the nation, one occasion being the sinking of the Armada in 1588. The ringing chamber is behind a glass window by Andrew Anderson which has as its theme Bach's chorale *Wachet Auf*, the words of which are based on Jesus' parable of the ten virgins.

116. OLDHAM, Lancashire

– 93 Werneth Hall Road, Oldham –

A plaque marks the house in which the composer Sir William Walton was born on 29 March 1902. Both his parents were singing teachers. His father, Charles, was one of the original intake into the new Royal Northern College of Music, his mother Louisa was an amateur contralto. Charles became organist and choirmaster at St John's Church, Werneth, a post he held for twenty-one years while teaching the organ and singing in the locality. Walton and his brother both sang in the St John's choir, Walton also learning the piano and, briefly, the violin. It was soon apparent he was musically gifted and when he was ten his mother took him to Christ Church Cathedral School in Oxford to audition: he got in, exchanging, as he later wrote, the 'nightmare' of school in Oldham for the 'odious' regime of boarding school where he was mocked for his Lancashire accent. It was while he was a chorister at Christ Church that he began to compose. The reason he later gave was that unless he cultivated an interesting personality, when his voice broke he would be sent back to Oldham, and he dreaded the thought. He never really liked Oldham and never returned there to live.

117. OSWESTRY, Shropshire

– 55 Willow Street, Oswestry –

A plaque outside denotes the birthplace of Sir Henry Walford Davies, composer, organist and Master of the

King's Music. Davies was born on 6 September 1869. His father was an accountant who played a prominent part in the musical life of Oswestry, playing the flute and cello. He was also choirmaster of Christ Church Congregational church. Davies grew up singing and playing any instrument he could find. He went first to school in Willow Street and then, between 1870 and 1880, to Oswestry College before being sent to St George's Chapel, Windsor, as a chorister. There he came under the influence of Sir Walter Parratt. He went on to study at the Royal College of Music, becoming a teacher of composition himself. Among his pupils were composer Rutland Boughton and conductor Leopold Stokowski. He held a number of organist posts in London before, in 1898, becoming organist of Temple Church. In 1917 he left the Temple to become the first director of music of the newly formed Royal Air Force for which he wrote *The Royal Air Force March Past*, still popular with brass bands today. Appointed Professor of Music at Aberystwyth University, he did much to promote Welsh music. On the death of Elgar in 1934, he became the Master of the King's Music. A radio personality towards the end of his life, Davies died in Bristol in 1941. Among his best-known compositions are the introit *God Be in my Head* and *Solemn Melody for organ and strings*. He also wrote an arrangement of the carol *O Little Town of Bethlehem* for the annual King's College, Cambridge, Festival of Nine Lessons and Carols. He was the person who commissioned Hubert Parry to write *Jerusalem*.

118. OUNDLE, Northamptonshire

– Apethorpe Hall, Apethorpe, Nr Oundle –

This 600-year old country house, one of the finest Jacobean buildings in Britain, was in such a poor condition recently that English Heritage put it on their list of critical properties and eventually bought it under a compulsory purchase order. A £4 million restoration programme is now under way while English Heritage looks for a new owner. Apethorpe Hall has had many royal visits and has entertained Elizabeth I, James I and Charles I. The musical interest here is the minstrels' gallery which contains an overmantel depicting King David playing a harp and contains the inscription:

> Rare and ever to be wished may sound here
> Instruments which faint spirits and muses cheer
> Composing for the body, soul and ear
> Which sickness sadness and foul spirits fear.

119. OXFORD

– Christ Church Cathedral –

Christ Church is both a cathedral and a college chapel. It was built by Cardinal Wolsey, Henry VIII's Chancellor, and originally called Cardinal College. The first organist and Master of the Choristers, appointed in 1526, was John Taverner, the personal choice of Cardinal Wolsey. Taverner was reluctant to accept the post but given no choice. He left when Wolsey fell from power. Another organist was William Crotch, a child prodigy who was offered the post when he was fifteen. By the time he was 22 he was the university's Professor of Music. William Walton was a choral scholar here from 1912 until 1918. Although he did not much like it, it was here he first received encouragement to begin composing.

– Magdalen College Chapel –

In the sixteenth century, Magdalen College was a centre of musical excellence with three of the era's finest composers holding the position of Master of the Choristers. Little is known about Richard Davy, John Mason and John Sheppard. Davy (c1465–1507) was a scholar at Magdalen before becoming choir master and organist in 1490. Nine of his compositions are in the *Eton Songbook* and he was the first composer we know by name to have set the *St Matthew Passion*. He possibly left Oxford for a post at Exeter Cathedral. If we know little about Davy, we know even less about John Mason (c1485–c1547). He appears to have been a singer in the household of Lady Margaret Beaufort, the mother of King Henry VII, and to have been at Magdalen College between 1508 and 1510. He went on to become Cardinal Wolsey's chaplain, accompanying him on a mission to Calais and Bruges. Only four of his works survive. John Sheppard (c1515–1558) was a singer as well as composer. He was at the college from 1543 until 1548, before becoming a Gentleman of the Chapel Royal. As a composer he was considered to be on a par with Thomas Tallis. He wrote *In manus tuas, Laudem dicite Deo, Spiritus Sanctus* and other pieces for performance in the Magdalen College Chapel. Daniel Purcell, brother of Henry, was organist here from 1688 to 1695. Other famous alumni from Magdalen College include Oscar Wilde, Lawrence of Arabia and John Betjeman.

— St Cross Church, Holywell —

John Stainer, who wrote the ever-popular cantata *The Crucifixion*, was churchwarden here for more than 30 years. He is buried in the Holywell Cemetery behind the church. Stainer was born in 1840 in Southwark, London, where his father was a schoolmaster. He joined the St Paul's Cathedral choir as a treble and sang at the funerals of the artist Turner and the Duke of Wellington. A prodigiously gifted organist, he was heard practicing in the cathedral by Sir Frederick Ousley who promptly offered him a job at St Michael's, Tenbury Wells. Stainer was aged just sixteen. He then moved to Magdalen College in Oxford, became the university organist and finally, organist at St Paul's and professor of music at Oxford. His music – apart from *The Crucifixion* now largely forgotten – was extremely popular, and as a church organist and choir trainer he set the highest of standards. Knighted for his services to music, he went on holiday to Verona where he died from a heart attack aged 60. The streets of Oxford were crowded for his funeral. There is a memorial window to him in the church, paid for by Lady Stainer.

— Sheldonian Theatre —

Designed by Sir Christopher Wren and not strictly speaking a theatre, the Sheldonian is based on drawings of ancient Roman theatres. Owned by Oxford University and seating 1,000 people, its principle function is as the location for the university's ceremonial and degree days. It is also an important centre of music-making. The Oxford Bach Choir has been rehearsing here every Monday for over 100 years;

Handel's *Athalia* received its premiere here in 1733; it was here that Haydn received an honorary degree in June 1791. His newly composed symphony was supposed to be performed in his honour but the orchestra couldn't play it and another had to be substituted, which is why Haydn's *Symphony No 92 in G Major*, written in Eisenstadt in Austria and first performed in Paris, is known as the Oxford Symphony. More recent recipients of honorary degrees include Herbert von Karajan and Dame Joan Sutherland. The organ case was designed by Wren although the instrument it houses is not the original.

120. PADSTOW, Cornwall

– Porthcothan, St Merryn –

In 1916, Philip Heseltine (later to achieve musical fame as Peter Warlock) stayed here with the writer DH Lawrence. Both men were conscientious objectors. Heseltine was going through a period of personal crisis and although he much admired Lawrence's writing and talked for a time about republishing some of Lawrence's work, the two men did not get on. There were rumours (as there were throughout his life, not least because of the pseudonym he adopted) that Warlock was heavily into the occult. The novelist Mary Butts claimed he had introduced her to the occult. He was certainly interested in flagellation. Warlock was the prototype for several characters in fiction including Halliday in DH Lawrence's *Women in Love*. Warlock threatened to sue but settled out of court.

– Primrose Cottage, St Merryn –

Malcolm Arnold moved here in 1966 with his second wife, Isobel Grey. He loved Cornwall and the Cornish people, becoming very closely involved with Cornish musical life. In 1968, he organised a festival of music by Thomas Merritt (1863–1908), a Cornish copper miner and organist, in Truro Cathedral, and that same year was elected a Bard of the Cornish Gorseth. Amongst the works Arnold wrote while living in St Merryn were the *Four Cornish Dances*, *The Peterloo Overture*, *The Padstow Lifeboat* (a march for brass band, dedicated to the local lifeboat crew), *Popular Birthday* (written for his friend William Walton's seventieth birthday concert), the *Concerto for Violin and Chamber Orchestra*, the *Concerto for Two Pianos* and the *Sixth Symphony*. Arnold was later to say that his stay in Cornwall was the happiest time of his life. His daughter Katherine recalls how on one beautiful day when Arnold was supposed to be busy composing, he suddenly appeared saying he had just written 'repeat everything' and they should all go to the beach. He and Isobel left Cornwall in 1972 and moved to Dublin.

121. PAINSWICK, Gloucestershire

– Clevelands, St Mary's Street, Painswick

This was the home from 1934 until his death on 24 February 1976 of the songwriter Charles Wilfred Orr. Orr had been born in Cheltenham on 31 July 1893. Having seen Elena Gerhardt in a concert, he fell in love with the voice and determined to become a songwriter.

He studied in London and was aided considerably by Delius, whom he met in a restaurant, and by Peter Warlock. However, his health was always poor, and he was advised by his doctors to leave London. He chose Painswick, home to the famous rococo gardens. CW Orr, as he was always known, was one of England's best songwriters. He made more settings of Housman's poetry than any other composer.

– Kingsmill, Painswick –

This is the cottage to which Gerald Finzi, having completed his studies in York with Edward Bairstow, moved in 1922, wanting to live in the country. He was twenty-one and stayed for four years until he found the country idyll too much. This is, however, where he began serious composition and among the works he wrote during this period were his *Violin Concerto* (which was conducted at its first performance in 1928 by Ralph Vaughan Williams), his first settings of Hardy (*By Footpath and Stile*) and the orchestral piece *A Severn Rhapsody*.

122. QUIDHAMPTON, Wiltshire

– The Daye House, Quidhampton, Wilton, Salisbury –

The Daye House on the Wilton Park estate, was leased in 1922 by Edith Olivier, daughter of the vicar of Wilton, a distant relative of Laurence Olivier and an author who filled the house with musical, literary and artistic friends, among them William Walton, Siegfried Sassoon, Cecil Beaton, Rex Whistler and Constant Lambert. Walton was a frequent guest and began his first symphony here in March 1932. He also wrote the song *Daphne*. The waspish Cecil Beaton didn't care much for him as he wrote in a letter to Edith Olivier in 1928: 'He is a good composer but oh such a worrying little wretch! I simply loathe and detest him for cringing so much and the mere thought of him sets my nerves on edge.' The house is private.

123. RICHMOND, Surrey

– 19 Denbigh Gardens, Richmond –

The home of Sir Malcolm Arnold in the early 1960s. Among the works written here were the *Guitar Concerto*, composed for Julian Bream, and the wonderfully haunting *Fifth Symphony*. Arnold left as a result of upheavals in his personal life – in particular his first marriage collapsing – and moved first to Thursley, a village near Haslemere in Surrey, and then in 1966 to St Merryn in Cornwall.

– Richmond Cemetery, Sheen Road, Richmond –

At the Richmond Park end of the cemetery Sir Andrzej Panufnik is buried. His gravestone has the geometric design he used for his Ninth Symphony, the *Symphony of Hope*, carved on it. Panufnik, born in Warsaw in 1914, is considered by many to be Poland's leading composer of the twentieth century. During World War Two, he wrote resistance songs and earned his living playing duets in Warsaw cafes with Witold Lutoslawksi. All his manuscripts from this time, including two symphonies, were destroyed in the Warsaw uprising. Unable to get on with the post-war communist regime, he went into exile in 1954, and as a consequence, his music was banned in Poland for twenty years. Settling in Britain, he became principal conductor of the City of Birmingham Orchestra then gave up conducting to concentrate on composition. Among his large and popular output were ten symphonies, two ballets, concertos for violin and cello, choral works and chamber pieces. It was during his daily stroll to Richmond along the banks of the Thames from his home in Twickenham that he would dream up most of his musical ideas. He also drew inspiration from the ancient oaks in Richmond Park. Panufnik was knighted in 1991, the year he died. His daughter Roxanna is a composer.

124. RUGBY, Warwickshire

– The Manor House, Ashby St Ledgers, Rugby –

The Manor House, scene of much of the plotting for the Gunpowder Plot when owned by the Catesby family, is actually in Northamptonshire. It later became the home of Viscount Wimborne and his wife, Lady Alice. In 1934, William Walton, who as a young man was a consummate sponger, fell in love with Lady Alice, twenty-two years his senior, and spent a lot of time here, moving in when Lord Wimborne died in 1939. He wrote the violin concerto here and when he took it to New York to show to violinist Jascha Heifetz, Lady Alice accompanied him. Among other works composed here were the march *Crown Imperial* and scores for the films *Henry V* and *Hamlet*. He started work on *Troilus and Cressida* but abandoned it to nurse the

mortally ill Lady Alice. She died in April 1948 aged 67. The
house is undergoing much needed restoration.

125. RUSTINGTON, Sussex

– Knightscroft House, Sea Lane, Rustington –

This was Sir Hubert Parry's country home from 1880 until
his death in 1918. It was in the music room that he wrote
Jerusalem, his famous setting of William Blake's poem. He
also wrote a hymn tune named *Rustington*. Among the
many famous visitors who stayed in the house was Dame
Nellie Melba. Parry died in Rustington on 7 October 1918.
Following a memorial service in St Paul's Cathedral, during
which were performed the motet *There is an old Belief*
(from *Six Songs of Farewell*, written at Rustington in
1916), and part of a chorale from his *Prelude for Organ
Works*, his ashes were placed in St Paul's crypt. In 1922 a
tablet was erected in his memory at the west end of
Gloucester Cathedral with lines especially written by Poet
Laureate, Robert Bridges. Knightscroft House has been
converted into flats and is not open to the public.

126. RYCOTE, Oxfordshire

– Rycote Chapel, Rycote –

Willoughby Bertie, the 4th Earl of Abingdon, who was born
on 16 January 1740, died in 1799 and is buried here. He was
an accomplished flautist and amateur composer, writing
mostly songs (frequently with his own lyrics) and glees. He

had been encouraged to compose by his friend Joseph Haydn, who dedicated a piece to him, as did JC Bach. The earl was a keen patron of music and together with his son-in-law Giovanni Gallini, a theatre manager and impresario, was responsible for bringing both Bach and Haydn to England. He helped establish the London concerts featuring Bach and Carl Friedrich Abel.

Rycote Palace, where Henry VIII was a frequent visitor and spent his fifth honeymoon (with Catherine Howard), was largely destroyed by fire in 1745 when Bertie was five. The family decamped to Wytham in Berkshire. In 1807, the palace was demolished and sold off in lots. Only part of the front façade remains and is now part of a rebuilt private house. The fifteenth-century chapel, the only original palace building that survives is situated off Rycote Lane and contains a fine example of a minstrel's gallery and some beautiful carvings, possibly by Grinling Gibbons. The organ is modern. Now administered by English Heritage, the chapel has somewhat erratic opening hours, so check first. www.english-heritage.org.uk

127. SAFFRON WALDEN, Essex

– 1 Audley Road, Saffron Walden –

This was the home of the composer and teacher Gordon Jacob. Born in London in 1895, Jacob enlisted in the Field Artillery at the beginning of the World War One and became a prisoner of war, one of only sixty survivors from a battalion of 800. After the war, he enrolled at the Royal College of Music, eventually becoming a professor there for forty years. Among his pupils was Malcolm Arnold. In 1958, when he and his wife were living in Brockenhurst, Hampshire, Jacob's wife died. His subsequent marriage to her twenty-one-year old niece, Margaret, when he was 63, set tongues wagging so they decided to move to Saffron Walden. Here Jacob continued his prolific output. He wrote in total more than 700 pieces, including two symphonies, twelve concertos, light music for radio, a ballet and an arrangement of the national anthem with fanfare for the Queen's Coronation in 1953. He died here on 8 June 1984, a few months short of his eighty-ninth birthday.

128. ST ALBANS, Hertfordshire

– The Cathedral and Abbey Church of St Alban –

Built on the site of the death of Britain's first Christian martyr, the Roman centurion Alban, the Abbey Church is all that remains of what was once a much larger complex. The church is the home of the St Albans International Organ Festival, founded in 1963 by Peter Hurford and held every two years over the course of a week in the summer.

The church is also important because of its connection with the distinguished medieval composer Robert Fayrfax who is buried in the Presbytery. The brass plaque that marks his grave is not the original, which was stolen, but a copy of a seventeenth-century brass rubbing. Fayrfax (or Fairfax, Fairfaux or Feyrefax) has only recently been rediscovered. He was born in Deeping Gate in Lincolnshire, on 23 April 1464. Nothing is known of his early years except that he became a Gentleman of the Chapel Royal sometime before December 1497 when he was granted a chaplaincy at Snodhill Castle in Herefordshire. A year later he became organist of St Alban's, a post he held for at least four years. As a Gentleman of the Chapel Royal he sang, in 1503, at the funerals of Prince Edmund, son of Henry VII, and Queen Elizabeth. He was the leading chorister at the King's funeral on 11 May 1509, sang at the coronation of King Henry VIII and at the 1520 Anglo-French summit at the Field of the Cloth of Gold just outside Calais. The King obviously thought highly of him because he was granted several royal benefices during the last decades of his life. Fayrfax's exact relationship with the Abbey after he ceased to be organist in 1502 is not known. It is possible he stayed on the music staff in an honorary capacity since he composed a mass in memory of St Alban and requested to be buried here. His tomb tells us that he died on 24 October 1521 at the age of 57 and was survived by his wife Agnes and their children. His surviving compositions reveal an extremely thoughtful, discriminating composer.

129. SALISBURY, Wiltshire

– The Cathedral –

Among organists here were John Farrant, father and son. John Farrant Senior (?–1602) was master of the choristers as well. He was also married to the Dean's daughter, a relationship that was far from happy. He treated her so badly that she complained to the Chapter. On 5 February 1592, in the middle of Evensong, Farrant, accompanied by a chorister, went to the Deanery, forced his way into the Dean's study brandishing a carving knife and threatened to cut the Dean's throat; fortunately he only managed to cut the Dean's gown. Recalling that Evensong was still in progress, Farrant and the boy returned to the cathedral and sang the anthem before Farrant fled to Hereford where he was made master of the choristers. His son John sang in Salisbury Cathedral choir as a child and later became the cathedral organist.

Another Salisbury organist to have a spot of bother was Michael Wise (c1648–87). Probably from Salisbury, Wise composed anthems and hymns and died on 24 August 1687 after quarrelling first with his wife then with a night watchman, who clubbed him to death.

The composer William Lawes, who was killed at the siege of Chester, was born in The Close in 1602.

130. SELSEY, West Sussex

It may be hard to believe but a blue plaque at the northern end of Selsey's East Beach, where the promenade meets Park Lane, marks the view across to Bognor Regis which inspired one of the best loved pieces of light music ever written. Eric Coates, England's finest composer of what is sometimes condescendingly called 'light music', loved this part of the country and over the years had at least six homes in the area including one in Park Crescent, Selsey, one in Sidlesham and another in Aldwick. As a child he had suffered from a weak chest and although he almost always composed at home in London, where the hustle and bustle of the city inspired him, he liked to get away as often as possible from the London smog to the fresh sea air of Selsey. The blue plaque marks the spot where, one summer's evening in 1930, out on his usual evening stroll, Coates stopped to admire the dark blue sea and Bognor, glowing pink, on the other side of the bay. It looked, he felt, just like the tropics and gave him the idea for writing *By the Sleepy Lagoon*, better known as the signature tune of the long-running radio programme *Desert Island Discs*. The widow of Roy Plomley, who devised *Desert Island Discs*, unveiled the plaque on 16 July 1998. Coates was on holiday in the area in 1957 when he suffered his fatal heart attack and died in nearby Chichester Hospital. He had been born in 1886 in the Nottinghamshire mining town of Hucknall where his father was a doctor. His parents wanted him to join a bank but instead he went to the Royal Academy of Music to study the viola, later becoming an orchestral musician. He was appointed principal viola of Henry Wood's Queen's Hall Orchestra where he played under such people as Elgar (an early champion of Coates' music), Holst and Richard Strauss. He was fired by Wood for putting in too many deputies while he went off to conduct performances of his own music. It was, he later said, one of the best things that could have happened to him because he put away his viola and became a full-time composer. It was the *Knightsbridge March* from his early *London Suite* that made his name when it was chosen by the BBC to introduce the radio programme *In Town Tonight*. More than 20,000 people wrote in to ask what it was and who had written it. Coates also went on to write the theme tune for *Music While You Work* and the famous *Dam Busters* march.

131. SETTLE, North Yorkshire

– Market Square, Settle –

A plaque on the wall of what is now a branch of NatWest bank but was formerly a doctor's surgery, commemorates the long friendship between Edward Elgar and Dr Charles Buck who lived here. They had met in Worcester when both were young men: Buck, a keen amateur musician, was playing in an orchestra Elgar was conducting. The two became lifelong friends and Elgar frequently visited Buck in Settle. In the summer of 1888, a time when Elgar was moving towards marriage with Alice Roberts, he decided to spend a few days with Buck. As he was leaving Worcester, Alice handed him a poem she had written called *Love's Grace*. When he reached Settle, Elgar reciprocated by writing a short piece of salon music and giving her the manuscript as soon as he got home. He made three arrangements of the piece to which he gave the name *Love's Greeting*, but it didn't sell. It was his publisher who suggested changing the name to *Salut d'Amour*. The piece became his first published work. There's no doubt Elgar knew the Settle area well. He played golf on the local course, went for long walks in the surrounding countryside, and drank in the Hart's Head Inn in Giggleswick.

132. SHERINGHAM, Norfolk

Martincross, The Boulevard, Sheringham –

Ralph Vaughan Williams and his wife Adeline moved to Sheringham in 1919 so that she could look after her invalid brother and he could begin work on his third symphony. The writer Patrick Hamilton, famous for *Hangover Square* and *Rope*, had also lived in the house.

133. SHIPLEY, West Sussex

– St Mary the Virgin Church, Shipley –

John Ireland, who died of heart failure in 1962, is buried here at his own wish, opposite the south door. He wanted to be buried within sight of Chanctonbury Ring and the Downs which had so inspired him. A stone plaque commemorates him with the words 'One of God's noblest works lies here'.

134. SHOREHAM-BY-SEA, Sussex

– 11 Atlantic Court, Ferry Road, Shoreham –

The final home of Havergal Brian, listed in the *Guinness Book of Records* as the composer of the longest symphony ever (the *Gothic*, 110 minutes duration, hundreds of performers). Brian also wrote a further 31 symphonies and remains one of the enigmas of music. Was he a neglected musical genius or a crazed megalomaniac turning out unperformable works? The few hearings his music have had would seem to indicate he was writing something worthwhile. He and his wife Hilda moved to this new block in January 1968. He had been living for the previous ten years in 1 The Marlinspike, Shoreham, a bungalow bought by his daughter and her husband into which Brian and Hilda had moved in November 1958. Although in his eighties, he wrote eighteen symphonies and two concertos there. In 1968 his daughter decided she needed the bungalow for her own family, so the Brians moved to Atlantic Court. Now in his nineties, he completed his thirty-first symphony, produced his *Legend for Orchestra Ave atque vale*, and his final work, the thirty-second symphony. He decided then to cease composing. But he was becoming increasingly deaf and unsteady on his feet. Returning to the block one day, having gone out to post a letter, he missed the entrance step, fell and never recovered. He developed pneumonia and, fifteen days after the fall, on 28 November 1972, he died. He was two months away from his ninety-seventh birthday. On the day of his funeral in Worthing, his children received a shock – he had been married before in the Potteries and there were five children from the marriage.

135. SLAITHWAITE, West Yorkshire

– 1 Station Road, Slaithwaite –

A plaque on a bungalow wall records that composer Haydn Wood, the man who wrote *Roses of Picardy*, was born on 25 March 1882, in the Lewisham Hotel, a hotel owned by his parents, which once stood on this site. When Wood was three, the family moved to the Isle of Man and the hotel was taken over by relatives. It stayed in the family until 1945 when it was sold to a brewery. A room in the hotel was named after Wood and there was a plaque inside commemorating his birth. It was demolished in January 1969. Wood's family was musical. His father, Clement, conducted the Slaithwaite brass band and, following the move to Douglas, Isle of Man, his older brother Harry, who taught Wood the violin, was known as Manxland's King of Music. At the age of 15 Wood enrolled at the Royal College in London where he soon established himself as a virtuoso player. He played the fiddle 'as if it were the easiest thing in the world, as easy as eating jam tarts' according to the *Musical Times*. As a violinist he toured the British Isles and overseas for eight years, before marrying the soprano Dorothy Court. They appeared in the music halls, Dorothy singing mostly songs he had written, Wood playing. He became a prolific composer of what became known as light music, in great demand as a conductor and appearing regularly on BBC radio. His output included more than 180 songs and ballads, orchestral suites, overtures, rhapsodies, marches, a piano concerto, violin concerto, variations for cello and orchestra, plus chamber music, incidental music and a symphony. He died in London on 11 March 1959.

136. SOUTH SHIELDS, Tyne and Wear

– St Hilda's Church, Market Place, South Shields –

In 1910, the composer Ernest Farrar, who had just spent six months as the organist of All Saints, the English church in Dresden, was chosen from more than seventy applicants to become St Hilda's new organist and director of music.

Vaughan Williams sent him a congratulatory letter. In addition to his church duties, Farrar became conductor of the local orchestra. Throughout his time at St Hilda's he was busy composing and wrote perhaps his best-known work, the song cycle *Vagabond Songs*. He occupied lodgings at 7 Park Terrace. In 1912, he left South Shields to take up a similar position at Christ Church in Harrogate. He returned to St Hilda's for his marriage to Olive Walton.

137. SPEEN, Buckinghamshire

– Valley Cottage, Speen –

The composer Edmund Rubbra moved to this village five miles from High Wycombe, shortly after he married French violinist Antoinette Chaplin in 1933. They knocked together two labourers' cottages and built a music room, a wooden building which still clings to the steep hillside above the cottage. It was here that Rubbra completed his first symphony and went on to write six more of the eleven he eventually composed. During World War Two, Rubbra was called-up into the army where he was asked to form a trio to perform classical music for the troops. This he did with cellist William Pleeth (who taught Jacqueline du Pré the cello) and violinist Joshua Glazier. An officer once introduced them as being at the top of the tree in their various combinations. On another occasion they were billed as Ed Rub and his Band and as soon as Rubbra announced a Haydn string trio, there was a rush for the exit. After the war, Rubbra was appointed lecturer at the newly formed music department at Oxford University, and kept the trio going for as long as he could. A convert to Catholicism, he also wrote, in addition to the symphonies, works for choirs, songs and motets, and chamber music. He was one of the composers who sparked a renewed interest in Renaissance music. He left Valley Cottage for Gerrards Cross in 1961.

138. STANMORE, Middlesex

– St John the Evangelist Church, Stanmore –

Five yards from the south door of the church is the grave of WS Gilbert, Sir Arthur Sullivan's librettist. His ashes were laid to rest on 2 June 1911, carried here by his friend Rowland Brown and by Herbert Sullivan, the composer's nephew, after cremation at Golders Green Crematorium. The simple ceremony was attended by a large number of distinguished mourners from the worlds of theatre, literature, the arts and the law. There were over three hundred wreaths including one from Whitelaw Reid, the American ambassador. Later the ashes of Gilbert's wife and their adopted daughter, Nancy Macintosh, were also laid to rest here. The grave is the work of Frederick Pomery ARA, who created the Lady of Justice bronze statue above the Old Bailey.

– St Lawrence's Church, Whitchurch Lane, Little Stanmore –

Handel played the organ in this delightful Baroque church, built on his estate by Lord Chandos. Although the organ has been restored, much of it is original. On Saturdays, Friends of the church are on hand to give a full guided tour of the building. In the graveyard is the tombstone of William

Powell, immortalised as the Harmonious Blacksmith. Powell was the village blacksmith, and also parish clerk at the time Handel was in the employ of Lord Chandos. Legend has it that during a sudden thunderstorm, Handel took refuge in the forge and that Powell was singing a catchy air while beating his anvil. It was upon this that the composer built his Harmonious Blacksmith variations. There is probably no truth in this account which did not become current until the early nineteenth century, and was fuelled by the discovery of Powell's anvil, later very profitably auctioned. A similar story is told about Handel visiting Whitchurch on the Welsh border and having to shelter from the rain in a smithy where he heard the blacksmith singing in Welsh.

139. STANWAY, Gloucestershire

– Stanway House, Stanway, Cheltenham, Gloucestershire –
One of the loveliest Jacobean houses in England, Stanway House was one of Percy Grainger's bases when he was on his searches in Gloucestershire for folk songs to record during the years 1907 to 1909. The owner, Lady Elcho, was a friend. The house is open to the public.
www.stanwayfountain.co.uk

140. STAPLEFORD, Wiltshire

– Thatcher's Cottage, Stapleford –
Vaughan Williams spent much of the summer of 1938 staying at what was then Rose Cottage, the home of

thatcher Jack Simper and his wife who ran a shop at the cottage and let out a bedroom with a small sitting room to paying guests. At the age of 66, Vaughan Williams rented the room for some months and began to compose his Fifth Symphony here. He would often walk the seven miles into Salisbury to meet up with his friend Sir Walter Alcock, organist of Salisbury Cathedral where they would play Bach together. Vaughan Williams' plans to return to the village the following summer were dashed by the war.

141. STEVENAGE, Hertfordshire

– Rook's Nest House, Weston Road, Stevenage –

Composer, pianist and writer Elizabeth Poston was born at Highfield in Walkern near Stevenage on 24 October 1905 (the site is now a park). In 1914, following the death of her stockbroker father, she, her brother and mother, moved to Rook's Nest House, where she lived for more than seventy years until her death in 1987. The house had been the childhood home of EM Forster and was the model for Howard's End. Poston fought hard to preserve its rural setting, the inspiration for so much of her work. She used much of her income from composition to help subsidise her fight against 'the cancer of concrete' as she called it. A very good pianist, she gave wartime recitals at the National Gallery. At the outbreak of war, she joined the BBC as director of music for the eastern service. One of her tasks was to use gramophone records to send coded messages to British agents. After the war she was an adviser on the setting up of the Third Programme (now Radio 3) and wrote extensively for radio and television, including the score for the 1970 TV production of *Howard's End* starring Leo Genn and Glenda Jackson. An expert on carols and folk song, Poston died on 18 March 1987. She left the house to her nephew who, while working abroad, rented it to Sir Malcolm Williamson, Master of the Queen's Music, and his partner Simon Campion. Williamson was suffering the effects of a stroke but did manage some composition including work on his choral symphony *The Dawn is at Hand*. He left the house in 1992.

142. STOKE-ON-TRENT, Staffordshire

– Holy Trinity Church, Watchfield Close, Meir, Stoke –

In 1892, when he was sixteen, the composer William Havergal Brian became organist of Holy Trinity. He also joined a men's choir, played the violin in local orchestras and started composing at the beginning of one of the most remarkable of musical careers. Brian had been born on 29 January 1876 at 35 Ricardo Street, Dresden, then a village outside Stoke, now an undistinguished part of the city suburbs. The son of a potter's turner, Brian moved house three times before he was three, including back to Ricardo Street. Both Ricardo Street houses have been demolished to become part of new council housing. Brian left school aged twelve to work in a colliery. After a year he gave that up to work as a clerk in a railway office. He also became the assistant organist of St James's Church, Uttoxeter Road, Longton. In 1896, when he was 20, Brian became organist of Odd Rode Parish Church not far from Stoke.

143. STONDON MASSEY, Essex

– St Peter's and St Paul's Church, Ongar Road, – Stondon Massey

The composer William Byrd, who lived locally, died in 1623 and was buried in the churchyard of this Norman church. Although no trace of his grave has been found, there is a modern memorial plaque to him in the church. Byrd was a well-known recusant and spent most of his time in retirement paying fines for not going to church. Unusually, however, he had it written into his will that he should be buried here: Catholics at that time could be refused burial in an Anglican churchyard.

Byrd lived in Stondon Place, a former farmhouse which he managed to acquire from the Shelley family. The Shelleys were well-known Catholics who had had their land confiscated by the Crown. Byrd, notwithstanding being a Catholic himself, acquired a lease on the house and 200 acres for £300 in 1593. He then bought the house outright despite attempts by the Shelleys to get it back. Byrd retired here in 1595 and died in the house on 4 July 1623. Stondon Place was radically rebuilt in 1707 and burnt down in 1877. Snooker star Steve Davis lives in a house on the site.

144. STORRIDGE, Worcestershire

– Birchwood Lodge, Storridge –

Birchwood Lodge is a four-square, unimpressive cottage in the woods just off the B4219 from Storridge to Longley Green. Elgar rented it in 1898 while living at Forli in

Malvern, as a summer retreat in which he could work (he couldn't see any views from his window in Forli and was desperate to work in the country). He loved the place and was extremely happy here, scoring *The Dream of Gerontius* and completing his oratorio *Caractacus*, a piece commissioned for the 1898 Leeds Triennial Festival and inspired by the British Camp, an Iron Age hill fort on top of the Malverns. Elgar conducted the first performance in October. He gave up the house in October 1903, having had his offer to buy it turned down. He also wrote four of the *Sea Pictures* here. Not open to the public.

145. STORRINGTON, West Sussex

– The White Horse Hotel, 2 The Square, Storrington, – West Sussex

In 1940, having completed his seventh symphony, Sir Arnold Bax, Master of the King's Music, moved into The White Horse which became his home for the rest of his life. It was not perhaps the wisest choice for a person who admitted to feeling washed up and was on the verge of alcoholism. Bax lived in an unheated room without a piano but he had, to all intents, given up composition. He did, however, have the energy to have two mistresses: Harriet Cohen and Mary Gleaves. A frequent visitor to The White Horse was John Ireland who lived a few miles away in Rock. Bax died in Cork in 1953, the last piece he wrote being a march for the Queen's Coronation.

146. SUTTON GREEN, Guildford, Surrey

− St Edward's Roman Catholic Church, Sutton Green −

One of the most successful songwriters of the Victorian era, Maude Valérie White, is buried here. She was born in France in 1855 and brought to England when she was one. Her mother was set against her becoming a musician but eventually allowed her to go to the Royal Academy where she became the first woman to win the Mendelssohn Scholarship and had her first song published. Despite the urgings of colleagues, White never went in seriously for instrumental pieces or large scale works. Fluent in English, French, German, Italian and Swedish, she worked as a translator and set songs in all those languages. Her output totaled around 200 songs many of them ranking with the finest. Her setting of Byron's *So We'll Go No More A'Roving* is considered a classic. She died in 1937.

147. TATTERSHALL, Lincolnshire

− Holy Trinity Collegiate Church −

The composer John Taverner, widely considered to be the most important English composer of the Tudor era, may well have been born in Tattershall in about 1490 or possibly 1495. His birthplace and date of birth both remain a mystery as does so much of his life. He certainly held office as a clerk fellow in the choir of the collegiate church built in Tattershall in 1438, alongside his renovated and improved brick castle, by Ralph Cromwell, the Lord

Treasurer. Taverner, who wrote masses, motets and songs for the church, left, rather reluctantly, in 1526 to work for Cardinal Wolsey, becoming the first organist and Master of the Choristers at what was then Cardinal College, Oxford, and is now Christ Church. Two years later Taverner became involved with a group of Lutheran heretics but escaped serious punishment for being 'but a musician'. In 1530, the year after Wolsey fell from favour, Taverner left Oxford to, it was always thought, become an agent of Thomas Cromwell and help in the dissolution of the monasteries. No one knows for certain if this is true. He eventually returned to Lincolnshire and settled in Boston. Holy Trinity also contains, close to the font, the grave of Tom Thumb.

148. TAUNTON, Somerset

– St Andrew's Church, Bishop's Hull –

Buried in the churchyard is William Crotch, organist, painter, pianist and probable composer of the *Westminster Chimes*. He had been born in Norwich in 1775 and was a child prodigy. At the age of three, helped by a pushy mother, he played for the King. He later became the first Principal of the Royal Academy of Music, retiring in 1832 and moving to the outskirts of Taunton to stay with his son. He died there on 29 December 1847.

149. TENBURY WELLS, Worcestershire

– St Michael's Parish Church –

The church and St Michael's College to which it is attached, were both founded in 1856 by Sir Frederick Arthur Gore Ouseley (1825–89) who is buried in the churchyard. Ouseley set up the college in order to provide a model for how Anglican church music should be sung and for 130 years, it was an important centre for church music, making a significant contribution to the musical life of Britain. Ouseley chose Tenbury Wells for his experiment because he wanted to be well away from London. The son of an ambassador to Persia, he had shocked his aristocratic family by becoming a priest. His great love was music: he wrote his first opera aged eight. He later became professor of music at Oxford and wrote oratorios, services, anthems, songs and chamber music. Friends who supported what he was doing did all they could to help and the library, which contained the original score of *Dido and Aeneas* as well as the score from which Handel conducted the first performance of *Messiah*, attracted scholars and musicians from around the world. Sixteen-year-old John Stainer, whom Ousley had heard practicing at St Paul's and promptly offered a job, was the college's first organist. When the school closed in 1985, the library was donated to the Bodleian in Oxford. St Michael's is now an international college.

150. THAXTED, Essex

− St John's Church, Watling Street −

Thaxted Parish church houses one of the few Georgian organs in Britain still in its original state. It was built in 1821 for a chapel in Bedford Row, Holborn, by Henry Cephas Lincoln. When the chapel roof collapsed in 1858, Thaxted bought the organ for £230. Both Gustav Holst and Vaughan Williams played the instrument and it is possible that the hymn *I Vow to thee my Country* (given the name *Thaxted* by Holst) was first performed here. Vaughan Williams was a frequent visitor to Thaxted to stay with Holst and would often help him with choir practice, the two men alternating between conducting and playing the organ. The organ is undergoing very necessary restoration.

− The Manse, 25 Town Street −

Holst's first home in the area was in the village of Monk Street, a few miles south of Thaxted, to which he moved in 1914 to work on *The Planets*. The cottage no longer exists. In 1917 he and his family moved into Town Street where a blue plaque, attached to the outside wall of what was his music room, marks his stay here until 1925. During that time he wrote his *Choral Symphony*, made a setting of the carol *Tomorrow shall be my Dancing Day* for the local choir, and wrote *The Perfect Fool*. As well as playing the organ in St John's church, he was heavily involved with local music. In 1916, his students from Morley College in London joined forces with the local choir to sing Bach and Byrd in the first Thaxted Festival.

151. **THURSLEY, Surrey**

It was to the village of Thursley, not far from Guildford, that Malcolm Arnold moved in 1962 following the breakdown of his first marriage. His stay was not very productive by his earlier standards. He did, however, write his *Five Pieces for Violin and Piano* here, his *Sinfonietta No 3,* and the score for a one act ballet, *Electra*. The architect Sir Edward Lutyens, whose daughter Elizabeth became a composer, grew up in the village.

152. **TINTAGEL, Cornwall**

The passionate forty-year long affair between pianist Harriet Cohen and composer Arnold Bax started in 1914 when she was nineteen and he was thirty-one. Cohen was to become the most talked about musician of her day and heavily involved with contemporary music. Vaughan Williams wrote his piano concerto for her, Bela Bartok his *Six Dances in Bulgarian Rhythms.* John Ireland wrote for her, Ernest Bloch, EJ Moeran and, of course, Bax. In 1917 the couple spent a six-week holiday in Tintagel and as a result Bax wrote a tone poem called *Tintagel*, describing his feelings about the place, the sea, and Arthurian legend, but even more about how he felt about Cohen. Although Bax left his wife, she refused to grant him a divorce: he and Cohen could not get married. When she did eventually die in 1947, Bax did not tell Cohen and it was almost a year later before she found out, discovering also that, for almost twenty years, Bax had been having a secret affair with Mary Gleaves. When Cohen heard the news, she dropped a tray of glasses, severing the artery in her right hand and effectively ending her career.

153. TOWCESTER, Northants

– Weston Hall, High Street, Weston, Towcester –

In 1714, an ancestor of the Sitwell family bought Weston Hall, then a small farmhouse and bakehouse with a paved courtyard in between, and over the years added to it. Sacheverell Sitwell inherited the house in 1929 and it was here that William Walton, who had become friendly with the Sitwells and was living in the stables, worked on *Belshazzar's Feast*. Sitwell later commented 'he made the most terrible din on the piano.' The house is still owned by the Sitwell family and is occasionally open to the public.

154. TRURO, Cornwall

– The Cathedral, 21 Old Bridge Street –

The first cathedral to be consecrated in Britain since the Reformation, Truro was completed in 1910. Among its treasures is a Father Willis organ, built in 1887 and one of the finest in the country. People come from all over the world to hear it. Willis built the organ in London and brought it to Cornwall by boat. It is set in an unusual stone vaulted chamber. A new console was built in 1963 situated above the stalls on the south side of the choir.

It was in Truro that the first Service of Nine Lessons and Carols was held in 1878. At that time the building was under construction and services were being held in a wooden building. The Rev GHS Walpole, the cathedral's Succentor, was concerned that many of the people coming to Midnight Mass on Christmas Eve were spending the evening in local public houses and arriving in a frame of mind far removed from the true meaning of Christmas. To provide a more fitting prelude to Midnight Mass, he organised a carol service to begin at 10pm. It was the Bishop, Edward White Benson, who suggested, for the following year, that nine short readings should be slotted in between the carols. These were read by officers of the church beginning with a choirboy and ending with the Bishop himself. In 1883 Benson became Archbishop of Canterbury and his carol service became more widely known. It was introduced to King's College, Cambridge by the new Dean, Eric Milner-White, in 1918, just after the end of World War One. The outgoing Provost had been a friend of the Benson family and knew all about the Truro experiments.

– St Kenwyn Church, Kenwyn Church Road, Truro –

Joseph Antonia Emidy (1770–1835), Britain's first black composer, is buried here. He was born in Guinea, West Africa, captured by slavers and taken as a child to Brazil. Adopted by Jesuit priests who recognised his musical talent and gave him a violin, he soon became an excellent violinist, able also to play the flute, cello and piano. Taken to Portugal, he became principal violinist of the Lisbon Opera where he was heard one night by a Royal Navy captain who arranged for Emidy to be kidnapped. He spent the next five years on board a Royal Navy vessel as the ship's fiddler. In 1799 he eventually left the ship in Falmouth where he made his living working as a music teacher and entertainer. He married a Cornish girl, with whom he had six children, and moved to Truro where he gave concerts in private houses and in the Assembly Rooms. Unfortunately, none of his compositions has survived. The only known picture of Emidy is in the Royal Cornwall Museum in Truro and there is a commemorative plaque to him in Falmouth Parish Church.

155. TWIGWORTH, Gloucestershire

– St Matthew's Church –

Composer and poet Ivor Gurney (1890–1937), who was born in Gloucester and sang in the cathedral choir, spent the last fifteen years of his life in mental hospitals as a result of being a manic depressive which may or may not have been brought on by his experiences during World War One. He died in the City of London Mental Asylum in Dartford from tuberculosis and is buried in the Twigworth churchyard. In October 2000, his grave was given a new headstone sponsored by the Ivor Gurney Society.

156. TWYCROSS, Leicestershire

– Gopsall Park, Twycross –

Handel was a frequent guest at Gopsall Hall, the home of Humphrey Jennens, a wealthy ironmaker, and got on so well with his son, Charles Jennens, that Charles became

Handel's librettist for six of his oratorios including Handel's masterpiece, *Messiah*. Indeed, the family rumour was that Handel wrote most if not all of *Messiah* in the Temple in the grounds of Gopsall Hall. There is no conclusive evidence that he did. The house that Charles subsequently built has gone, pulled down in the 1950s after being severely damaged when requisitioned during World War Two, and the estate, owned by the Queen, has reverted mostly to private farmland. It is, however, possible to see the ruins of the Temple by using a public footpath onto the estate from near the Gopsall Hall Gatehouse entrance in the village of Shackerstone. The organ Handel was commissioned to install in the Music Room of Charles's new house, on which he played, is now in St James's Church, Great Packington.

157. WADHURST, Sussex

– Tidebrook Manor, Wadhurst –

Sir Michael Tippett moved here in 1950, having been helped to buy the house by his mother. She moved in with him as did Tippett's then boyfriend, artist Karl Hawker, and a cockney family of conscientious objectors whom Tippett (himself jailed in Wormwood Scrubs for three months because of his refusal to have any sort of involvement with the war) had befriended. The house was dilapidated, the roof leaked and there was no electricity. It was a mad household and the cockney family had to go when they hinted at blackmailing Tippett about his relationship with Hawker (homosexuality then being illegal). Surprisingly in such a chaotic atmosphere, Tippett was able to compose. He completed his opera *The Midsummer Marriage* and wrote several major orchestral works including the *Fantasia Concertante on a theme of Corelli*, the piano concerto, his *Second Symphony* and much of *King Priam*. He also wrote a number of smaller pieces including a hymn tune for the local Salvation Army band which was run by the man in the High Street where Tippett got his fish and chips. He called the tune *Wadhurst*. Tippett and his mother left for Corsham in 1960.

158. WALTHAM ABBEY, Essex

– Waltham Abbey, Church of the Holy Cross – and St Lawrence

The present Abbey church is the fourth on the site, the first being founded in 1030. In 1540 it became the last abbey to be dissolved by Henry VIII. The last organist before the dissolution was Thomas Tallis. Tallis had been born in about 1505 and was probably at Waltham Abbey for two years. When the abbey closed he moved to Canterbury Cathedral. The current Flight and Robson organ dates from 1819 although it has been much enlarged. It was on this instrument that William Cummings set the words *Hark! The Herald Angels Sing* to Mendelssohn's now famous tune. The resulting hymn was heard for the first time in the abbey on Christmas Day 1852.

159. WASHINGTON, West Sussex

– Rock Mill, Washington –

John Ireland first came to Sussex in the 1920s and fell in love with the landscape, the villages such as Amberley, Ashington, Shipley and Steyning, and the history of the area, all of which had a profound influence on him. His inspiration for the piano concerto and the *Legend for Piano* both came from a fascination with the ancient hill fort of Chanctonbury Ring. Both pieces were first played by his pupil Helen Perkin, to whom he dedicated the works and with whom he fell in love. His offer of marriage was turned down, however, and when Perkin married someone else and went to live in Australia, he took her name off the scores. In 1953, when Ireland, who had rented a flat on a local farm in 1949, decided to retire, this part of the Sussex Downs was the obvious area for him to search for a house. Driving past the converted windmill at Rock, a building he had driven past many times, he noticed a 'for sale' board outside and promptly bought it. It became his home until his death on 12 June 1962. Ireland would frequently drive over to The White Horse in Storrington to meet Arnold Bax, now Master of the Queen's Music. Since Bax had no car, Ireland would drive him around the region trying to show his friend, who was obsessed with Celtic mythology, why Sussex was on a par. Among other visitors to Rock Mill were Arthur Bliss, Geoffrey Bush, Alan Bush and William Alwyn. Ireland is buried in the graveyard of Shipley church.

160. WEEDON LOIS, near Towcester, Northamptonshire

– The Church of St Mary and St Peter –

Dame Edith Sitwell, who lived at nearby Weston Hall and inspired William Walton to write *Façade*, is buried here. Her memorial stone is by Henry Moore.

161. WELLS, Somerset

– Wells Cathedral –

Thomas Linley Senior is buried here. The monument to him also commemorates his two daughters, Elizabeth (who eloped to marry the playwright Richard Brinsley Sheridan) and Mary. Linley was born in Wells and began his working life locally as a carpenter. But he soon switched to music and went to Bath to study. He spent a large part of his career in Bath working as a conductor and singing teacher.

162. WEOBLEY, Herefordshire

– St Peter and St Paul Church, Church Street –

Ella Mary Leather (1874–1928), folk-song collector, is buried in the churchyard of this picturesque black-and-white village in North Herefordshire. Born in the nearby village of Dilwyn, where her family were gentry farmers, Leather moved to Weobley following her marriage to local solicitor Francis Leather. They lived in a house overlooking Castle Green. In her mid-twenties, she became interested in the folklore and songs of the area and began collecting them. One of her principal sources at first was William Colcombe, the last man in Weobley to wear a smock, who gave her more than thirty traditional songs and carols. Through her interest she got to know Vaughan Williams and introduced him to many local people. They worked together from 1908 until 1912, then later in 1922, helping save many traditional songs, especially those of the local gypsy community. She also became very friendly with Lucy Broadwood and Cecil Sharp, with whom she joined forces to collect folk songs. In 1912 she wrote the influential *The Folklore of Herefordshire*, and also a description of how in the same year she and Vaughan Williams went to hear some gypsies singing. 'We saw Harriet again at Monkland, near Leominster, where she and several of her fifteen children were hop-picking. After some trouble Dr and Mrs Vaughan Williams and I found their camp in a little round field at dusk, on a fine September evening. There were several caravans, each with its wood fire burning, the Stephens and other families being there, besides Alfred Price Jones, whom we were seeking. His wife was very ill, and we found him with her under an awning near one of the fires. He agreed to sing so we all sat down on upturned buckets kindly provided for us by the gypsies, and while Dr Vaughan Williams noted the tune, his wife and I took down alternate lines of the words. It is difficult to convey to those who have never known it the joy of hearing folk songs as we heard that pathetic ballad; the difference between hearing it there and in a drawing room is just that between discovering a wild flower growing in its native habitat and admiring it when transplanted to a botanic garden.'

163. WETHERDEN, Suffolk

– St Briavels, Stowmarket Road, Wetherden –

Michael Tippett's parents settled in the peaceful village of Wetherden, north-west of Stowmarket, soon after Tippett had been born in London on 2 January 1905. The cottage in which they lived is sixteenth-century and was his home until the age of thirteen when he won a scholarship to Fettes College in Edinburgh. He loathed the school and so was moved to Stamford School in Lincolnshire where he took up the piano and decided he wanted to be a composer.

164. WHITCHURCH, Shropshire

– The Old Town Hall Vaults, St Mary's Street, Whitchurch –

A plaque outside what was once the Cornmarket Inn commemorates the birth here of the composer Sir Edward German on 17 February 1862. The Whitchurch Heritage and Tourist Information Centre makes a feature of German with excerpts of his music, information on his life and even the regalia he wore when he was knighted, on display.

German, whose real name was German Edward Jones, was considered Sir Arthur Sullivan's heir. He was the son of a brewer and liquor retailer who played the organ at church. As a boy, German played the violin and was leader of the Whitchurch orchestra. He went to the Royal Academy and there began his composing career writing both serious music as well as light operas. He became music director of the Globe Theatre in 1888 and provided incidental music for many productions. He wrote symphonies, orchestral suites, symphonic poems, songs and piano music. In 1904 he wrote one of his best-loved pieces, the *Welsh Rhapsody*. In 1900 he was invited to complete *The Emerald Isle* following Sullivan's death and went on to write *Merrie England* in 1902 and *Tom Jones* in 1907. He also wrote the *Just So Song Book*, settings of Rudyard Kipling poems. He stopped composing in about 1912 but continued to conduct until 1928, the year he was knighted.

German died on 11 November 1936 and is buried in Whitchurch Cemetery, off Mile Bank Road, Whitchurch. Signs from the entrance direct visitors to his grave.

165. WILTON, Wiltshire

– Wilton House –

Hubert Parry married into the Herbert family who owned Wilton House. While staying here in 1887, he composed *Blest Pair of Sirens* for his friend Charles Villiers Stanford who ran the Bach Choir. The work was to establish Parry as a major force in English music.

166. WIMBORNE, Dorset

– Long Crichel House, Long Crichel, near Wimborne –

A Queen Anne house and former rectory, which Eardley Knollys, music critic Desmond Shawe-Taylor and Eddy Sackville-West (later joined by the writer Raymond Mortimer) bought in August 1945 as a country retreat and turned into a mecca devoted to the arts, a sort of male salon. Among the many guests who stayed here were Lord Berners, Benjamin Britten, Lennox Berkeley, Nancy Mitford, Graham Greene, Laurie Lee and the German soprano Elisabeth Schumann. Not open to the public.

167. WINCANTON, Somerset

– Pen Pits, Penselwood –

A country house built for Sir Arthur Bliss by the architect Peter Harland in 1934. Fifty yards from the main house, in the woods, Harland built a music room where Bliss worked on the scores for his opera *The Olympians*, and his ballets *Miracle in the Gorbals* and *Adam Zero*. He gave up the house in 1955.

168. WINCHESTER, Hampshire

– 26 St Swithen Street and 1 St John's Terrace –

These were the homes of Sir George Dyson when he became director of music at Winchester College, the oldest public school in England. The school has been on the present site in its current buildings for over 600 years. Born in Halifax, Yorkshire, in 1883, Dyson completed his studies with a four year period abroad, then signed up for the army. He saw action in the trenches and his book on grenades became a classic. Invalided out of the army, he joined the Air Ministry and became involved with their military band, before beginning the round of teaching in a succession of public schools. In 1924 he became director of music at Winchester College and began to write copiously for the forces he had at the school. His output included a symphony, a violin concerto, two large choral works, *Three Rhapsodies for String Quartet*, liturgical settings which are still in use today, and the popular *The Canterbury Pilgrims*. He also wrote pieces for the Three Choirs Festival. In 1937 Dyson left Winchester College to become Director of the Royal College of Music, a position he held until 1952. He was knighted in 1941 and continued to live in Winchester at 1 St John's Terrace until his death in 1964.

– Winchester College –

Other organists at Winchester College include Jeremiah Clarke (c1670–1707), famous for the trumpet voluntary so often attributed to Purcell. He was organist from 1692 until 1695, when he moved to London to become the organist of the Chapel Royal. He committed suicide in St Paul's Cathedral graveyard after his passion for a lady of rank went unrequited and was buried in the crypt. Thomas Weelkes spent time at the College as did Samuel Sebastian Wesley who became organist when he was organist at the Cathedral. Standards at the College had sunk so low that when the doddery old incumbent died, Wesley, who had only been at the cathedral for a year, was asked to take over the College as well. He became the last person to combine the two posts and lived at 8 Kingsgate.

169. WINDSOR, Berkshire

– Windsor Castle –

Windsor Castle dates from the Norman Conquest and has had a long connection with music, many famous musicians having been summoned to the castle to perform, especially during Queen Victoria's reign. These include Franz Liszt, who played for George IV during the summer of 1825 when he was fourteen, and for Queen Victoria sixty years later, when he was seventy-four; Edvard Greig; Mascagni, who conducted a performance of *Cavalleria Rusticana*, the Queen's favourite opera; Jacques Offenbach playing his cello; Anton Rubinstein; Saint-Saëns; Sousa; and Richard and Cosima Wagner. Mendelssohn received his summons in 1842 and listened to the Queen singing his songs. Six months before his death he played for the royal couple again and arranged his *Lied ohne Worte* for them as a duet. Haydn visited the castle as a tourist in 1792. The Royal Collection contains many items of musical interest, although the bulk of the music in the Royal Library at Windsor was sent on permanent loan to the British Museum in 1911 and made an outright gift to the museum by HM Queen Elizabeth II in 1957. Some manuscripts have remained at Windsor however. They include some of Prince Albert's compositions together with works by Mozart and Mendelssohn.

– St George's Chapel, Windsor Castle –

The present building, home to the Order of the Garter founded by King Edward III, dates from the fifteenth century. The chapel has had a long line of distinguished musicians in charge of its music. Richard Farrant held office from 1564 until his death in 1581. Born about 1530, Farrant was a composer, choirmaster, theatrical producer and playwright. He resigned from being a member of the Chapel Royal choir when offered the post in Windsor. As well as his duties at St George's, he staged plays for the Queen. Little of his music or dramatic writing has survived.

John Marbeck (c1510–85), sometimes known as Merbecke or Merbeck, may have been born in Yorkshire or Windsor, where he became a boy chorister. In about 1541 he became organist of the chapel. A theologian as well as a composer (he produced the standard setting of the Anglican liturgy and is known today for his setting of the Mass *Missa per arma iustite*) he was convicted of heresy and condemned to death by burning but thanks to the intervention of the Bishop of Winchester, spared. Some years later he was back at the chapel. Nathanial Giles, who was born in 1588 and is first heard of as the organist at Worcester Cathedral, was organist from 1555. He was also organist at Westminster Abbey and, with Ben Johnson, ran a children's theatre at the Blackfriars Theatre. He died on 24 January 1633 and is buried in the chapel as are John Mundy, who died here in 1630, and Nicholas Staggins, Master of the King's and Queen's Musick, who died on 13 June 1700. Sir Walter Parratt, one of the most influential of British organists, became chapel organist in 1893 and held the post until his death on 27 March 1924. He had also been appointed Master of the Queen's Musick in 1893 (a post he was succeeded in by Edward Elgar). Parratt, who had been born in Huddersfield in 1841, lived in Horseshoe Cloisters and his ashes are buried in the north choir aisle close to the organ.

170. WOLVERHAMPTON, Staffordshire

– Molyneux Stadium –

The home of Wolverhampton Wanderers Football Club better known as Wolves. A plaque at the ground commemorates the fact that Sir Edward Elgar was a loyal Wolves' supporter. He composed what was probably the first football chant when he set to music the words of a phrase from a newspaper report of a match. He regularly visited Wolverhampton to stay with his friend the Rev Alfred Penny, rector of St Peter's Church, and attended matches with Dora, the rector's daughter.

171. WORCESTER, Worcestershire

The city of Worcester is associated above all with Sir Edward Elgar (1857–1934), who was born in nearby Lower Broadheath and spent much of his childhood in the city.

– The Crown Hotel, Broad Street –

The meeting place of the Worcester Glee Club which Elgar joined in 1873 and was appointed conductor of in 1879.

– 2 College Precincts, Worcester –

Elgar's parents had spent eight years living here before their move to Lower Broadheath. When, in 1861, they moved back into Worcester because the family needed more room, this was where they chose. Elgar was four, his father still earning his living as a piano-tuner. The family lived here for two years before moving to live above the music shop in the High Street.

– Loretta Villa, 35 (now 12), Chestnut Walk –

When he was 22, Elgar moved out of the family's High Street home and in with his newly married sister Pollie. Here he began writing a weekly piece or arrangement for the wind quintet he'd set up. Practices took place in the shed behind his father's music shop. During this period Elgar became music director of the county lunatic asylum in Powick, a progressive institution that believed in the recuperative powers of music.

– 4 Field Terrace, Bath Road –

When Pollie and her husband moved to the Potteries in 1883, Elgar moved in with his other sister Lucy and her husband. He left in 1889 when he married Alice.

– 10 High Street –

A blue plaque on the Gifford Hotel in a modern shopping arcade marks the site of the music shop owned by Elgar's father. As a young man William Elgar had managed to make enough money from piano-tuning (thanks largely to obtaining a contract to look after the pianos of the widowed Queen Adelaide who lived at Great Witley Court), that he was able to open his own shop in 1863. Elgar lived here until 1879 when he was twenty-two, the longest he spent in any single home. He wrote many of his early compositions here. Also in the High Street, looking towards the Cathedral, is a statue of the composer by local sculptor Kenneth Potts, unveiled by the Prince of Wales in June 1981. On the ground alongside is a memorial slab with an inscription by Michael Kennedy summarising the composer's achievements and his strong links with the city. This was unveiled by the Mayor on 23 February 1984.

– Elgar Court, Rainbow Hill, Worcester –

A block of flats now occupies the site of Marl Bank, Elgar's final home. Following the death of his wife Alice in 1920, Elgar wrote 'There is no work left for me to do: my active creative period began under the most tender care and it ended with that care.' He spent the last few years of his life conducting when he felt like it, talking to old friends, working on the occasional composition, and restlessly moving from one house to the next when the lease ran out. He finally settled on Marl Bank, with its views of the city and countryside beyond, in 1929. Among his final compositions written here were *The Severn Suite*, *Pomp and Circumstance March No 5* and the *Nursery Suite*. He also began to sketch out his Third Symphony. In the garden Elgar kept a piece of the stone parapet from the old Worcester Bridge acquired when the new bridge was being built in 1932. It was subsequently removed to the village of Broadheath. Elgar died in the local hospital in 1934. Marl Bank was demolished in 1969.

– The Guildhall –

It was here that Elgar received his Freedom of the City in 1905 from the then Mayor, his childhood friend, Hubert Leicester. A portrait of the composer by Philip Burne-Jones, hangs here and a bronze bust by Donald Gilbert can be seen.

– St George's Roman Catholic Church, Sansome Place –

Although a Protestant, Elgar's father William played the organ here. His mother attended the services to keep William company and was in due course converted to Catholicism. She persuaded William to follow suit, and when Elgar (their fourth child) was born, he was baptised and brought up a Catholic. When, after only a year, the young Elgar turned his back on the solicitor's office to which he had gone from school, in order to become a composer, he worked in his father's shop and became assistant organist here, taking any casual employment he could get as a violinist. He followed his father into the Three Choirs Orchestra and later succeeded him as St George's organist in 1885.

– The Cathedral –

Worcester cathedral is one of the three cathedrals which participate in the Three Choirs Festival (the others being Hereford and Gloucester). In the 1884 Festival, Elgar played as a violinist under Dvorák. The cathedral contains a Gerontius memorial window unveiled at the opening of the 1935 Festival, the year after Elgar died. Among the cathedral's organists have been Nathaniel Patrick who died in 1595 and wrote much church music, some of it still in use today; Nathaniel Giles who composed madrigals and church music and held the post from 1581 until 1585 before going on to become organist of the Chapel Royal; and Thomas Tomkins, who was born at St David's, Pembrokshire, in 1573 and died at Martin Hussingtree in 1656. He held office from 1596 until 1646, when Puritanism, which banned organ and choir music, deprived him of his position. Tomkins wrote instrumental music, church music and some wonderful madrigals. The Tomkins family has been described as producing more musicians than any other family in England. Thomas had five brothers, all of whom were musicians and altogether twelve members of the family are mentioned in Grove. One of Thomas's nephews became organist of Worcester cathedral when musical services were resumed after the Restoration. Other notable organists have included William Hayes (1705–77), a composer of glees, canons and catches who held office from 1731 until 1734 before taking up a similar position at Magdalen College, Oxford, and Sir Ivor Atkins, who held the post from 1897 until 1950. Atkins (1869–1953) worked in a number of cathedrals as an assistant organist before coming to Worcester. He was one of the conductors of the Three Choirs Festival and composed songs, church music, service settings and anthems. Together with Elgar, he prepared an edition of Bach's *St Matthew Passion*. He died in Worcester.

172. WRINGTON, near Axbridge, Somerset

– Glencairn, Wrington –

After the outbreak of World War Two, the BBC music department was transferred from London to Bristol as part of the preparations for an expected German bombing of London. Sir Henry Walford Davies, who had become a well-known personality on radio, moved into this house. Davies was a great teacher and communicator as well as composer. He first went in front of the microphone in 1924 and it was not long before he was being heard every week broadcasting such programmes as *Music for the Ordinary Listener* or *Everyman's Music*. He died here suddenly on 11 March 1941 aged 71 and his ashes were interred in the grounds of Bristol Cathedral.

173. WYCK RISSINGTON, Gloucestershire

– St Laurence's Church, Wyck Rissington –

This gem of a church, which dates from the thirteenth century if not earlier and contains a fourteenth-century stained glass crucifixion and sixteenth-century panels depicting the Mysteries of the Gospels, is where seventeen-year-old Gustav Holst got his first professional engagement as a musician. Born in nearby Cheltenham in 1874, he became the church's organist and choirmaster in 1892. The organ was then hand-pumped. Holst lived in the last cottage on the left of the lane leading out of the village towards the Fosse Way. He also became the choirmaster of the Bourton-on-the-Water choral society. The money may not have been much but it taught him a lot about the workings of choral music. 1892 was also the year that, inspired by the music of Arthur Sullivan, he wrote his first operetta, *Lansdown Castle*. This received its first performance in the Cheltenham Corn Exchange the following year and was sufficiently well received for Holst's father to finally agree he could go to music college and study composition.

174. YORK, Yorkshire

– Castle Museum, Tower Street, York –

One of Britain's leading folk museums based on the collection made by Dr John Kirk, a general practitioner in Pickering on the edge of the North Yorkshire moors. Kirk collected anything he thought might disappear (from shop goods to farm machinery) but since his wife was a musician, he began to amass a collection of woodwind instruments dating from the early eighteenth century to the early twentieth which is one of the finest, and least known, collections in Britain. He found the instruments in church bands, town bands and privately, and there are now well over a hundred including minstrel instruments such as a serpent, bassoon, and an ophicleade (a member of the bugle family). There is a virginal of 1651, a 1789 harpsichord, a Johannes Player spinet, a Victorian harmonium 'with patent mouse-proof pedal' and harps as well as wind instruments. Kirk handed over the entire collection to the city in 1932 and the museum opened on its present site in 1938.

www.yorkcastlemuseum.org.uk

– York Minster –

The sixth window of the North Nave Aisle, known as the Bellfounders Window, was given to the Minster in the early 1300s by Richard Tunnoc, a noted citizen of York, goldsmith and bell-founder. The borders show silver- and gold-coloured bells (the orange ones are early twentieth-century insertions). The lower panels show the craft of bell making (left panel), tuning and casting (right panel), while the central panel shows Tunnoc presenting the window to St William of York. Tunnoc died in 1330 and is buried in the Minster.

One of the earliest organists at the Minster was John Thorne, a leading Tudor composer who died in 1573. Little is known about Thorne other than that he suffered for his faith under Queen Elizabeth I and was only allowed to continue in his job because he was such a talented musician. A few of his church compositions have survived and those that do demonstrate a considerable talent. Thorne also wrote poems and had sufficient reputation as a logician to have it mentioned on his tombstone in the Middle Aisle of the Minster:

> Here lieth Thorne, musician
> Most perfect in his art
> In logic's lore who did excel
> All vice who set apart
> Whose Life and conversation did all men's Love allure,
> And now doth reign above the skies in joys most firm and pure, who dyed December 7 1573.

Edwin George Monk held the position of organist for nearly a quarter of a century from 1859 until 1883. Born in Frome, Somerset, in 1819, Monk was an important member of that group of church musicians who led a revival of Anglican church music during Victorian times. He had been the organist and music-master of Radley College before accepting the York job. A composer in his own right, he also edited hymn and chant books. He died at Radley in 1900.

Thomas Tertius Noble, born in Bath in 1867, became the Minster's organist in 1897 and held the post for sixteen years, leaving to become the organist of St Thomas's Church, New York. His church music was extremely popular in its day but has gone out of fashion. He was succeeded by Edward Cuthbert Bairstow. Bairstow was born in Huddersfield in 1874 and had been assistant organist at Westminster Abbey before moving to York, a post he was to hold until his death in 1946. He became Professor of Music at Durham University in 1929 and was knighted in 1932. He composed songs, part songs, organ music and church choral music.

www.yorkminster.org

175. ZENNOR, Cornwall

– The Tinners Arms, Zennor –

The only pub in the village is where DH Lawrence stayed in 1916 while he and Frieda were waiting for the cottage they had rented to be ready. Composer Peter Warlock (1894-1930) stayed here the following year. He and Lawrence had had a falling out and although Warlock tried hard to rekindle the friendship, Lawrence was having none of it. The unpleasant character of Halliday in *Women in Love* is based on Warlock. Meanwhile Warlock, who, it is claimed, dabbled in the occult while in Cornwall, learnt Cornish and wrote two carols set in the language. He also wrote his Folk Song *Preludes* for piano, based on Celtic melodies.

LONDON

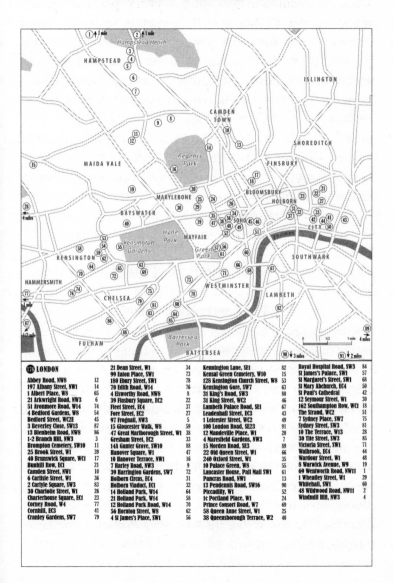

~ Abbey Road, NW8 ~

Abbey Road Studios, with the pedestrian crossing outside, are probably the best known music studios in the world thanks to the Beatles. A plaque records that Sir Edward Elgar opened them on 12 November 1931, conducting a *Pomp and Circumstance* march. He made his famous recording of the violin concerto with sixteen-year-old Yehudi Menuhin the following year.

~ 197 Albany Street, NW1 ~

Composer Constant Lambert lived here from 1947 until his death in 1951. Lambert, born in 1905, was something of a whizz kid. He was the son of an Australian painter of Russian extraction, and an outstanding composer who never achieved his potential in an all too brief life. Educated at Christ's Hospital, he wrote his first orchestral pieces when he was thirteen. At the age of twenty he was invited by Diaghilev to write a score for the Ballet Russes. He enjoyed enormous popularity especially after the first performance of his best-known piece, *The Rio Grande*. This was written when he was living at 59 Oakley Street. Lambert was one of the first to incorporate jazz into 'serious' music. But the poor reception of his subsequent work made him feel a failure as a composer and, in the last fifteen years of his life, he only wrote two major works. Instead he earned his living as a conductor and was especially good at ballet. A founder of the Vic-Wells company (which became the Royal Ballet), he had an affair with the seventeen-year-old Margot Fonteyn. Having been very ill as a child, Lambert had a fear of doctors and failed to get his diabetes diagnosed. He was also an alcoholic, which contributed to his death two days before his 45th birthday. His ashes are interred at Brompton Cemetery.

– 1 Albert Place, W8 –

The home from 1901 until 1922 of Sir Arthur Somervell, pioneer of music teaching in schools and a superb songwriter. Somervell was born in the Lake District in 1863, the son of the founder of K Shoes. He was a successful composer of choral music, much of it written for amateur choral societies, and also wrote concertos for piano and violin, five operettas and some chamber works. He is chiefly remembered today for song cycles such as *Maud* (based on the poems of Tennyson), and was the first person to set AE Housman's *A Shropshire Lad*. He also lived at 105 Clifton Hill in St John's Wood. When he died in 1937 he was buried in Windermere.

– 21 Arkwright Road, NW3 –

Tobias Matthay (1858–1945) lived here from 1902 until 1909. Matthay was a teacher, pianist and composer. A professor at the Royal Academy of Music, he devised his own method of teaching which laid great stress on touch controlled by weight and relaxation, publishing his theories in *The Art of Touch* (1903). He established his own school in 1906 and among his pupils were Myra Hess, Harriet Cohen and Ethel Kennedy. Together with Frederick Corder, professor of composition at the Royal Academy, he co-founded the Society of British Composers in June 1905.

~ 51 Avonmore Road, W14 ~

Shortly after his marriage to Alice, Edward Elgar moved to London and lived here from March 1890 to June 1891. His hope of bursting onto the London musical scene didn't quite work out so they returned to Malvern. The Elgars spent the next twenty years in Malvern and in Hereford before returning to London again. It was in this house that he composed his concert overture *Froissart*.

~ 4 Bedford Gardens, W8 ~

A blue plaque marks where Frank Bridge (1879–1941) lived for ten years. Born in Brighton, Bridge's first home after his marriage in 1908 was in Chiswick where he wrote the *Suite for Strings*, the *String Sextet* and, possibly his best work, *The Sea*. In 1914 he moved to Bedford Gardens where he wrote his second String Quartet and the tone poem *Summer*. Bridge had become so active as a player and conductor that he had little time left for composing. To cut down on his playing, he and his fellow-members of the English String Quartet decided to give more private concerts and fewer public ones. One of these private concerts was played a few doors away in the house of Majorie Fass who was to become a good friend. When the Bridges had a cottage built in Friston in Sussex, Fass had one built next door. They all moved to Friston in 1924.

~ Bedford Street, Covent Garden, WC2E 9ED ~

St Paul's Church, known as the Actor's Church, is most famous for the portico which fronts the west side of Covent Garden piazza, the place where Professor Higgins first meets Eliza Doolittle in *My Fair Lady*. It was designed by Inigo Jones, surveyor of works to Charles I and a theatrical designer, and opened in 1633. Alterations were made in 1795 following a fire and further renovations were carried out in 1871.

There is a memorial tablet to Thomas Arne, who was born a stone's throw away in King Street and was baptised and buried in the churchyard, although his grave has vanished. There is a memorial to William Linley and his mother noting that 'this is a family endowed with genius' and a tablet commemorating Constant Lambert (1905–51).

– 44 Belsize Park Gardens, NW3 –

This is one of the few places Delius stayed in London for any time. Although always considered English, Delius, whose parents were German, lived most of his adult life in France. He came to London at the beginning of World War One, then again to Belsize Park in 1917 when his house in Graz was taken over by French troops. During this time he wrote *On Hearing the First Cuckoo in Spring* and most of the *Violin Concerto*. Strings had to be pulled to get the soloist for the premiere, Bandsman Albert Sammons, off having to play at an all-night army ball.

– 3 Beverley Close, Barnes, SW13 –

The home of composer Herbert Howells. In 1936 Howells took over as Director of Music at St Paul's Girls School from Gustav Holst, staying in the post until 1962. Howells had been born in Lydney in 1892, and been Professor of Composition at the Royal College since

1920. Although he wrote a piano concerto and composed for orchestras, he was more noted for his small scale works, especially his chamber music, organ pieces and choral music. The year after his appointment to St Paul's (where, apparently, he made the girls go weak at the knees) his son Michael died suddenly, aged nine. Howells wrote a choral requiem for him, *Hymnus Paradisi*, which is probably his best-known work. Howells died in 1983. He was Julian Lloyd Webber's godfather.

– 13 Blenheim Road, NW8 –

The baritone Sir Charles Santley (1834–1922) lived here from about 1912 until his death. Santley had a long and distinguished career. He made his debut as an opera singer in Italy in 1857 and gave one of his last recitals in 1915 at the Mansion House in aid of Belgian refugees. He sang Valentine in the first British performance of *Faust* and Van der Decken in *The Flying Dutchman*, the first Wagner opera to be performed in an English-speaking country.

– 1-2 Branch Hill, Hampstead, NW3 –

The house in which the singer Paul Robeson stayed from 1929 until 1930 when he was in London playing the title role in *Othello*. The play caused considerable controversy because the production required him to kiss Peggy Ashcroft who was playing Desdemona, and the idea of a black man kissing a white woman was anathema to many people. Recent research has shown that Ashcroft and Robeson also had an off-stage romance. The controversy didn't hurt the box office: *Othello* ran for 295 performances.

– Brompton Cemetery, Finborough Road, SW10 –

The last resting place of the great Austrian tenor Richard Tauber. Tauber had settled in London and lived at 297 Park West in the Edgware Road. He died in 1948. Constant Lambert's ashes are interred here, as is his son Kit Lambert, first manager of The Who, and the American opera singer Blanche Roosevelt. Arthur Sullivan's mother, father and brother are buried here. The family had intended that Sullivan should be buried with them but Queen Victoria would not allow it, insisting he be buried in St Paul's Cathedral.

– 25 Brook Street, W1 –

The home for thirty-six years of George Frideric Handel (born in Halle, Germany, in 1685) who died here on 14 April 1759. It was newly-built when Handel acquired it in 1723, and was originally number 57. In the music room on the first floor, Handel wrote some of his greatest works including *Messiah*, the *Coronation Anthems*, *Music for the Royal Fireworks* and *Israel in Egypt*. During the twenty-four days it took him to write *Messiah*, Handel did not leave the house, food being brought to him by a servant. The house remains much as it was in 1759 although in the late nineteenth century an extra floor was added and in 1906 the ground floor was converted into a shop. The house has been restored by the Handel House Trust and is now a museum.

Rock guitarist Jimi Hendrix (1942–70) lived next door at No 23 from 1968 until 1969, moving out the year before he died of a drug overdose aged 27.

www.handelhouse.org

– 40 Brunswick Square, WC1 –

The Coram Foundation. In 1739 Captain Thomas Coram, of the merchant navy, opened a Foundling Hospital, since renamed the Coram Foundation. In 1746, the governors appealed for funds to complete the chapel. King George II gave £2,000, plus half as much again for a preacher. But more than twice the King's contribution was raised by one man: George Frideric Handel. In May 1749 he offered to give a concert to raise funds. Thereafter, until ill-health prevented it, he personally supervised an annual fund-raising concert, performing such works as *Messiah*, *Music for the Royal Fireworks*, excerpts from *Solomon* and other pieces including a specially written Foundling Hospital anthem, *Blessed are the Poor*. His efforts raised a stupendous total of £7,000. On Handel's death in 1759, the Hospital inherited 'a fair copy of the score and all parts of my oratorio called *The Messiah*'. This manuscript is on show, as is the portable organ used by Handel when touring the work, presented to the hospital by the composer. There is a bust of Handel by Louis Francis Roubiliac.

www.foundlinghospital.org.uk

– Bunhill Row, EC1 –

Bunhill Fields Cemetery was specifically for dissenters and among the many interesting people interred here are John Bunyan, William Blake, Daniel Defoe, Hugh Pugh, the Welsh harpist and Isaac Watts (1674–1748), the prolific hymn-writer, whose best-known hymns include *O God, our help in ages past* and *When I survey the wondrous cross*.

– Camden Street, Camden Town, NW1 –

In the rather confusingly named St Martin's Gardens, opposite St Michael's Church, for which the gardens were once the graveyard, lies Charles Dibdin (1745–1814), the famous songwriter, who lived in nearby Arlington Street. Dibdin's lasting fame is as a composer of sea songs, which did much to make the navy popular and are still sung today. It was said that he was responsible for more people joining the Royal Navy than the press gangs. During his lifetime he was a popular performer of his own material and also wrote innumerable music dramas. Among his best known songs are *Tom Bowling* and *The Belles of Aberdovey*. Dibdin died in 1814. On his gravestone were words from *Tom Bowling* but the grave has been vandalised and the inscription can no longer be read. A memorial cross, erected by voluntary subscriptions, still stands in front of the grave. There is a memorial to him on the tower of Holyrood Church in Southampton (where he was born) and a statue of him in Trinity College of Music, Greenwich.

– 6 Carlisle Street, W1 –

John Christopher Smith (1712–63) lived and died here. Smith was a pupil and friend of Handel, acting as his amanuensis after Handel's sight failed. He was also a composer in his own right, particularly of opera. His adaptation of *A Midsummer Night's Dream* (entitled *The Fairies*) was successfully produced at Drury Lane in 1754 by David Garrick.

– 2 Carlyle Square, Chelsea, SW3 –

The home of Osbert Sitwell and the house to which William Walton moved after he left Oxford in 1919. Walton lived here, on and off, until 1932, and it was here that he wrote *Façade*, the piece which made his name. The work was given its premiere in the drawing room on 24 January 1922 with Edith Sitwell reciting and Walton himself conducting.

~ 30 Charlotte Street, W1 ~

Now the Etoile Restaurant, this was the home from 1805 to 1810 of the songwriter and composer Charles Dibdin. Dibdin, who wrote more than forty operas and innumerable musical dramas, worked extensively with David Garrick, only to be fired following a row (an occurance that happened to him more than once). He was given a £200-a-year pension by Prime Minister William Pitt to write anti-French songs. He retired to Cranford in Middlesex, but when his pension was stopped, was forced to come back to work at the Lyceum. He died in poverty and is buried in Camden Street.

~ Charterhouse Square, EC1 ~

The Charterhouse (or to give its full title, Sutton's Hospital in Charterhouse), was formerly a monastery then a charitable school. John Christopher Pepusch (1667–1752), who was organist here and is best-known today for being the person who arranged the music for John Gay's *The Beggar's Opera*, is buried in the chapel. Another Charterhouse organist was William Horsley (1774–1858), who wrote the hymn tune *There is a Green Hill Far Away* and was a friend of Mendelssohn. Visits need to be booked. www.thecharterhouse.org

– Corney Road, Chiswick, W4 –

Buried in Chiswick Old Cemetery is Henry Joy, a soldier in the British Army who, according to the inscription on his tombstone, was Trumpet Major of the 17th Lancers and, on 25 October 1854, sounded the charge for the notorious Charge of the Light Brigade during the Battle of Balaclava. This claim is strongly disputed by descendents of Billy Brittan, Lord Cardigan's trumpeter, and it seems they might have a better claim. Joy was the Earl of Lucan's trumpeter and although Lucan was General in overall charge of both the Light and Heavy Brigades, he did not take part in the charge, staying with the Heavy Brigade. Joy, who was probably by Lucan's side throughout the battle, almost certainly sounded the advance for the Heavy Brigade to proceed to what Tennyson memorably called the Valley of Death but went no further. After serving in the Crimea, Joy became a messenger in the War Office until he retired. He died on 17 August 1893.

– Cornhill, EC3 –

St Michael's Church, Cornhill, contains a Renatus Harris organ dating from 1684, considered by many to be the finest organ in England. It was played by Purcell and by William Boyce who was organist here from 1736 until 1768. In the nineteenth century, Richard Limpus, founder of the Royal College of Organists, held the post. There is a plaque on the organ in memory of Harold Darke (1888–1966), who was organist here for fifty years and is best known as the composer of the carol *In The Bleak Midwinter*.

– Cranley Gardens, South Kensington, SW7 3BB –

In 2001, what was formerly St Peter's Church, reopened, following extensive renovation, as the St Yeghiche Armenian Church. Sir Arthur Sullivan was organist at St Peter's from 1867 until 1872. The curate at that time was the Rev Clement Schofield, who later became chaplain at Eton School and has always been credited with writing the popular hymn tune St Clement (*The Day Thou Gavest*). Recent research has shown that the tune was almost certainly written by Sullivan (who also wrote the tunes for *Onward Christian Soldiers* and *Nearer, My God, to Thee*). The church is used regularly for concerts given by international artists.

– 21 Dean Street, W1 –

The site of Caldwell's Assembly Rooms where the eight-year-old Mozart played the harpsichord accompanied by his twelve-year-old sister, in 1764.

– 99 Eaton Place, SW1 –

A plaque marks the house where, on 23 June, Frederic Chopin (1810–49) gave the second London recital of his 1848 concert tour of England and Scotland, arranged for him by former pupil Jane Stirling. On an earlier holiday in London in 1837, he had been impressed: 'One can have a moderately good time in London if one doesn't stay too long. There are extraordinary things: Imposing toilets too narrow to turn round in. And the English! And the houses! And the palaces! And the pomp, and the carriages! Everything from the soap to the razors is extraordinary.' The 1848 February Revolution in Paris, which led to the establishment of the Second Republic, lost Chopin almost overnight all his pupils and all his concert dates. Jane Wilhelmina Stirling (a former pupil to whom he had dedicated his *Op 55 Nocturnes* some years earlier) invited him to visit her and her sister, Mrs Katherine Erskine, in Scotland, playing a few money-raising concerts on the way. He arrived in London on Good Friday and was taken to 48 Dover Street (no longer there) where Stirling and Erskine had booked him an apartment. His drawing room was large enough to accommodate the three grand pianos placed at his disposal by Pleyel, Broadwood and Erard, and he soon found himself a selection of pupils, charging them a guinea a lesson. He needed the money: his rooms cost 40 guineas a month. He left London to begin his Scottish tour in August.

– 180 Ebury Street, SW1 –

Wolfgang Amadeus Mozart (1756–91) paid only one visit to London, in 1764, when his father Leopold took him and his sister Nannerl on a concert tour of Europe. Mozart was eight, his sister twelve; both were child prodigies. The family reached London in April and took lodgings in Cecil Court, St Martin's Lane, with a Mr John Couzens, a barber. The building no longer survives although Cecil Court, the home of book and ephemera sellers, does. Within five days of their arrival the Mozarts were summoned to court. King George III and Queen Caroline were so captivated, they made them return to the palace twice more, and the King even stopped his carriage to wave to them when they were out in St James's Park looking at the deer and the women plying their trade.

During the summer of 1764 Leopold became ill with a throat infection contracted at an open-air concert they had given in Grosvenor Square for the Earl of Thanet. The family decided to move to the country for Leopold to recover. They chose Chelsea, then a little village, and moved into a doctor's house in Five Fields Row (now Ebury Street). Since Leopold was really suffering, he forbade the children to play the piano and so to while away the time, Mozart wrote his first symphony, out of his head, with Nannerl helping him with the orchestration. That finished and Dad still unwell, he embarked on his second symphony as well as writing a number of short pieces collected in an album known as *The Chelsea Notebook*. Queen Charlotte was so impressed when Mozart presented the album to her that she gave him fifty guineas. The house, which has a blue plaque outside and is not open to the public, has hardly changed since Mozart's day, although the view, described by Leopold as 'one of the most beautiful views in the world', certainly has. After seven weeks in Chelsea, Leopold had recovered his health, and they moved to Frith Street, Soho, taking lodgings over a corset maker's shop at number 20 (then 15 Thrift Street) almost directly opposite where Ronnie Scott's Jazz Club is now. The house in which they stayed was demolished in 1858. Leopold, who was always very money-conscious, advertised Mozart's appearances with a challenge inviting Londoners to try his son's 'surprising Musical Capacity, by giving him anything to play at Sight, or any Music without Bass, which he will write upon the Spot.'

But the Mozarts' popularity and novelty value was fading and the family was forced to move to cheaper premises in the City, lodging at the Swan and Hoop Inn in Cornhill where Mozart gave daily performances between twelve and three o'clock until they finally left London in July 1765.

– 59 Eccleston Square, Pimlico, SW1 –

The home for twenty-six years of the pioneering conductor and orchestral reformer, Sir Michael Costa. Costa was born in Naples in 1808. He came to England in 1829 to help put on a work at the Birmingham Festival by his teacher Zingarelli. The festival committee refused to let him conduct because he was only twenty-one, but Costa still decided to stay. He became conductor at the King's Theatre in London and soon made an enormous impact with his new, tough approach to orchestral playing. He was much admired by such composers as Meyerbeer and Verdi for the results he got. In 1847, he helped set up the Royal Italian Opera at Covent Garden and for the next twenty-two years, conducted almost every performance they gave. Although he wrote prolifically as a young man, Costa abandoned composition to concentrate on conducting. He was the first professional conductor in Britain and one of the first to use a baton. The plaque outside his house was unveiled by Antonio Pappano, Musical Director of the Royal Opera.

– 70 Edith Road, W14 –

From 1912 to 1927 this was the home of the remarkable Goossens family. Originally Belgian, their grandfather (Eugene) had come to England to conduct opera. Their father (another Eugene) was a violinist and conductor who gave his son (Eugene) the violin to learn. Leon was given the oboe, Adolph the French horn, and Sidonie and Marie the harp. Eugene, who was born in 1893, played in the Queen's Hall orchestra and became Beecham's assistant conductor. Giving up the violin to concentrate on conducting he founded his own orchestra and gave the first British performance of *The Rite of Spring* in Stravinsky's presence. In the early 1920s he left for the United States, spending almost twenty-five years there. In 1942, he invited composers to come up with a patriotic fanfare for the war effort. Aaron Copland delivered the *Fanfare for the Common Man*. From 1947 to 1956, Goossens was in Australia conducting the Sydney Symphony Orchestra and running the New South Wales music conservatory. The year after he was knighted, disaster struck when some letters he had written to his kinky mistress were made public. Stopped at Sydney airport, he was discovered to have porn in his suitcase and was fined £100. He fled back to England in disgrace having resigned all his appointments. Former pupil Richard Bonynge visited him in London and found him 'destroyed'. Goossens, whose compositions included two symphonies, two operas, two string quartets and an oboe concerto for his brother, died in 1962 and is buried in the St Pancras and Islington Cemetery, High Road, East Finchley. Leon was the finest oboist in England, Adolph was killed on the Somme, while Sidonie, a founder member of the BBC Symphony Orchestra, became the oldest person to play at the Last Night of the Proms when she appeared playing *The Last Rose of Summer* in 1991 at the age of 95. She died ten years later.

– 4 Elsworthy Road, NW8 –

The conductor Sir Henry Wood (1869–1944) lived here from 1905 until 1937. Wood will forever be associated with the Proms which he started in 1895 and conducted for fifty years. Born in London, he became a deputy organist by the time he was ten and organist at St Sepulchre by fourteen. He wanted to be a singing teacher and that is what he became. However, invitations to conduct operas, sometimes for obscure companies, led to him becoming a full-time conductor. He took charge of the British premiere of Tchaikovsky's *Eugene Onegin* and helped Sullivan prepare the scores for *The Yeomen of the Guard* and *Ivanhoe*. Wood's quest to bring classical music to as many people as possible led to the foundation of the Proms through which he was to have an enormous and lasting influence on British music-going. The Promenaders gave him the affectionate nickname of Timber. Visitors to the house included Saint-Saëns, Reger, Sibelius, Delius (who stayed a month), Janáček and Bartók.

– 39 Finsbury Square, EC2 –

Now Citygate House, headquarters of the financial news and data company Bloomberg. On this site stood Seyd's German Guesthouse where the Austrian composer Anton Bruckner (1824–96) stayed from 29 July to the end of August 1871, when he was in London representing Austria in a series of recitals to inaugurate the organ of the Royal Albert Hall. Camille Saint-Saëns represented France. Bruckner's six recitals were so well received that he had to give a further four at Crystal Palace, playing, on 19 August, to 70,000 people. He was so thrilled with his reception that he began work on his *Second Symphony* during this period. He had previously visited London in 1869 as an organ virtuoso.

– Fleet Street, EC4 –

St Bride's Church is where the madrigalist Thomas Weelkes (c1576–1623), is buried close to the Bride Lane tavern in which the first meetings of the London Madrigal Society were held over a century later. He died on a visit to London to stay with a friend named Drinkwater – an ironic surname in view of the fact that Weelkes was an alcoholic. His grave has vanished but there is a plaque in the crypt erected by madrigal lovers to commemorate his tercentenary.

Maurice Greene (1695–1755) was the organist of St Dunstan-in-the-West (between Chancery Lane and Fetter Lane) for two years before becoming organist at St Paul's Cathedral in 1718 and organist of the Chapel Royal of George II. Greene was Master of the King's Musick and later Professor of Music at Cambridge University. He composed songs, theatre music and much church music. John Reading (1686–1764), who as a chorister of the Chapel Royal had sung at the funerals of Purcell and Queen Mary, was also organist here. Reading was not an outstanding composer himself but has been important to musical history by preserving British organ music at a time when it was undergoing rapid change. Handel and Mendelssohn both played the original Renatus Harris organ here.

Temple Church, off Middle Temple Lane, Fleet Street, got its name from the days when this area was the headquarters of the Knights Templar. Originally there were three Temples – Inner, Middle and Outer – but only two, the

Inner and Middle, remain today, home to the legal profession. In the seventeenth century, John Playford (1623–86) had a shop in the West Porch of Temple Church of which Samuel Pepys was a customer. Playford made an extremely important collection of popular music called *The Dancing Master*. In 1683 the church was the scene of the 'battle of the organs'. Both the Inner and Middle Temples agreed the church should have an organ but disagreed violently as to who should build it. It was decided there should be a competition. The Middle Temple asked Bernard Smith (1630–1708) to provide their instrument, with the Queen's organist Giovanni Draghi as his champion. The Inner Temple went for Renatus Harris (1652–1724) with John Blow and Henry Purcell as organists. There were accusations that Harris had vandalised the Smith organ, and it took five years before the dispute was resolved by the Lord Chancellor who chose the Smith organ. This remained in the church until it was destroyed by bombing in 1941. For many years in the eighteenth century, the Temple organist was the blind musician John Stanley (1734–86). Such was his prowess, particularly at improvisation, that the Sunday morning services were frequently attended by up to fifty other organists wanting to hear him play, including Handel.

Also off Middle Temple Lane, is Middle Temple Hall, where the first performance of Shakespeare's play *Twelfth Night* took place in front of Queen Elizabeth I on 2 February 1601.

– Fore Street, Barbican, EC2 –

St Giles without Cripplegate is the church where Oliver Cromwell got married, Daniel Defoe worshipped and Shakespeare may well have been a parishioner. It is one of the few remaining medieval churches in the City of London. It survived the Great Fire of 1666 but not the German bombs of World War Two. Only the tower was left standing. The church was restored during the building of the Barbican. The original Renatus Harris organ, on which Handel is supposed to have played (a claim made by most city churches), was destroyed by the bombs. The current 1733 organ was brought from nearby St Luke's in Old Street when that church was demolished as unsafe in 1960. Composer Henry Smart, who was organist from 1824 until 1844, definitely played on the original organ as did Thomas Morley, who compiled *The Triumphs of Oriana*, and was organist here. One of Morley's contributors, John Milton, the father of the poet, is buried here. Milton senior was born in Stanton St John, near Oxford, in about 1583. Disinherited by his wealthy Catholic parents for becoming a Protestant, he moved to London, became a scrivener, and soon amassed his own fortune. He died in London in March 1647, aged eighty-four. A cultured amateur composer, he wrote mainly church music and madrigals. He was buried next to his son, the poet. The church is the home of the St Giles' International Organ School.

www.stgilescripplegate.org.uk

– 20 Frith Street, W1 –

Site of the premises where the Mozart family lodged in 1765.

– 97 Frognall, NW3 –

Kathleen Ferrier (1912–53), the contralto, lived in Flat 2 from 1942 until 1953, virtually the whole of her professional career. In 1937 she accepted her husband's wager to enter the Carlisle Festival and won both the piano and vocal competitions. She then began serious vocal training and moved to London in 1942. Many concerts followed and her last public appearance was in February 1953 when she sang in *Orfeo* at Covent Garden, conducted by Sir John Barbirolli. She had to withdraw, however, when she broke her leg while on stage (in true trouper tradition, she carried on). She died shortly afterwards.

– 15 Gloucester Walk, W8 –

Jean Sibelius stayed here in 1909 when he was in London to conduct a concert of his music. His music had always enjoyed a warm reception in Britain and he first visited in 1905. While here he completed his string quartet and made the acquaintance of Debussy. His only complaint about London was that the woman in the apartment below kept playing the *Moonlight Sonata* while he was trying to write his quartet. He made two further visits during the twenties and stayed at the Langham Hotel in Langham Place.

– 47 Great Marlborough Street, W1 –

A plaque on the wall of this modern office building records that Franz Liszt stayed in a house on this site in both 1840 and 1841.

– Gresham Street, EC2 –

The Guildhall is the centre of government for the City of London. It was here on 16 November 1848, that Chopin gave his last public performance as one of the artists appearing at a fundraising 'Grand Dress and Fancy Ball and Concert in aid of the Funds of the Literary Association of the Friends of Poland.' But the audience preferred to dance rather than listen to Chopin. His appearance was not even reported in the press the next day. It was to be his last public appearance anywhere.

– 14A Gunter Grove, Chelsea, SW10 –

Known as 'The Studio', this was the home of composer John Ireland who, for twenty-two years, was organist and choirmaster at nearby St Mark's Parish Church. It was for the choir that he composed the hymn tune *My Song is Love Unknown*. He was also teaching composition at the Royal College where his pupils included Benjamin Britten and EJ Moeran. Always a shy, retiring person, leading, it seemed, an uneventful life of church, college and composition, Ireland astonished his friends by marrying Dorothy Philips, one of his students. He was 47, she was 17. The marriage only lasted two years and there has been speculation that it was never consummated. Although he did write full-scale works such as the *Piano Concerto*, the *Legend for Piano and Orchestra*, and overtures, Ireland excelled at writing smaller pieces, especially songs, drawing much of his inspiration from the landscape of Sussex. He lived in Gunter Grove from 1908 until his retirement to Washington, Sussex, in 1953.

– Hanover Square, W1 –

St George's Church, just off the southern end of the square, was completed in 1724 after three-and-a-half years of building. It was one of the fifty churches built when parish boundaries were changed as a result of London's expansion. Its parish ran from Regent Street in the east (then called Swallow Street) to the Serpentine in the west, and south from Oxford Street to cover the areas now known as Mayfair, Pimlico and Belgravia. In 1725, the year the church was consecrated, it was still possible to shoot snipe at the western end of Brook Street. George Frideric Handel, who lived at 25 Brook Street, attended the church regularly until his death in 1759. Even when blind and suffering from arthritis he still made it to services. He advised on the building of the organ and wrote a theme for the applicants for the post of organist to extemporise on. His involvement with the church led to him being given his own pew. Of that original organ, only the case remains. The first organist appointed was Thomas Roseingrave (1691–1766) who had been born in Winchester where his father was organist at the Cathedral. His father later moved to St Patrick's Cathedral in Dublin, where Thomas's own musical talents were first recognised. He was sent by the Dean to study in Italy where he became a friend of the Scarlattis and an admirer of the work of Palestrina. On his return to England in 1717, he did much to promote Domenico Scarlatti's music. Settling in London, he became well-known as a virtuoso organist, teacher and composer as well. Roseingrave's collection of voluntaries and fugues is considered to be the earliest printed collection of English organ fugues. He was organist at St George's until forced to retire in 1737 because of mental instability brought on by the fact that the father of a female pupil with whom he was madly in love refused to let his daughter marry a musician.

~ 10 Hanover Terrace, NW1 ~

Now the official residence of the Provost of University College London, this was the home of Ralph Vaughan Williams (1872–1958) from 1953 until his death. He moved here following his second marriage and completed his Eighth and Ninth Symphonies here. He also wrote the violin sonata, a concerto for tuba and several songs. Visitors included Percy Grainger, Arthur Bliss, Arthur Benjamin, Gerald Finzi, Elizabeth Maconchy, Grace Williams, Leopold Stokowski and many others.

~ 7 Harley Road, NW3 ~

This was the home of singer Dame Clara Butt (1873–1937), from 1901 until 1929. Clara Butt first went to London from Bristol, where she grew up, when she won a scholarship to the Royal College of Music. She made her debut at the Royal Albert Hall two years later. Her striking appearance (she was 6 feet 2 inches tall) and powerful contralto voice were to make her one of the most popular singers of her day. Saint-Saëns wanted her to sing Dalila for him, Elgar wrote *Sea Pictures* for her. She came to epitomize the Last Night of the Proms. In 1900 she married the baritone Kennerly Rumford and the following year they moved into Harley Road as the house's first occupants.

~ 39 Harrington Gardens, SW7 ~

This was the home of Sir William Schwenck Gilbert (1836–1911) from 1883 until 1890. Here he wrote the librettos for *The Mikado*, *The Yeomen of the Guard* and *The Gondoliers*. The house was built especially for him, paid for by the success of *Patience*. It contained central heating, a bathroom on every floor and a telephone, making it one of the most modern houses in London.

– Highgate Cemetery, Swains Lane, N6 –

Best known for being the last resting place of Karl Marx. However, among musicians lying here is Carl Rosa (1842–89), founder of the opera company that bore his name and responsible for introducing many operas then unknown on the British stage. He mounted productions of more than 150 operas including the first production of Wagner's *The Flying Dutchman* in English. He also encouraged British composers to write opera. Arthur Sullivan, Richard D'Oyly Carte and Sir Charles Villiers Stanford were among those at his funeral.

– Holborn Circus, EC4 –

St Andrew's Church managed to escape the Great Fire, but being in a poor state was nevertheless restored by Christopher Wren. Daniel Purcell (1660–1717), brother of Henry, was the organist here from 1713 until his death four years later when Maurice Greene took over temporarily before his appointment to St Paul's. John Stanley (1713–86), the blind organist who was also organist at Temple Church, held the position for sixty years, from 1726 until his death in 1786. He succeeded Handel as a governor of the Foundling Hospital and continued the tradition started by Handel of holding an annual fund-raising performance of *Messiah*. Stanley was buried in the churchyard but his grave is not marked. The church was destroyed by bombs during World War Two and was rebuilt stone-by-stone to Wren's original designs.

– Holborn Viaduct, EC1 –

The church of St Sepulchre-without-Newgate, standing at the eastern end of Holborn Viaduct, is the largest parish church in the City of London and is known as the Musicians' Church. Badly damaged in the Great Fire of 1666, its interior was rebuilt in the style of Wren. The organ, built originally by Renatus Harris in 1670, still contains much that is original, including the casing with Charles II's monogram. The young Henry Wood (1869–1944) learnt to play on this instrument and at the age of 14 became deputy organist. Both Samuel Wesleys (father and son) played here and it is probable that Handel and Mendelssohn did also. Sir Sydney Nicholson (1875–1947), organist of Westminster Abbey (where he is buried), composer and founder of the Royal School of Church Music, was organist here in the 1930s. The side chapel, known as the Musicians' Chapel, contains a St Cecilia window commemorating Sir Henry Wood, whose ashes are buried beneath a slab in the floor below. Two panels show Wood playing the organ as a boy and conducting one of the Promenade Concerts of which he was founder. Another window, erected in 1963, is to the memory of John Ireland. The medallions contain pictures of places connected with Ireland's life and music, while below is the beginning of his anthem *Many Waters Cannot Quench Love*. Over the top are the closing bars of perhaps his most famous song, *Sea Fever*. The window was designed by Brian Thomas who was also responsible for the window in memory of Australian diva, Dame Nellie Melba. Here you can pick out the Australian arms, the insignia of a Dame of the British Empire, Covent Garden opera house and the Royal Albert Hall. The portrait of Melba is surrounded by all the singing birds of Australia, and in the bottom right-hand corner a Peach Melba, the dessert named in her honour. The window above the chapel altar, known as the Magnificat window, is dedicated to Walter Carroll (1869–1955), a highly respected church musician and teacher, who wrote piano and violin music for children. In the Musicians' Chapel is a book of remembrance in which the names of hundreds of professional musicians are inscribed. Practically everything in the chapel has been given by or in memory of a musician. Every chair has a name-plate on it; and all the kneelers, embroidered voluntarily in many parts of the world, commemorate individual musicians including Dennis Brain, Elgar, Kathleen Ferrier, Eugene Goossens, Myra Hess, Hubert Parry and Ernest Read. The blue carpeting in front of the high altar, some kneelers and one of the altar fronts (a green one) were given in 1969 in memory of the conductor Sir Malcolm Sargent. At the entrance to the church another remembrance book lists all those bandsmen who gave their lives in World War Two.

– 14 Holland Park, W14 –

Home of the Harding family. Charles Copeley Harding was a Birmingham businessman who had married the Swedish soprano Louise Alvar, daughter of a Swedish MP. Alvar, a tall, striking blonde, kept a flourishing musical and literary salon at her home in not just one of the most expensive residential districts in London but the world. Among her guests were Sir Edward Elgar, Lord Berners, Sir Henry Wood, Hugo von Hofmannsthal (the librettist of Strauss' comic opera *Der Rosenkavalier*), Joseph Conrad, TS Eliot and the Italian composer Gian Francesco Malipiero. In 1919

Manuel De Falla stayed with them for a month leading up to the premiere at the Alhambra Theatre of his ballet *The Three-Cornered Hat* (sets and costumes designed by Pablo Picasso). Maurice Ravel always stayed with them when in London. Louise Alvar was a noted interpreter of Ravel's songs and in 1926 accompanied the composer on a tour of Scandinavia. The Harding's yellow Rolls-Royce was a familiar sight in Holland Park taking their son to school.

– 21 Holland Park, W14 –

The home of Sir Arthur Bliss from 1896 until 1923 when he left for an extended stay in the United States. Bliss, born in Barnes in 1891, had only just started at the Royal College when World War One began. He immediately enlisted, was commissioned into the Grenadier Guards, and saw action on the Western Front, where he was gassed. After the war he became known as an enfant terrible, writing concertos for voices without words and in 1922, one of his most popular pieces, *The Colour Symphony*. He later began writing film scores, the best of which was for HG Wells' *Things to Come*. He returned to live in London in the late twenties and a blue plaque on East Heath Lodge, 1 East Heath Road, Hampstead NW3, recalls that this was the house in which he lived from 1929 until 1939 and where he wrote *Things to Come* and many other pieces. Bliss was again in the States at the outbreak of World War Two, returning in 1941 to become deputy then Director of Music at the BBC. In 1948 he moved to 15 Cottesmore Gardens W8, where he worked on the *Violin Concerto*, his first opera *The Olympians*, and *Meditations on a Theme of John Blow*. Bliss was knighted in 1950 and appointed Master of the Queen's Music in

1953. He gave up the house in Cottesmore Gardens in 1955 (the same year he left Pens Pit in Somerset) and moved to 8 The Lane, Marlborough Place NW8, where he stayed for the rest of his life. He died in 1975.

– 12 Holland Park Road, W14 9LZ –

Leighton House was the home of the artist Lord Frederic Leighton and is now a museum owned by the Royal Borough of Kensington and Chelsea. Leighton was born in Scarborough in 1830 and studied art throughout Europe. Queen Victoria bought one of his early paintings and his fortune was made. In 1864 he commissioned this house/studio from architect George Aitchison, moving in in 1866. He was knighted in 1878, the year he became President of the Royal Academy, and eight years later became the first painter to be given a peerage. He died the day after he was given it, making it the shortest peerage ever. For many years Leighton was at the centre of London's art world and used to hold musical soirées in his studio at which the finest performers of the day would appear. These included the violinist Joseph Joachim, Clara Schumann, Charles Hallé and singers Pauline Viardot, Adelaide Sartoris and Amelie Joachim. Concerts are still held in the house.

www.leightonhouse.co.uk

– 56 Hornton Street, W8 –

On the corner with 50 Holland Street, a blue plaque marks the home from 1894 until 1916 of Irish composer Sir Charles Villiers Stanford. By the time he moved here, Stanford was a senior figure in the British musical establishment. He was conductor of the Bach Choir, professor of music at Cambridge, professor of composition at the Royal College, and a prolific composer. Among those who visited him here were Tchaikovsky, Dvořák, Saint-Saëns and Bruch. He wrote his fifth and sixth symphonies here, the second piano concerto, the first four *Irish Rhapsodies*, *Songs of the Sea*, *Songs of the Fleet* and the opera *Shamus O'Brien*. Now forgotten, this enjoyed a long run in the West End.

– 4 St James's Place, SW1 –

Chopin stayed here in 1848 from the beginning of November until 23 November, following his Scottish tour with Jane Sterling. He arrived back in London on 31 October and stayed first in Golden Square with the piano manufacturer Henry Broadwood before moving to St James's Place. As a blue plaque records, it was from here that he went to the Guildhall to take part in a fundraising concert on 16 November. He was already ill with tuberculosis and had to be helped from his bed to get there. It was to be his last public appearance. The front of the house has been rebuilt as a facsimile of the seventeenth-century original but the interior is little changed.

– Kennington Lane, SE11 –

The small area of grassland known as Spring Gardens is all that remains of what was once London's most exciting, glamorous and popular playground. The twelve-acre Vauxhall Pleasure Gardens consistently made money for its investors during its 200-year existence. It opened in the 1660s but enjoyed its heyday in the middle of the eighteenth century when owner Jonathan Tyers remodeled the gardens to produce an English Versailles. Part of Tyers' dream was to introduce good music to the poorer, uneducated visitors. Huge orchestras, under the direction of Thomas Arne, performed especially composed operas, cantatas and oratorios in the rotunda. Outside in the gardens, smaller ensembles played on the bandstands while some musicians even played in the bushes. 'Vauxhall is particularly adapted to the taste of the English nation,' wrote Boswell, 'there being musick, vocal and instrumental, but not too refined for the general ear.' It was in the Gardens that the public dress rehearsal of Handel's *Music for the Royal Fireworks* was given in 1749. Performed by 100 musicians, it attracted a crowd of more than 12,000 and caused a three-hour carriage jam on Westminster Bridge. The gardens closed in 1859 after the site was dissected by the new railway line to the south coast.

– Kensal Green Cemetery, Harrow Road, W10 –

Among the many musicians buried in Kensal Green Cemetery are the composers of what became known as the English Ring: William Vincent Wallace (1812–65), Sir Michael Balfe (1808–70) and Sir Julius Benedict (1804–85). Other residents include Philip Cipriani Potter (1792–1871), pianist, composer and Principal of the Royal Academy of Music, who became acquainted with Beethoven in 1817; Henry Russell (1812–1900) who composed some eight hundred songs including *A Life on the Ocean Wave*; Sir Michael Costa (1808–84); the conductor and teacher Henry Wylde (1822–90); Sir John Goss (1800–80) organist of St Paul's Cathedral; the virtuoso cellist Robert Lindley

(1777–1855); songwriter George Linley (1798–1865); and the Afro-Polish violinist George Bridgetower (c1778–1860). Bridgetower was the son of a Barbadian in the service of Prince Esterhazy, Haydn's patron, and first came to England as a child to play concerts in London, Bath and Bristol. Such was his renown that he was summoned to play for the King and Queen. The Prince Regent, later King George IV, was so impressed he paid for Bridgetower's tuition, during which Bridgetower played in the orchestra that gave the first performances of Haydn's London symphonies, with Haydn in charge. In 1803, in Vienna, he met Beethoven and with Beethoven playing piano, gave the first performance of the Violin Sonata No 9. Even though Bridgetower had to play the second part looking over Beethoven's shoulder because the copyist had not finished writing it out in time, Beethoven was delighted and dedicated the piece to him. Shortly afterwards, Beethoven accused Bridgetower of insulting one of his lady friends and removed his name from the score, replacing it with that of Kreutzer. The sonata is now known as the Kreutzer even though Kreutzer said it was far too difficult to play. Bridgetower died in poverty in Peckham.

The composer and conductor Sir George Smart (1776–1867) is also buried here. It was at his Great Portland Street house (number 91 which became 103 and is now demolished) that Mendelssohn stayed when in London for the first performance of *Fingal's Cave* and Carl Maria von Weber died in 1826. Weber was in London to write an opera for Covent Garden and came even though he was suffering from a throat disease and was essentially unfit to travel, because he needed the money. He was installed on the second floor, with piano, but did not like London, complaining that it was expensive: the only thing cheaper than in Germany, he wrote home, was a haircut. Weber conducted the first performance of *Oberon* in April and was supposed to conduct its run, but was so exhausted he decided to cut short his stay and return to Germany. However he died during the night of 4 June. He was buried in St Mary's Catholic Chapel, Moorfields. Twelve years later his successor as conductor of the Dresden Choral Society, Richard Wagner, arranged for his body to be returned to Dresden.

– 128 Kensington Church Street, W8 –

The home of Muzio Clementi (1752–1832). Clementi is remembered chiefly as the composer of the original theme on which Beethoven based his variations. Born in Rome, he was brought to England by Sir Peter Beckford of Stepleton House, Blandford Forum, who became his patron. Clementi spent most of his musical life in England and made a considerable fortune conducting, playing and teaching (one of his most famous pupils being John Field). He had given up performing and devoted himself to composition while living here between 1820 and 1823. In 1823 he sold the lease to the organist and composer William Horsley (1774–1858). Mendelssohn, a friend of the Horsley family, was a frequent visitor to the house.

– Kensington Gore, SW7 –

A blue plaque outside Albert Hall Mansions, the red-brick apartment block alongside the Royal Albert Hall, commemorates the fact that the conductor Sir Malcolm

Sargent lived at number 9 for the last twenty years of his life. Sargent was throughout that time chief conductor of the Promenade Concerts, famous for his Last Night speeches as much as for his music-making. He was one of those conductors who divided opinion between those who thought the Flash Harry nickname was appropriate and those who felt he could do no wrong. Sargent was born in 1895 and went to Stamford School (where Tippett was later a pupil). He died here on 3 October 1967.

– 17 Kensington Square, W8 –

The London home of Sir Hubert Parry (1848–1918). He moved into the house in 1887 and remained until his death. Parry, whose music is now rarely performed (apart from *Jerusalem*) was a major influence on the musical life of Victorian England, both as a composer and as Director of the Royal College of Music, a post to which he was appointed in 1895. While living at Kensington Square, he wrote his *Symphonic Variations*, the anthem *I Was Glad*, *Songs of Farewell*, and many other pieces.

– 31 King's Road, SW3 –

The eccentric Australian pianist and composer Percy Grainger, who wrote some of the most quintessentially English folk songs – *Handel in the Strand, Country Gardens* – lived here from 1908 to 1914. Having studied in Europe, Grainger arrived in London in 1901 and lived in a number of apartments in the Chelsea area. He later claimed to have lost his virginity at 16 Cheyne Walk, formerly Rossetti's home, with his patron, Mrs Lowery, in 1902. He was 20, she slightly more mature. Grainger became fascinated by English folk song, becoming the first person to capture such songs on wax cylinders. He was known as the jogging pianist because of his habit of running to the concert hall so that he would be exhausted during the performance.

– 31 King Street, WC2 –

A blue plaque commemorates the fact that the composer Thomas Arne (1710–78) was born and brought up here. Arne was the son of an upholsterer and coffin-maker. On one occasion, young Arne's violin teacher turned up to give him a lesson and found the boy practicing with his music stand on a coffin. The teacher wondered how he could concentrate on his music. There might, he said, be a corpse in the coffin. Arne replied that there was and lifted the lid to show him. The teacher fled from the house and never returned. Arne's father, a keen amateur musician, was a friend of Handel, and both his sister and brother were singers who appeared in his stage shows. He became one of the leading lights of West End theatre, working extensively at Drury Lane with the actor David Garrick. Arne is best remembered today for having written *Rule Britannia*. He also lived in Great Queen Street from 1735 until 1748, and in Bow Street where he died. Arne was a great ladies' man, who would often prowl the local streets on the pick up. His pupil Dr Burney wrote of him: 'he never could pass by a woman in the street, to the end of his Life, without Concupiscence or, in plain English, picking her up.' There is a memorial to Arne in St Paul's Church, Covent Garden where he was baptised and buried, although his grave can no longer be identified. St Paul's is known as the Actor's

Church and contains memorial plaques to a wide range of famous stage names.

– Lambeth Palace Road, SE1 7LB –

At the junction with Lambeth Road, next to Lambeth Palace, the London home of the Archbishop of Canterbury, stands the restored church of St Mary at Lambeth, now the Museum of Garden History. The derelict church was chosen because its graveyard contains the family tomb of the Tradescant family, where John Tradescant, father and son, famous seventeenth-century gardeners responsible for bringing many new species of plant to England, are buried. Also in the graveyard are the tombs of Captain Bligh of *Bounty* fame, six archbishops, and Elias Ashmole, who founded the Ashmolean Museum in Oxford. So too is the grave of the soprano Nancy Storace (1766–1817), Mozart's first Susanna in *The Marriage of Figaro*. She was the sister of operatic composer Stephen Storace (1762–96), the children of an Italian double-bass player who had settled first in Dublin, then in London, where they were both born. She made her stage debut when she was ten in *Le Ali d'Amore* by Rauzzini, her teacher. She continued to study in Venice and began to appear regularly on the stage. Together with her brother, she moved to Vienna in 1784 where she was engaged at the Imperial Theatre, they became friendly with Mozart, and Stephen was imprisoned for quarreling with an officer. She moved back to London in 1788 and continued to enjoy a successful career. A plaque on the wall in the café area commemorates her.

226

– Leadenhall Street, EC3 –

Historically the location of Lloyd's of London and the East India Company, it was, according to legend, from Leadenhall Street that Dick Whittington stole away, stopping at Highgate to be summoned back by the sound of Bow bells. Today it contains the church of St Katherine Cree. The church survived the Great Fire and the Blitz, and contains a restored Renatus Smith organ, parts of which date from 1686. It was played by Purcell, Handel and Wesley.

– 1 Leicester Street, WC2 –

Formerly the Hotel du Commerce and then Manzi's Seafood Restaurant , this is where Johann Strauss the Elder (1804–49), father of the Waltz King and composer of the *Radetzky March*, stayed on his first visit to London in April 1838. He was here with his twenty-eight piece orchestra to take part in Queen Victoria's coronation celebrations, for which he composed his *Queen Victoria Waltz*. Strauss played at the State Ball held at Buckingham Palace in May, and was playing outside the Reform Club on coronation day itself, 28 June, as the Queen's procession went past, competing with the military and brass bands that were churning out endless *God Save the Queen*s. On this trip, Strauss and his orchestra played 72 concerts, often giving three a day. He returned to tour England again in 1849, dying from scarlet fever not long after returning to Vienna. A plaque commemorates his 1838 visit.

– 100 London Road, Forest Hill, SE23 3PQ –

On the South Circular Road, the A205, at Forest Hill, is the Horniman Museum, named after its founder Frederick Horniman. Horniman, a Member of Parliament, made his money from tea: he was the first person to sell it pre-packaged. On his travels he began collecting artefacts that interested him – anything from a totem pole to Egyptian bone clappers in the shape of hands dating from 1500 BC. Wanting to teach the inhabitants of Forest Hill something about the cultures of the world, Horniman opened his collection to the public in his home and it is now one of the foremost collections anywhere. It contains an impressive and important collection of over 7,000 musical instruments and 1,000 documents. Recent acquisitions include the Wayne collection of 600 concertinas and the Boosey and Hawkes collection, bought, together with their archives when instrument manufacturers Boosey and Hawkes closed their Edgware factory. In order to preserve them the instruments are not usually played but occasionally recitals are given and there are recordings and videos played alongside the exhibits. Admission to the museum is free.

www.horniman.ac.uk

– 2 Manchester Square, W1 –

The home of composer Sir Julius Benedict (1804–85) for more than forty years. Benedict, the son of a Jewish banker, was born in Stuttgart in 1804. He studied with Hummel and Carl Maria von Weber of *Der Freischütz* fame. It was Weber who introduced him to both Beethoven and Mendelssohn. He began his career as an operatic conductor first in Vienna then in Naples, where his first two operas were staged not very successfully. In 1835, at the suggestion of Maria Malibran, he arrived in London where he became musical director of the opera at Drury Lane. This was the time when Balfe was riding high. In 1850, Benedict was Jenny Lind's accompanist on a tour of the USA. He continued writing operas, the most successful of which was *The Lily of Killarney* based on Dion Boucicault's blockbuster play, *The Colleen Bawn*. *The Lily of Killarney*, which was written here, together with Wallace's *Maritana* and Balfe's *The Bohemian Girl*, were popularly known as the English Ring. Benedict conducted the Norwich Festival for more than thirty years. He was knighted in 1871 and died in this house.

– 12 Mandeville Place, W1 –

A plaque commemorates the fact that Sir (Francesco) Paolo Tosti lived in a house on this site (where the Mandeville Hotel now stands) from 1886 until his death in 1916. Tosti was a composer of popular songs and a renowned singing teacher. Born at Ortano sul Mare on the Adriatic coast on 9 April 1846, he began his musical life as a violinist, before studying singing and composition. When Princess Margherita of Savoy (later Queen of Italy) heard one of his ballads at a concert, she invited him to become her singing teacher. In 1875 Tosti made his first visit to London, returning every year until 1880, when he decided to settle here. He became singing teacher to Queen Victoria's younger children and professor of singing at the Royal Academy of Music. He received a knighthood in 1908 after becoming a British citizen two years earlier. In 1912, he retired to Italy, living mostly in Rome where he died on 2 December 1916. Tosti wrote some 350 songs and ballads many of them extremely popular and still included in recitals by today's leading tenors. They include *Forever*, *Goodbye*, *At Vespers*, *That Day*, *La Serenata*, *Lamento d'Amore* and *Malia*. Writing a salon ballad 'alla Tosti' became many a composer's ambition.

– 4 Maresfield Gardens, NW3 –

From 1918 until 1924, this was the home of Cecil Sharp, leader of the English folk song movement. Sharp, after whom the Folk Song Society headquarters on the edge of Regent's Park is named, was born in Camberwell in 1859, the son of a slate merchant with a love of the arts. Encouraged by his father, he decided to emigrate to Australia where he worked in the Chief Justice's office in Adelaide, and involved himself in local music. In 1892 he returned to England to become a music teacher. This was at the time when an interest in folk song was beginning to sweep Europe, and Sharp, on his bicycle, began collecting English folk songs (and, having seen Morris dancers near Oxford, folk dances). His pioneering work inspired such composers as Vaughan Williams, EJ Moeran and Percy Grainger. There is a blue plaque.

– 15 Morden Road, Blackheath, SE3 –

French composer Charles Gounod (1818-93) stayed here in 1870, from the beginning of October until 10 November, then again for two weeks in 1874. He had left France with his family after war had been declared on Prussia and stayed in London until 1874. In France, he had concentrated on writing opera: *Faust* and *Romeo et Juliette* being two of them. In London he became addicted to oratorio, then considered by the English to be the height of musical expression. On his return to France, Gounod wrote *The Redemption* and *Mors et vita*.

– 42 Netherhall Gardens, Hampstead, NW3 –

The site of the house Elgar named Severn House, in which he lived from 1912 until 1921. In 1910 the Elgars were living in Hereford, with Elgar commuting to London whenever he needed to, renting small properties in which to stay. It was tiring so they decided to buy a London house, settling on a large Queen Anne building in Hampstead with a music room large enough to give recitals. They moved in on New Year's Day, 1912. The house's proximity to central London meant, however, there were always people to see. Elgar did manage some composition – he worked on the cello concerto and wrote his symphonic study *Falstaff* – but decided he had to get a country retreat where he wouldn't be disturbed. He chose Brinkwells at Fittleworth in Sussex. Severn House was demolished in 1938 and numbers 42 and 44 built on the site. There is a plaque on number 42.

– 47 North Side, Clapham Common, SW4 –

The home of music publisher George Augener and the house where Edvard Grieg (1843–1907) stayed when in London. Grieg first came to England as a teenager in 1862, then, between 1888 and 1906, when his music had become the most popular in England by a living composer, on a series of concert tours accompanied usually by his singer wife, Nina. He was lionised wherever he went and the concerts at which he played or conducted were invariably sold out. He also visited the universities of Oxford and Cambridge to be awarded honorary doctorates. His accommodation in Clapham was on the second floor with a music room overlooking the common. Augener would fly a Norwegian flag outside the house whenever Grieg was in residence. On his last visit to London, Grieg was invited to play for King Edward and Queen Alexandra at Buckingham Palace. The King was seated next to the Norwegian ambassador whom he knew well and they immediately fell into a deep conversation even though Grieg was playing. Grieg stopped. 'When you have finished,' he said, 'I will finish.'

~ 22 Old Queen Street, W1 ~

Close to St James Park in the heart of Westminster, this was the London home of Frank Schuster, a wealthy banker and patron of the arts who did much to foster Elgar's career. 'He was always the most loving, strongest and wisest friend man could have,' Elgar wrote after Schuster's death. Schuster and his sister loved throwing lavish parties and it was here that a young conductor named Adrian Boult first met Elgar. Fauré stayed here when in London and other visitors included Ivor Novello and Richard Strauss.

~ 240 Oxford Street, W1 ~

Now part of Marble Arch Underground Station, this was the site of the pastry shop above which Vincent Novello was born on 6 September 1781. Novello became a brilliant organist and people flocked to hear him and his choir at the Portuguese Embassy Chapel in nearby South Street. During the 25 years he was there, he introduced to Britain the masses of Mozart and Haydn and the organ works of JS Bach. Requests for the music his choir was performing began to grow and being unable to find a publisher, Novello decided to print it himself. The success of *The Portuguese Collection*, as it was called, encouraged him to continue printing music at his own expense and led to the founding in 1829 of the famous music publishing house of Vincent Novello. The Novello family lived in their Oxford Street home for many years and among the many eminent musical visitors were Felix Mendelssohn, the celebrated diva Maria Malibran, and the legendary genius of the double-bass, Dragonetti.

– 10 Palace Green, W8 –

The residence of the Norwegian Ambassador, its library contains a charcoal drawing of the composer Frederick Delius by Edward Munch. Although not open to the general public, those wishing to see the portrait can apply to the Royal Norwegian Embassy for an appointment.
www.norway.org/embassy

– Lancaster House, Pall Mall, SW1 –

In 1848 there was a revolution in France. Overnight Chopin found his wealthy students and concert promoters in Paris had vanished and he was broke. It was his former pupil Jane Stirling (who was madly in love with him) who suggested he should make a concert tour of England and Scotland. He duly arrived in London and moved into 48 Dover Street where three pianos were delivered for him to practice on. He then began the round of private house concerts, appearing first at Lord Falmouth's house in St James's Square and then at 99 Eaton Place. He was paid £300 for the two concerts. He then gave a recital in Pall Mall at Lancaster

House (then called Stafford House) for the Duchess of Sutherland. The concert took place in the State Rooms on the first floor and was attended by Queen Victoria, Prince Albert and the Duke of Wellington. Lancaster House now belongs to the nation but is not open to the public.

~ Pancras Road, NW1 ~

The churchyard of St Pancras Old Church is where Johann Christian Bach, the eleventh and youngest son of Johann Sebastian, was buried. JC, sometimes known as the English Bach, was born in Leipzig in 1735. His father was fifty so it's hardly surprising they didn't always see eye-to-eye on matters musical. Taught by his father (he was fifteen when JSB died) and then by an elder brother, Bach carved out a nice career for himself as a composer and a performer. He lived in Italy for some time, becoming organist of Milan Cathedral and converting to Catholicism. Then, in 1762, he came to London for the premieres of three of his operas. These were so well received he decided to stay, becoming music master to Queen Charlotte, wife of King George III. He died in London on New Year's Day 1782. The site of his grave has disappeared but there is a memorial to him in the churchyard gardens. There's a grave, too, of his friend Carl Friedrich Abel, who had also settled in London as a private musician to Queen Charlotte. Bach and Abel, who was considered to be the last great viol de gamba player, gave recitals together.

~ 13 Pendennis Road, Streatham, SW16 ~

A plaque records that Sir Arnold Bax was born here on 8 November 1883. He was brought up, though, in Ivy Back, a mansion in its own grounds on Haverstock Hill, Hampstead. Coming from a wealthy middle-class family, Bax never had to get a job. Instead he could indulge his passion for music and poetry. Reading the poetry of WB Yeats introduced him to Ireland and Irish culture, a fascination that lasted until his death in Cork in 1953.

– Piccadilly, W1 –

Green Park, on the southern side of Piccadilly, was where Handel's *Music for the Royal Fireworks* was first performed in 1749 as part of the celebrations marking the end of the War of Austrian succession. Shortly after the Treaty of Aix-la-Chapelle had been signed in October 1748, workmen began to erect an enormous wooden structure in Green Park, 410 feet long, 114 feet high, designed in the Palladian style with colonnades and a central triumphal arch over which were statues of Greek gods and a bas relief of King George II. Handel was commissioned to provide suitable music to accompany a firework display for which Italian experts were being brought in. The King had originally been against any music at all but eventually agreed, hoping 'there would be no fidles'. During the course of writing the piece Handel decided not only to incorporate fiddles but caused a furore by reducing the number of trumpets and horns from sixteen to twelve. He eventually compromised with nine trumpets, nine horns, twenty-four oboes, twelve bassoons and three pairs of kettle drums. The performance took place at 6pm on 21 April (following a public rehearsal in Vauxhall Gardens when over 12,000 people attended, jamming Westminster Bridge for three hours). There is no evidence that the firework display (which was generally regarded as poor) coincided with the music, which is probably just as well since a firework landed on the pavilion next to which the orchestra had been playing. Although it was a damp evening, the wooden building caught fire and burnt to the ground. The designer promptly drew his sword on the Comptroller of Fireworks and had to be disarmed. Handel's music went on to become one of the most popular pieces in the repertoire.

Le Meridien Hotel, on the northern side of the road, just off Piccadilly Circus, formerly the Piccadilly Hotel, stands on the site of St James' Hall, a purpose-built concert hall which opened in 1858 at a cost of £40,000. Here Richter conducted Brahms, and Camille Saint-Saëns gave the world premiere of his popular Third Symphony in May 1886. The hall was demolished at the turn of the century and the hotel built on its site. When it was the Piccadilly Hotel, the Russian composer and pianist Sergei Rachmaninov used to stay here.

St James's Church on the southern side of Piccadilly, opposite Le Meridien, was built by Sir Christopher Wren and completed in 1684. It soon became the most fashionable church in London (the poet William Blake, whose poem 'Jerusalem' was famously set by Parry, was baptised here in 1757) and in 1690 Queen Mary donated to the church a Renatus Harris organ from the Chapel Royal in Whitehall Palace. John Blow, the organist at Westminster Abbey, and his pupil Henry Purcell, were responsible for overseeing its installation and, although we have no concrete evidence that they did, both men must surely have played the instrument. The casing is by the Dutch-born sculptor and wood carver

Grinling Gibbons, as is the altarpiece and, possibly, the font. The conductor Leopold Stokowski was organist here until he emigrated to the United States in 1905. Although the church was badly damaged in the Blitz during World War Two, the organ and Gibbons casing had been removed for safety. They were returned when the church was rededicated after rebuilding in 1954. Regular lunchtime and evening concerts are held here.

– 1c Portland Place, Regent Street, W1 –

The Langham was re-opened as a hotel in 1991 after almost fifty years of BBC occupation following bomb damage during World War Two. Originally opening its doors in 1865, it was London's first great luxury hotel and the first with hydraulic lifts. It had six hundred bedrooms but a mere thirty-six bathrooms. The hotel's proximity to The Queen's Hall on the other side of Portland Place, one of London's premier concert venues and home of Sir Henry Wood's famous Promenade Concerts from 1895 until 1941 when the building was destroyed by enemy bombing, meant that a number of eminent musicians stayed here. They include Sir Edward Elgar (who used the hotel as his London base after he left his London house and moved to Malvern), Toscanini, Sibelius, Janácek and Dvorák. The site of the Queen's Hall is now an office block and there is a plaque just inside the BBC's Henry Wood House marking the location of The Queen's Hall.

– Prince Consort Road, South Kensington, SW7 –

The Royal College of Music, opposite the steps up to the Royal Albert Hall, houses an important collection of over

800 instruments dating from the late fifteenth century to the present day, and covers not just Western instruments but Asian and African too. Gifts to the college since its foundation in 1883 have included the collections of the Rajah SM Tahor, King Edward VII, Sir George Donaldson, AJ Hipkins, EAK Ridley and Geoffrey Hartley. The museum is open to the public and admission is free.

www.cph.rcm.ac.uk

– 58 Queen Anne Street, W1 –

A blue plaque records that Hector Berlioz (1803–69) stayed here in 1851. Berlioz visited London five times. On his first trip in 1847, he stayed at 76 Harley Street, (now demolished and where number 27 is today), the home of Louis Jullien, founder of Promenade Concerts and Director of the Grand English Opera Company of Drury Lane, who had invited Berlioz to conduct his opera company. The sixth-month engagement ended disastrously when Jullien went bankrupt and Berlioz was thrown out of the house by the bailiffs. He managed to find alternative lodgings at 26 Osnaburgh Street before returning to Paris in a fury. He returned in 1852, 1853 and 1856 to conduct concerts, always staying in the Marylebone area. He was in London in 1851 (his second trip) as a member of the jury judging the quality of musical instruments submitted to the Great Exhibition by manufacturers from throughout Europe. He found the task onerous, performing day after day 'the stupid job of examining the musical instruments… It splits your head to hear these hundreds of wretched machines, each more out of tune than the next.' He stuck to his task, however, even after all the other French judges had packed their bags and left, 'in order to see justice done… France comes out ahead beyond any possible comparison… The rest is more or less in the class of penny whistles and pots and pans.' Berlioz stayed in Queen Anne Street, the home of a professor of music, from 10 May until 28 July. The Beethoven Quartet Society gave regular performances in the drawing room, as Berlioz recorded: 'My apartment being situated above the main staircase, I could easily hear the whole performance by simply opening my door. One evening I heard Beethoven's Trio in C Minor being played. I opened my door wide. Come in, come in, welcome proud melody!' This house is the only one in which Berlioz stayed that is still standing.

– 38 Queensborough Terrace, W2 –

The composer Sir William Sterndale Bennett lived here from 1865 until 1873, two years before his death. Born in Sheffield in 1816, he was brought up in Cambridge by his grandfather following his father's death. At the age of seven he became a chorister at King's College. As a young composer and pianist he enjoyed a very high profile in Germany. He was friends with Mendelssohn and also got to know Robert Schumann who raved about his *Third Piano Concerto* at its premiere in Leipzig and said Bennett was the most musical of Englishmen. Bennett's early work was youthful and exuberant. He wrote six piano concertos, other works for piano and orchestra, piano pieces, chamber music, songs and a symphony, at the same time gaining an increasing reputation as a conductor. He was appointed professor of music at Cambridge University and then, in 1866, became Principal of the Royal Academy of Music, virtually giving up composing. Bennett's great-great-grandson is Charlie Simpson, vocalist and guitarist with Fightstar (formerly with Busted).

– Royal Hospital Road, SW3 –

The Royal Hospital, home of the Chelsea Pensioners, was founded in 1692 by King Charles II and built by Christopher Wren. The buildings include a chapel which has had only fourteen organists since its foundation, one of them being Dr Charles Burney, the musicologist and father of novelist Fanny, who held the post from 1783 until his death in 1814. Burney wrote a *General History of Music*, published between 1776 and 1789, which revealed an extraordinary breadth of knowledge, much of it gained while travelling in Europe. He was a friend of Haydn, who stayed in the organist's apartments at the Royal Hospital during two of his London visits, and it was through Burney's recommendation that Haydn was awarded an honorary Doctorate of Music by the University of Oxford in 1791. It appears that in the nineteenth century, the Royal Hospital followed the custom common in city churches in the eighteenth century, of employing female organists, who were expected to resign if they got married. The organ in the chapel retains the original Renatus Harris casing but is a modern instrument. Visitors are welcome at Sunday Services. The chapel can be visited during the day.

www.chelsea-pensioners.co.uk

– St Alfege's Church, Greenwich, SE10 –

St Alfege's is the Greenwich parish church, built on the site of the martyrdom of St Alfege. Nearby Greenwich Palace was one of the places where the Chapel Royal performed and where Queen Elizabeth I held lavish parties. Thomas Tallis, who served as organist of the Chapel Royal under four monarchs, is buried here. His tomb carries the inscription 'As he did live, so also did he die, In mild and quiet Sort. (O! happy man).' Richard Bower, who served as Master of the Children of the Chapel Royal from 1545 until 1563, is also buried here.

– St Botolph's Without Aldgate, Aldgate High Street, EC3 –

This houses what is generally regarded to be the oldest church organ in London, if not the country. The original was built by Renatus Harris between 1702 and 1704, and a plaque inside the church records that it was 'the gift of Mr Thomas Whiting to the hole [sic] parish.' Although it survived the Great Fire, the church fell into disrepair and a new building (the current one) was put up, designed by George Dance who built the Mansion House. This opened in 1744 with the Harris organ rebuilt by John Byfield, Harris's son. The instrument was greatly enlarged in the mid-nineteenth century and survived the building being hit by a bomb during World War Two (the bomb stuck in the roof and failed to go off). In 2002 it was decided to rebuild the organ to its original 1744 specification, the work being undertaken, after a considerable period of fundraising, by the Nottinghamshire firm of Goetze and Gwynn and completed in May 2006. The result is one of the most historically accurate of eighteenth-century organs. Anyone wanting to play the organ should contact the parish office during office hours on 020 7283 1670.

www.botolph.org.uk

– St James's Palace, Pall Mall, SW1 –

St James's Palace is still the most senior palace in Britain – even though a monarch has not lived here for centuries – and the Chapel Royal and Queen's Chapel (designed by Inigo Jones) are the two most important Chapels Royal. The term Chapel Royal was not originally used for buildings but was a choir that would sing services wherever and whenever the monarch required them. Sir Arthur Sullivan, as a young boy, was a chorister here, while among the organists in charge of the choir have been Thomas Tallis, Orlando Gibbons, William Byrd and Henry Purcell. Purcell had a suite of rooms in the palace in which the poet John Dryden used to hide to avoid his creditors. Handel was appointed official composer to the Chapel Royal by George II in 1723, and later composed *Zadok the Priest* for George's coronation. The Chapel Royal and the Queen's Chapel are open to the public only for services.

www.royal.gov.uk/TheRoyalResidences/TheChapelsRoyal

– 45a St John's Wood High Street, W8 –

This is the flat to which Benjamin Britten moved in 1943 the year after he and Peter Pears returned from the USA. It was here that he wrote *Peter Grimes*, one of the most important operas of the last century. They left in 1946 for Snape. Between 1970 and 1976, if Britten needed to be in London, he would stay at 8 Halliford Street N1, where there was a studio in which the bulk of the opera *Death in Venice* was written.

– St Margaret's Street, Westminster SW1 –

St Margaret's Westminster is the official church of the House of Commons. The musical life of the church and of Westminster Abbey has often been intertwined. John Blow was organist in both churches and Edward Purcell, son of Henry, was organist here from 1726 until 1740. John Hingston, who died in 1688 and was composer and organist to Oliver Cromwell, is buried here. Blow was his pupil, Purcell his apprentice. After the Reformation Hingston became a viol player at court and official court instrument repairer. Also buried here is Nicholas Ludford (c1490–1557), one of the leading composers of his generation. He lies next to his first wife Anne. Ludford, whose surviving music is to be found in two choirbooks in the libraries of Lambeth and Caius College, Cambridge, was the organist and verger at St Stephen's, Westminster, part of the old palace of Westminster, from about 1521 until ten years before his death. He lived rent-free in lodgings owned by St Stephen's and had an annual income of more than 46 pence a week (£10 a year). His principal task was to provide music for the royal chapel (which was later destroyed by fire in 1834). A staunch Roman Catholic, Ludford gave up composition after the Reformation and became a church warden at St Margaret's.

– St Mary Abchurch, Abchurch Lane, EC4 –

The present church was rebuilt after the Great Fire of 1666 by Sir Christopher Wren and is well worth a visit in its own right. No trace of the medieval building remains and so the grave has been lost of the sixteenth-century musician Thomas Whythorne who was buried here. Composer of the first known duets in England, he achieved modern prominence as a result of EJ Moeran's *Whythorne's Shadow*, an orchestral rhapsody based on one of his part songs. Whythorne's autobiography, first published in 1961, counts as the first musical autobiography and gives a vivid account of life as a sixteenth century working musician.

– St Paul's Cathedral –

The present St Paul's is Christopher Wren's masterpiece, replacing an earlier building destroyed in the Great Fire of 1666. Clearly no trace of the building in which two eminent musicians played the organ before the Great Fire remains. They were John Redford and Thomas Morley. Little is known about Redford who held the post in the middle of the sixteenth century, wrote compositions mainly for the choir and himself, and died in 1547. Morley (1557–c1603) held the post from around 1591. A Gentleman of the Chapel Royal, he was possibly a friend of Shakespeare for whose plays he composed songs. He was given the monopoly of music printing by Queen Elizabeth's government in 1598 and held it until his death. He wrote church music, instrumental music, lute songs and many madrigals. He also wrote a *Plaine and Easie Introduction to Practicall Musicke* (1597) which remains the best guide to sixteenth-century musical practice, and edited *The Triumphs of Oriana*, a collection of madrigals in honour of Queen Elizabeth I.

Organists and composers who have played in the present building include Handel, who practiced on the organ regularly, and Jeremiah Clarke, who held the position of organist from 1695 until his death in 1707. Clarke wrote the trumpet voluntary now known as *The Prince of Denmark's March* and traditionally attributed to Purcell. He was master of the choristers and shot himself in the cathedral precincts after being rejected by his lover. Although buried in the cathedral, the site of his grave is unknown. Maurice Greene (1695-1755), who was organist from 1718 until 1755, is buried in the crypt next to William Boyce. There is a tablet on the wall of the north transept listing the cathedral organists beginning with John Redford in 1530 and including Thomas Attwood, a pupil of Mozart, Sir John Goss, Sir John Stainer, Sir George Martin, Charles Macpherson, Sir Stanley Marchant and Sir John Dykes Bower. In the same alcove as this tablet but further along the wall is a statue of Sir Arthur Sullivan who is buried in the crypt. Opposite, is a memorial to Sir John Stainer. Also buried in the crypt are Sir John Goss and Maria Hackett. There is a monument to Goss, sculpted by William Thornycroft. Maria Hackett (1783-1874) worked tirelessly visiting the cathedrals of England, to check on and try to improve conditions for choirboys, which, in the nineteenth century were dreadful. The choristers of St Paul's, for example, were so badly paid they had to double as choristers at the Chapel Royal, which meant dashing across London between services. Their education also left much to be desired. Goss recalled he was only taught 'as much reading, writing and arithmetic as could be acquired between half-past twelve and two on Wednesdays and Saturdays.'

Other memorial tablets commemorate Ivor Novello (1893-1951) and Thomas Attwood (1765-1838). Attwood was a boy chorister of the Chapel Royal. He travelled Europe under the patronage of the Prince of Wales and for two years lived in Vienna, studying with Mozart. His compositions from that time, with Mozart's comments, have survived. In 1796, he became the St Paul's organist.

During his time here he became a good friend of Mendelssohn, who stayed with him on two occasions in 1829, one being the first British performance of Mendelssohn's music for *A Midsummer Night's Dream*. Mendelssohn had given the manuscript to Attwood who managed to leave it in a cab. It was never recovered. When informed what had happened, Mendelssohn simply sighed, sat down and wrote the whole lot out again from memory. Mendelssohn frequently played on the cathedral organ when staying with Attwood. On one occasion he was playing after the afternoon service and the congregation made no attempt to leave. The vergers switched off the bellows, much to Mendelssohn's annoyance. Attwood was a noted writer of anthems and a successful theatre composer. He became a professor at the Royal Academy in 1823 and taught members of the Royal family. A portrait of him hangs at the Royal College of Music.

Also in the crypt is a tablet in memory of Sir George Martin (1844–1916), who studied with Stainer and succeeded him as organist in 1888. Martin wrote much church music including a *Te Deum* sung on the steps of the cathedral when Queen Victoria celebrated her Diamond Jubilee, a composition which helped him obtain his knighthood. There are memorials, too, to Sir John Dykes Bower (1905–68), who was organist from 1936 until 1967, and John Battishill (1738–1801). Battishill was a theatre musician who gave up writing for the stage after his actress wife ran off with a member of the company. He never composed again, preferring to study the classics, and is buried in St Paul's because of his dying request to be placed near to that great man, Dr Boyce.

William Boyce (1710–79) lived in Kensington Gore for the last thirteen years of his life. A fine organist, like most composers of the time, he wrote for a wide range of musical genres including the theatre and the King's orchestra, of which he had charge. His own career as a performer was cut short when he developed deafness. Instead he concentrated on completing the collection known as *Cathedral Music* started by Maurice Greene. Containing anthems and church services, the first part was published in 1776, the final part in 1778, the year before his death. Boyce is buried in St Paul's, as are Sir Hubert Parry and Charles Macpherson (1870–1927), organist from 1916.

Two other musicians are buried here, although their graves are unmarked. Philip Hayes (1738–97), organist of Magdalen College, Oxford, and Professor of Music (both positions formerly held by his father, William, a well-known composer of catches and glees) is buried here because he died suddenly while on a trip to London. Philip wrote glees, catches and canons as well and had a reputation for being one of the worst tempered men in England, and one of the fattest. He was nicknamed Phil Chaise because of his habit of taking up both seats of a chaise. It seems possible that he was the first person to write a piano concerto. The pianist David Owen Norris believes the fourth of Hayes' *Six Concertos for Organ, Harpsichord and Fortepiano*, was written in 1769 for the square piano before the grand piano took over.

– 12 Seymour Street, W1 –

The home of Irish composer Michael William Balfe (1808–70) from about 1861 to 1865. Balfe, who has been called the English Rossini, is chiefly remembered for his opera *The Bohemian Girl* and his drawing-room ballad setting of Tennyson's poem *Come into the Garden Maud*. He had an incredible career, however, becoming the first British composer to achieve universal international recognition during his lifetime. Born in Dublin, he was a child prodigy on the violin, joining the orchestra of the Theatre Royal, Drury Lane, when he was fifteen. He studied composition in Paris with Cherubini who introduced him to Rossini. Rossini was so impressed with his voice that he insisted Balfe should sing Figaro in a revival of *The Barber of Seville*. Balfe had an equally high-profile career as a singer particularly in Italy (he appeared at La Scala, Milan) where he was highly regarded as a composer. He also had a glittering career as a conductor. *The Bohemian Girl*, together with Verdi's *Ernani*, became the most performed operas of their time. Balfe composed several of his most famous works in Seymour Street including the three operas: *The Puritan's Daughter*, *Blanche de Nevers* and *The Armourer of Nantes*. In 1864 he moved to Rowney Abbey, near Ware, Hertfordshire, where he became a gentleman farmer and died on 20 October 1870. He is buried in Kensal Green cemetery. There is a statue of him in the foyer of Drury Lane, a memorial in Westminster Abbey and a memorial window in St Patrick's Cathedral, Dublin.

– 162 Southampton Row, WC1 –

A plaque on the wall outside what is now the Bloomsbury Park Hotel commemorates the conductor Sir John Barbirolli's birth in an upstairs apartment here on 2

December 1899. Giovanni Barbirolli came from a musical family. Both his father and uncle played violin in theatre and cinema orchestras and had played at La Scala, Milan. Barbirolli, too, became a string player and was in the cello section of the London Symphony Orchestra when Elgar's cello concerto was first performed. But he decided he wanted to become a conductor. For thirty years he was principal conductor of the Hallé Orchestra. He was also Musical Director of the New York Philharmonic and Houston Symphony. In Barbirolli Square, Lower Moseley Street, Manchester, there's a statue of him by Byron Howard. He died in London on 29 July 1970.

– The Strand, WC2 –

The Savoy Hotel was built by Richard D'Oyly Carte from the profits made by Gilbert and Sullivan's *HMS Pinafore*. From the outset the hotel was designed to cater for every whim of the rich and famous. Johann Strauss led the Savoy orchestra, Anna Pavlova appeared in cabaret, Philip Heseltine, who became better known as the composer Peter Warlock, was born in the hotel in October 1894. It was in the grill room that the Peach Melba was first created for Dame Nellie Melba when Puccini brought her here after the first night of *Manon Lescaut.* Another singer who stayed here was the renowned soprano Luisa Tetrazzini. She was a large lady who managed to crack the pedestal of her toilet. Other famous musicians who have stayed include Leonard Bernstein and Igor Stravinsky.

The Savoy Theatre, next to the hotel entrance, was built by D'Oyly Carte as home for the Gilbert and Sullivan Savoy Operas. It was one of the most advanced buildings in

London and the first public building in England to be lit by electricity. The theatre opened with *Patience* on 10 October 1881 and also saw the first nights of *Iolanthe*, *The Mikado*, *The Yeomen of the Guard* and *The Gondoliers*. The Savoy Chapel in Savoy Hill alongside the hotel, contains a stained glass window dedicated to D'Oyly Carte's memory. It is also supposed to contain the grave of Matthew Locke (1630–77) but no trace of the grave has been found. Locke was one of the composers who wrote what is generally regarded as the first English opera, *The Siege of Rhodes* in 1656. He was Composer in Ordinary to King Charles II after the Restoration of the monarchy, and musician in residence in the Tudor palace which stood on the site of the present Somerset House.

In Victoria Embankment Gardens between the back of the Savoy Hotel and the river Thames, there is an impressive statue of Sir Arthur Sullivan by the Welsh sculptor Sir William Goscombe John.

– 7 Sydney Place, South Kensington, SW7 –

A blue plaque commemorates the fact that the Hungarian composer Bela Bartok (1881–1945) stayed here whenever he was in London between 1922 and 1937. It was the home of his avid admirers, Sir Duncan and Lady Wilson. Bartok gave a recital in the house.

– Sydney Street, Chelsea, SW3 –

St Luke's Church is the Chelsea Parish Church. As a twenty-four year old, the composer and teacher John Goss became organist here in 1824 and held the post for fourteen years. The composer John Ireland, who lived in nearby Gunter Grove, was organist here for twenty-two years, until 1926.

– 10 The Terrace, Barnes, SW13 –

Home of Gustav Holst from 1908 to 1913, while Director of Music at St Paul's Girls School, Hammersmith, a position he held from 1906 to 1934. His appointment to the post enabled him and his wife to leave their rooms in Shepherd's Bush and rent this Regency house overlooking the river. Holst had a music room at the top of the house and also a sound-proof study at St Paul's where he wrote his *St Paul's Suite* for strings and most of his masterpiece, *The Planets*.

– 30 Tite Street, SW3 –

A blue plaque marks the final home of the composer Peter Warlock (Philip Heseltine). It was here, when the apartment was numbered 12a, that he died on 17 December 1930. He was found dead from gas poisoning. There has always been controversy as to whether Warlock intended to kill himself or whether his death was a horrible accident. The gas came from a pipe from which a fire had recently been disconnected, and it has been suggested that the tap was faulty. This theory was raised at the inquest and the coroner visited the flat to see for himself. He doubted whether the tap could have been turned full on by accident. Certainly a proper plug was missing and it does appear that the fire removal was done by a 'cowboy'. Although prone to depression, a letter Warlock sent to his mother shortly before his death does not indicate he intended doing away with himself: '… some stuff of mine that I have never heard, is being sung at Westminster

Cathedral, and at the Brompton Oratory on Christmas Eve and Boxing Day and I should like to attend the performances,' he wrote.

– Victoria Street, SW1 –

On the corner of Victoria Street and The Broadway, directly opposite New Scotland Yard, home of the Metropolitan Police, stands a memorial to Henry Purcell. Sculpted by Glynn Williams it is called *The Flowering of the English Baroque* and was commissioned in 1994 by Westminster City Council. The 14 foot high bronze was unveiled by Princess Margaret, Countess of Snowdon, on the tercentenary of Purcell's birth. He was born in nearby Marsham Street in a house on a site where government buildings now stand.

– Walbrook, EC4 –

The Church of St Stephen Walbrook is another of the City's many Wren churches which replaced one destroyed in the Great Fire. During the rebuilding, the tomb of John Dunstaple (c1390–1453) was lost. Dunstaple or Dunstable was regarded by his contemporaries as the 'Prince of Music'. He was much admired throughout Europe, especially by the Italians. He was clearly a wealthy man, owning properties in England and in Normandy where he had served with the Duke of Bedford, Henry V's brother. As well as being a fine, innovative musician, he had a reputation as an astronomer, astrologer and mathmetician.

– Wardour Street, W1 –

Novello House was built in 1906 for the music publishing firm Novello and Company, founded by Vincent Novello.

The building was designed by Frank Loughborough Pearson, son of James Pearson who led the Gothic revival, and is now Grade II listed. The building's chief glory lies behind the mullioned windows. Inside the oak-paneled Sales Hall, with carvings in the style of Grinling Gibbons, scores were laid out for the public to look at during the day. In the evening music was performed, often by musicians placed in the mezzanine gallery. Roubilliac's statue of Handel, now in the Victoria and Albert Museum, used to stand outside the Hall.

– 8 Warwick Avenue, W9 –

A green plaque marks the home for almost fifty years of the composer Sir Lennox Berkeley. He had been born in Boar's Hill, Oxford on 12 May 1903, the younger child and only son of Captain Berkeley RN, the eldest son of the seventh Earl of Berkeley. Captain Berkeley had not succeeded to the earldom since his parents were not married at the time of his birth and illegitimate children could not inherit. Berkeley was brought up mostly in and around Oxford and at various boarding schools. He had his first compositions played while a pupil at St George's School, Harpenden. He also had several compositions performed while at Merton College, Oxford, where he read French. He became Ravel's minder when the French composer received an honorary doctorate from Oxford University in 1928 and showed him some of his work. Ravel advised him to study with Nadia Boulanger, which he did. He later became friendly with Benjamin Britten, with whom he moved into a converted windmill in Snape. His first symphony was performed at the Proms in 1943. In 1946, while working at the BBC, he married Frieda Bernstein, his secretary, and the following year, after Berkeley had become Professor of Composition at the Royal Academy, they moved to Warwick Avenue. The house quickly became a salon for musicians and writers, among them Richard Rodney Bennett and John Tavener. Berkeley's son Michael is also a composer.

– 69 Wentworth Road, Golders Green, NW11 –

A plaque marks the house where the Russian pianist and composer Nicholas Medtner (1880–1951) lived. Nikolay Karlovich Medtner was born in Moscow of German descent, a younger contemporary of Rachmaninov and the composer and pianist Alexander Scriabin. A prizewinner at the Moscow Conservatory, Medtner decided to forsake performing for composition, a decision that horrified his family. He also married his brother's wife after his brother generously divorced her so he could. Leaving Russia in 1921 after the Revolution, he lived first in Germany then France. Neither country took to his romantic piano works, considering them old fashioned, and so, in 1935, he moved to London where he felt he would get a more sympathetic reception. At the outbreak of World War Two, he and his wife went to live with one of his pupils in the Midlands where he completed his *Third Piano Concerto*. Medtner wrote four piano concertos in all, many songs in Russian and German, and many piano pieces, all in the Romantic tradition. After years of neglect, his music is gradually coming back into fashion and many people put him on a par with Rachmaninov, who championed his music and helped him financially. He died in 1951 and is buried in Hendon Cemetery.

– Westminster Abbey –

Westminster Abbey is the church in which the monarch is crowned. Music has always played an important part in the life of the Abbey and many important pieces were first heard here.

Among the Abbey's distinguished organists and Master of the Choristers has been Henry Purcell (1659-95). He was appointed to the post at the age of 19 when still at Westminster School, making him the only schoolboy organist in the Abbey's history. John Blow, who taught Purcell, was organist from 1669 to 1680, and again from 1695 after Purcell died, until his own death thirteen years later. Orlando Gibbons (1583-1625) held the post as did his son Christopher Gibbons (1615-76). Christopher, who composed anthems, string fantasies and music both sacred and secular, was a leading figure in re-establishing the Abbey's musical tradition after the Reformation and is buried here.

In the nave of the Abbey, a floor stone commemorates Sir William Herschel (1738-1822), the well-known astronomer and discoverer of the planet Uranus who was also Director of Music in Bath and had Haydn to stay in his house in Slough. In the North Aisle behind the organ, known as the Musicians' Aisle, stones commemorate Sir Edward Elgar (1857-1934), Ralph Vaughan Williams (1872-1958), whose ashes are here, and Herbert Howells (1892-1983). Sir Charles Villiers Stanford (1852-1924) and Sir William Sterndale Bennett (1816-75) are both buried here while Benjamin Britten is commemorated with a memorial stone and James Turle (1802-82), organist at the Abbey from 1831 until 1882, with a stained glass window. Henry Lawes, who died in 1662, is buried here (although his grave has been lost) as are Purcell and William Croft, who succeeded him as organist. In the South Walk lie William Shield, Johann Salomon and Muzio Clementi. William Shield was Master of the King's Musick; Salomon, the impresario who brought Haydn to London and Clementi 'the master of the pianoforte'. There are many other musicians buried here or with memorials including Pelham Humfrey, Handel, Charles Burney, Samuel Arnold (1740-1802), Thomas Greatorex, Michael Balfe and William Walton.

– 1 Wheatley Street (formerly Great – Chesterfield Street), W1

This was the home of Charles Wesley, the divine and hymn writer, from 1771 until his death in 1788. His sons Charles (1757–1834) and Samuel (1766–1837) both became musicians. Charles was a fine organist; Samuel was called the English Mozart by William Boyce and championed the works of JS Bach. They both gave subscription concerts in the house until Samuel left the family circle in 1784 to become a Roman Catholic.

– Whitehall, SW1 –

The Banqueting House, designed by Inigo Jones in 1619 for King James I, is all that remains of Whitehall Palace after a disastrous fire in 1698. The hall has always been an important performing space. Many masques were first seen here and also Handel's *Te Deum* (written for the Treaty of Utrecht) received its first performance here. After the fire, on the orders of the king, the Banqueting Hall became a Chapel Royal.

www.hrp.org.uk/banquestinghouse

– 48 Wildwood Road, NW11 –

A blue plaque marks the home of concert pianist Dame Myra Hess, who will always be remembered for the morale-boosting war time concerts she staged in the National Gallery.

– Windmill Hill, Hampstead, NW3 –

Fenton House is a late eighteenth-century property owned by the National Trust. It houses the Benton Fletcher Collection of Early Keyboard Instruments, one of the most important collections in Europe. Benton Fletcher was an army officer who began assembling a collection of instruments a century ago. They now range from a Ruckers harpsichord and Italian virginals dating from around 1540 to a clavichord built by Arnold Dolmetch. The instruments are kept in playable order and anyone wishing to play them should contact the Keeper of Instruments in writing.

www.nationaltrust.org.uk

WALES

THE HARP

There has been an unbroken tradition of harp playing in Wales for at least nine hundred years. King Griffith of Wales was the first to appoint a royal harper in the eleventh century and at one stage the harp was the only possession Welsh law did not allow to be seized for debt. But the story of the harp goes back long before that. It is the oldest string instrument for which there is irrefutable evidence and was played by the Ancient Egyptians.

Harps have undergone many changes over the centuries, from the hand-cradled harps used by thirteenth-century troubadours to today's sit-down-to-play concert instruments. Leading composers began to write for the instrument during the Renaissance but traditional harps only gave them an octave of sound (the equivalent of the white notes on a piano.) Composers wanted the black notes as well. This led to the invention of the triple harp or, as it became known, the Welsh Harp, with three rows of strings. The two outer rows would play the diatonic scale (a scale in the major or minor key), while the central string would provide the chromatic scale (a scale that has notes in it which are not in the basic key). The harp became such a popular instrument in the eighteenth and nineteenth centuries that many wealthy households employed a house harpist and it became tradition for the monarch to appoint a royal harpist. John Thomas was the last to be appointed by Queen Victoria and even though Nansi Richards, who died in 1976, was appointed Royal Harper of the Prince of Wales (later King Edward VIII) at his investiture in 1911, the tradition lapsed.

In 2000, Prince Charles, the present Prince of Wales, revived the post in order to foster and encourage young musical talent in the Principality. The first appointee was Catrin Finch who held the post for four years and has since become an international star. She was followed by Jemima Phillips, who played at the wedding of the Prince to the Duchess of Cornwall in 2005 but achieved headlines for all the wrong reasons when she was found guilty of handling stolen goods and sentenced to attend a drug rehabilitation clinic. The third royal harpist, student Claire Jones, was appointed in 2007.

177. ABERYSTWYTH, Ceredigion

– Nanteos Mansion, Rhydyfelin –

This Grade I listed eighteenth-century Palladian house, three miles south east of Aberystwyth, now restored as a bed and breakfast hotel and venue for weddings and receptions, was once, according to legend, the home of the Holy Grail. Apparently the monks of Glastonbury, where the olivewood cup had been taken by St Joseph of Arimathea, brought it to Wales when their monastery was dissolved in 1539 by Henry VIII. They settled, with the Grail of course, at Strata Florida abbey. Three years later, with Henry's men on the march again and coming their way, they sought refuge at nearby Nanteos, the country home of the Powell family. To help disguise them, they were put to work on the estate. When the final monk was on his deathbed, he left the cup in the safe-keeping of the Powell family. The house was rebuilt in 1739 by Thomas

Powell, MP for Cardiganshire, and for two centuries the cup was on show, attracting pilgrims by the thousand including apparently, in 1855, Richard Wagner, who was invited to see it by the then heir to the house, George Powell. George was a masochistic homosexual with a fondness for the birch and the works of the Marquis de Sade. It was seeing the cup that apparently gave Wagner the idea of writing his opera *Parsifal*. Local legend even claims he wrote part of the opera in the upstairs music room. Because so many pilgrims were taking bites out of the cup, it was removed from show and is now, according to local gossip, in a Hereford bank vault.

Not only has Nanteos been the home of the Holy Grail, it is also haunted. Every Christmas for sixty-nine years, harpist Gruffydd Evans would entertain the Powells and their guests. He was 92 when he died and was buried in Llanbadern Fawr cemetery. The sound of his harp can still be heard in the music room and in the woods surrounding the house.

www.nanteos.co.uk

178. ANGLESEY

‒ Y Craigwen, Menai Strait, Anglesey ‒

This was the home of composer William Mathias, the noted conductor and pianist. He was born in Whitland in 1924, and became a lecturer at Bangor University in 1959. In 1968, he joined the music department in Edinburgh but returned to Bangor two years later to become Professor of Music, moving into this house overlooking the Menai Straits. It was here he did most of his composition. His output was extremely varied, ranging from operas (he wrote three) to symphonies (three) to piano concertos (three). He wrote extensively for the Anglican choral tradition, including the anthem *Let the People Praise Thee O God* for the wedding of Diana and Prince Charles. This was heard live by one billion people worldwide – which has to be one of the biggest audiences ever for the premiere of a piece of classical music. Two days before his death in 1992, Mathias was working on a new symphony for the Santa Fe Symphony Orchestra.

179. BARRY, Glamorgan

– 16 Wenvoe Terrace, Barry –

This was the birthplace on 19 February 1906 of composer Grace Williams. Both her parents were schoolteachers but from an early age she wanted to be a musician. She was taught at the Royal College by Vaughan Williams and wrote many of her early pieces while a student, including the *Sinfonia Concertante* and *First Symphony*. During the war Royal College students were evacuated to Grantham in Linconshire, where she wrote the piece that made her name: the *Fantasia on Welsh Nursery Tunes*. After the war she taught at Camden School for Girls in London then worked on educational programmes for the BBC. Suffering from depression, she returned to Barry to live in a flat in her parent's house at 9 Old Village Road, working occasionally for BBC Wales but attempting to earn her living as a freelance composer. She destroyed the manuscript of her first symphony but wrote a second and also wrote the opera, *The Parlour*, given its world premiere by Welsh National Opera on 5 May 1966 at Cardiff's New Theatre. Williams died on 10 February 1977.

180. BETWS Y COED, Conwy

– Craig-y-Dderwen Riverside Hotel, Betws y Coed –

Elgar and his wife stayed in this Victorian country house, close to the town centre and overlooking the River Conwy, during the summers of 1901 and 1903, when it was a private house. They were guests of their friend Albert E Rodewald, a textile magnate from Liverpool whose passion was music. Largely thanks to him, the Liverpool orchestras had been raised to a standard whereby they could give performances of works by Elgar, Strauss and Wagner. The first of Elgar's Pomp and Circumstance Marches (*Land of Hope and Glory*) was dedicated to Rodewald. While here in 1903, Elgar, as well as going cycling in the area and on sightseeing trips in Rodewald's car at a 'frightful pace', completed the scoring of *The Apostles*. A couple of months later, Rodewald died unexpectedly as the result of influenza, aged only 43. Elgar was very cut up about it and not long afterwards began to produce the sketches for what became the second movement of the *Second Symphony*, a movement described by Alice Elgar as 'a lament for Rodey'. The house became a hotel in the 1920s.
www.snowdoniahotel.com

181. BLAENAU FFESTINIOG, Gwynedd

~ Llechwedd Slate Caverns ~

In the Victorian village atop these fascinating slate mines is
the house where David Francis, the blind Harpist of
Merionnydd, was born in 1865 and died in 1929. His
Bardic name was Y Telynor Dall o Feirion and he had a
great influence upon subsequent Welsh harpists. Francis
suffered from arthritis which, towards the end of his life,
made it very difficult for him to play. Instead he taught,
being especially in demand just before the annual
Eisteddfod. His last pupil was Jane Williams who won a
major prize at the 1929 National Eisteddfod in Liverpool,
the last time it was held outside Wales. In September of
that year, he took to his bed, never to play the harp again.
On 15 September, his visitors included Eleanor Dwyryd,
another of his pupils. 'One string is broken on the harp,' he
told her. 'When the third string goes it will be time for me
to say farewell.' He asked Eleanor to play something for
him. As she put her hands to the harp, a second string
broke. Francis took his wife's hand while Eleanor played
on. The third string broke. 'The strings are broken,' said
Francis. They were his last words.

182. CARDIFF

~ 1 Colchester Avenue, Penylan ~

This was the home of the Welsh composer and conductor
Arwel Hughes. The father of conductor Owain, he was born
near Wrexham on 25 August 1909, and attended the Royal

College of Music in London where he studied with Vaughan Williams. He returned to Wales in 1935 to join the BBC's Music Department, where his duties included conducting many first performances of works by composers such as Grace Williams, David Wynne and Alan Hoddinott. He also wrote much incidental music for radio and television himself. In 1965 he became Head of Music for BBC Wales, a post he held until his retirement in 1971. Among his many compositions were oratorios, a popular *Fantasia for Strings* and a symphony. He also wrote two operas, *Menna* and *Serch Yw'r Doctor*, both given first performances by Welsh National Opera. *Serch Yw'r Doctor*, based on a Molière play, was performed in Welsh at the Eisteddfod and broadcast in English. Hughes was responsible for the music for the investiture of the Prince of Wales. He died on 23 September 1988.

– Llwyn-yr-Eos, 95 Cowbridge Road –

A blue plaque marks the house in which the composer, dramatist, singer and actor Ivor Novello was born on 15 January 1893. The Welsh name of the house means Grove of the Nightingale. Novello's real name was David Ivor Davies. His father, David Davies, was a tax inspector, his mother, Clara Novello Davies, a well-known singer and teacher who founded the Welsh Ladies Choir and had taken her stage name from Clara Novello. Ivor won a singing scholarship to Magdalen College Choir School in Oxford, and it was there he began to write songs under the name Ivor Novello. Once he had left school, the family moved to London and in 1914, Novello's song *We'll Keep the Home Fires Burning* made him famous overnight.

– The National Museum Cardiff, Cathays Park –

The museum houses the Snetzler organ taken from Wynnstay Hall, Ruabon, near Wrexham, upon which Handel is known to have played. The instrument, with a case by Robert Adam, dates from 1774 and was built for the London home of Sir Watkin Williams Wynn, a Welsh patron of the arts. It was there at 20 St James's Square (in a house that still exists) that Handel played it. The organ was altered by Samuel Green in 1783 and moved in 1863 to Wynnstay Hall, North Wales, the Williams Wynn country seat. It was acquired by the National Museum when the current Victorian Wynnstay Hall was converted into apartments. It is used for concerts.

183. CARMARTHEN, Carmarthenshire

– St Peter's Parish Church –

The church has interesting royal connections: William Devereux, first Earl of Essex and father of Queen Elizabeth I's favourite, is buried in the chancel as is Charlotte Dalton, granddaughter of George III and Hannah Lightfoot, herself the daughter of a London shoe-maker. They allegedly married in secret when he was Prince of Wales. The church also has an impressive eighteenth-century piped organ built by George Pike England on the orders of George III. The King had intended the organ for the Chapel Royal in Windsor but changed his mind and it ended up in Wales.

On 13 November 1817 the composer Henry Brinley Richards was born in nearby Lower Market Street. His father, also Henry, ran a music shop in the town, was organist at St Peter's and chief organiser of local musical events. Richards, destined to become a doctor, soon showed musical talent however, and in 1834 won a prize at the Cardiff Eisteddfod for his arrangement of *The Ash Grove*. As a result, the Duke of Newcastle put up the money for him to go to the Royal Academy of Music where he subsequently became a professor. After completing his London studies, Richards enrolled as a pupil of Chopin in Paris and the two became good friends. Richards, regarded by many as the finest piano-player in Britain, set up the Royal Academy's local examination system. He was also a prolific composer though known today only for his song *God Bless the Prince of Wales*. He never lost his interest in Welsh music, becoming patron of the National Eisteddfod of Wales and joining with Lady Llanover in trying to popularise the triple harp. He died in London on 1 May 1885 and is buried in Brompton Cemetery.

184. COWBRIDGE, South Glamorgan

Llandough Castle in Llanfair village, two miles from Cowbridge, is where the French composer Gabriel Fauré stayed in August 1898 as a guest of Mrs George Campbell Swinton. He wrote part of his *Seventh Nocturne* here.

Elizabeth Swinton was a well-known Edwardian socialite (there is a lovely portrait of her in the Art Institute of Chicago by their mutual friend John Singer Sargent), who married George Campbell Swinton, a Scottish politician who became chairman of the London County Council and chairman of the town-planning committee of Delhi. Their great-granddaughter is the Oscar-winning actress Tilda Swinton. Llandough Castle (not much remains of the original fourteenth-century fortified manor house which has been rebuilt and modernised several times) was just one of their many homes. At the age of 32 she bravely decided, against the advice of family and friends, to become a professional singer under the name Elsie Swinton. Sargent was in the audience at her first concert. She enjoyed some success and among those with whom she worked were Hamilton Harty, Percy Grainger and Fauré. Fauré, in particular, became a fervent admirer. Recently discovered letters between the two suggest that their relationship may have been more than friendship. She finally gave up singing after World War One because of family pressure, and concentrated on doing good works. She did, however, keep up her involvement with musicians for whom she held open house, among them Stravinsky, Prokofiev, Szymanowski and Artur Rubinstein. The house is a private home and not open to the public.

185. DEVIL'S BRIDGE, Dyfed

– Cae Bach, Devils' Bridge –

The English composer Geoffrey Bush wrote *Music for Orchestra* while on holiday here in 1967. One of the work's themes spells out, in German notation, the name of the cottage. Bush, the son of a crime fiction writer, was born in London on 23 March 1920. He became a chorister at Salisbury Cathedral and began composing at the age of ten. While at Lancing College he met John Ireland who became his mentor. His studies at Oxford were interrupted by the war which, as a conscientious objector, he spent looking after unruly evacuees in Wales. He also spent much of his time composing. After the war, he divided his time between teaching (he was a great champion of British composers) and composition. Among his best-known work is *A Christmas Cantata*, a setting of carols very popular with amateur choirs. He also wrote six operas, two symphonies, a number of chamber pieces and many fine songs. He died in London in 1998.

186. LLANDYSSIL, Powys

– Cefn Bryntalch –

This important Grade II Queen Anne revival house, built in 1869, was the family home of composer Peter Warlock's stepfather, Walter Buckley Jones. In 1921, Warlock (1894–1930) began editing *The Sackbut*, a new music magazine, in London. It was deliberately controversial; so much so that his financial backer decided to pull out. The magazine closed and a penniless Warlock was forced to go home to mother at Cefn Bryntalch. This become his base for the next three years where he completed *The Curlew*, the song cycle of poems by WB Yeats which is generally considered to be his masterpiece, and the *Lillygay* cycle. He also made numerous transcriptions of early music and completed a biography of Delius. Bartok stayed here in 1922 on his way back to London having played a concert at University College, Aberystwyth, on 16 March for which he was paid £15. It was as a result of Bartok's influence that

Warlock decided to write *Lillygay*, his most consciously folk-influenced piece. Warlock also played the organ in the Victorian parish church of St Tyssil, sometimes deputising for the church organist.

While the house, on the B4386 four miles west of Montgomery, is not open to the public, the grounds sometimes are. An application has been made to convert the house into a residential arts centre.

187. LLANGRANOG, CEREDIGION

– The Village Gardens, Llangranog, –

The gardens, close to Gerwn Waterfall, contain a slate memorial commemorating the visit to the village of Edward Elgar in August 1901 and the inspiration it gave him. Elgar had been invited to Llangranog, where she had rented a house, by Miss Rosa Burley, the head of the Malvern school where Elgar taught the violin. Elgar had his meals with Miss Burley and her other guests, but slept in a neighbouring cottage. The Burley house may well have been the one next to the Pentre Arms which is now a part of the pub.

According to Elgar's own account, he was out walking on the seashore one day, thinking about writing a piece for string orchestra, when he heard the distant sound of singing from a group on a hillside across the bay. He couldn't hear what it was they were singing but did pick up on the frequent drop of a third, something he felt typified Welsh music. For some time he contemplated using this in a Welsh overture, but it found its way instead into the

Introduction and Allegro for Strings as the second subject. The piece was first performed at the Queen's Hall in London on 8 March 1905.

188. LLANOVER, Abergavenny, Monmouthshire

– St Bartholemew's Church, Old Llanover –

Augusta Hall, Lady Llanover, is buried here alongside her husband, Benjamin Hall. She was born in the big house, Ty Uchaf, on the Llanover estate which had been bought by her parents. Her husband was an MP for 22 years and became the first Commissioner of Works. He was elevated to the peerage and Big Ben was supposedly named after him. Although English, Lady Llanover was passionate about all things Welsh. She insisted that the servants, estate workers and even aristocratic guests should wear Welsh costumes, and when she and her husband decided to rebuild Llanover House, it was not just as a family home but as a centre for Welsh culture. She supported collectors of Welsh folk music, in particular Maria Jane Williams (1795–1873), helping her publish *The Ancient Airs of Gwent and Morgannwg*. She did much to revive interest in Welsh harps, in particular the triple harp of which the Puritans had disapproved because of its association with dancing. Lady Llanover encouraged harp manufacture, gave harps as prizes at Eisteddfodau and employed harpists on the estate, including John Wood Jones (1800–44), the partially blind Thomas Griffiths (1815–87) and his daughter Susanna. Musicians, poets and artists were also invited to stay and play. They included the composer and instrumentalist John Parry (1776–1851), his son, the popular composer, singer and entertainer John Orlando Parry (1810–79), the pianist and composer Brinley Richards, and John Thomas, harpist to Queen Victoria. John Thomas (1826–1913) had studied at the Royal Academy with Cipriani Potter, taught at the Royal College and was the composer of several harp pieces still popular today. He also wrote an opera, a symphony, two cantatas, two concertos and quantities of chamber music. Lady Llanover was 94 when she died in1896, still organising concerts and working on her projects. Llanover House was demolished in 1936 but the grounds are occasionally opened to the public.

www.llanovergarden.co.uk

189. MERTHYR TYDFIL, Mid Glamorgan

– 4 Chapel Row, Chapel Banks, Merthyr Tydfil –

The Welsh composer Joseph Parry, the man who wrote *Blodwen*, the first grand opera in Welsh, was born in this terraced ironworker's cottage on 21 May 1841. He was one of eight children and at the age of nine followed his father down the pit. When he was thirteen the family left Merthyr for the United States, settling in a Welsh community in Danville, Pennsylvania, where Parry worked alongside his father in a steel mill. He also began composing and showed such talent that the local people clubbed together to raise the money to send him to the Royal Academy of Music in London. After graduating from the Academy, he continued his studies in Cambridge and then, in 1872, became the first professor of music at the university in Aberystwyth. His famous hymn tune of that name, sung to the words *Jesus Lover of My Soul*, was written there and a plaque commemorates his time there. He left Aberystwyth to found a private music school in Swansea before accepting a post at the university in Cardiff. Parry was a prolific composer writing ten operas, three oratorios, five cantatas, numerous anthems and songs (including the gorgeous *Myfanwy*), piano pieces and a composition that is generally considered to be the first commissioned specifically for a brass band. His opera *Blodwen*, first performed in 1878, was given more than five hundred performances in under twenty years but is now never staged. If Parry is known for anything today, it is for *Myfanwy* and *Aberystwyth*. He died in 1903 and is buried in St Augustine's Church, Penarth. Parry's birthplace is now a museum.

www.visitmerthyr.co.uk

– Cyfarthfa Castle Museum, Cyfarthfa Park, – Brecon Road, Merthyr Tydfil

The museum houses a collection devoted to the Cyfarthfa Band, founded in about 1840 by Robert Crawshay. As well as instruments there are also manuscripts, cap badges, photos, paintings and ephemera connected with the band. There are also instruments from other South Walian bands and Welsh harps.

www.visitmerthyr.co.uk/Cyfarthfa

190. NEATH, West Glamorgan

– Craig-Y-Nos, Brecon Road, Pen-y-cao, Neath –

This mock-Gothic castle in the upper Swansea Valley was bought by the Victorian diva Adelina Patti in 1878. She paid £3,500 for what was to become her home base for some thirty years, the place she went to relax and recuperate after wowing audiences around the world. Patti was a Spanish opera singer, as famous in her day as Queen Victoria. She was also the highest paid, with one tour to the United States alone earning her £100,000. Having bought Craig y Nos, she managed to get a railway station built nearby and remodeled much of the castle, including adding a 150-seat theatre. On her death, at the castle in 1919, her third husband, a Swedish baron twenty-six years her junior, sold off the house and returned to Sweden. Patti was buried in Paris, close to Rossini's grave in the Père Lachaise cemetery. The castle became a hospital, a home for the elderly and has now been turned into a luxury hotel specialising as a venue for weddings. The theatre, in which Patti used to sing to her many famous guests even after retiring from the stage, is now listed and used to stage operas.

www.craigynoscastle.com

191. NEWTOWN, Powys

– Gregynog Hall, Tregynon, Newtown –

There has been a house on this site since at least the twelfth century. The present building, set in 750 acres of garden, is about 150 years old and was bought in 1920 by Gwendoline and Margaret Davies, sisters of the first Lord Davies, a politician and Welsh benefactor. Avid collectors of paintings (their collection of Impressionist pictures was bequeathed to the National Gallery of Wales), they wanted to develop the hall as an artistic and cultural centre. The Gregynog Press they founded became world-famous. In 1932 they started the Gregynog Music Festival with Adrian Boult conducting. The festivals lasted until 1938 and among the musicians who took part were Ralph Vaughan Williams, Gustav Holst and Edward Elgar. Gwendoline died in 1951, and in 1960, Margaret, who died three years later, bequeathed the house and grounds to the University of Wales which runs it as a residential centre and has restarted the music festival every June.

www.wales.ac.uk

192. PENARTH, Vale of Glamorgan

– St Augustine's Church, Penarth –

Joseph Parry, probably Wales's best-known composer, is buried in St Augustine's churchyard. He spent his last years teaching music at the University College in Cardiff, and living in a house in Penarth called Cartref, where he died on 17 February 1903. Every July, the church, which dominates the Penarth headland, holds a week-long festival of organ and choral church music.

193. PONTYPRIDD, Mid-Glamorgan

– Mill Street, Pontypridd –

A plaque marks the site of Ty'r Factory, the home next door to their cloth factory, in which the James family were living in 1856 when father Evan and son James sat down one Sunday afternoon in January to come up with what has since become the Welsh National Anthem: *Hen Wlad fy Nhadau* (*Land of My Fathers*). Evan, the father, wrote the words, James the music. James James, who had been born in 1833, was a publican who played his harp for the dancing in the pub; his father a wool merchant and weaver who was also a poet. The song, originally called *On the Banks of the Rhondda*, received its first performance in the Methodist Capel Tabor in Maesteg sung by sixteen-year-old Margaret John. It was originally written in 6/8 time but had to be slowed down when sung by large crowds. It was the first song ever to be recorded in Welsh when singer Madge Breese recorded it in London for the Gramophone Company in 1899. Lasting for one minute and 17 seconds, the recording was pressed onto a single-sided 7-inch disc. The original score is in the National Library of Wales. Ynysangharad Park in Pontypridd contains a memorial to Evan and James James, sculpted by Welsh sculptor Sir William Goscombe John. The two figures represent Poetry and Music and were unveiled before a crowd of 10,000 in 1930.

Another famous Welsh musician lived in Pontypridd: John Hughes, composer of the great hymn tune *Cwm Rhondda* (*Bread of Heaven*).Approached by the organist of the Capel Rhondda Welsh Baptist Church to write a hymn tune for the inauguration of their new organ, Hughes, who played the organ at the first performance in 1907, set some words by William Williams in English! The words have been changed since and the hymn has become the Welsh rugby anthem, sung around the world. Hughes, who died in 1932, is buried in the graveyard of the Salem Baptist Chapel near Tonteg, where he was organist and choirmaster.

194. RHYD-Y-MWYN, CLWYD

– Coed Du Hall, Nant Alyn Road, Rhyd-y-Mwyn –

This was the home of John Taylor, a mining engineer, entrepreneur and host for Felix Mendelssohn when he stayed for a week at the end of August 1829, on his Grand Tour of Britain. Mendelssohn had been in Scotland and was planning on going to Ireland but the weather was so bad he changed his mind and moved in with the Taylors instead. The house, as he described it, was a country house on an expensive cut lawn surrounded by flowers. Two of the three piano fantasies he wrote, one for each of Taylor's three daughters, were inspired by flowers. He also began work on an organ piece for his sister's marriage in October and a theatre piece to celebrate his parents' silver wedding. He enjoyed his time with the Taylor family, in particular going for long walks with Susan, the middle sister and his favourite. The house is now a hospital. A blue plaque attached to the property's wall commemorates Mendelssohn's visit.

195. ST ASAPH, Denbighshire

– St Asaph Cathedral –

The smallest cathedral in Britain and home to the annual North Wales International Music Festival, founded in 1972 by the composer William Mathias who ran it until his death on 29 July 1992. Mathias is buried in the cathedral grounds.

www.stasaph.co.uk

196. ST DAVID'S, Pembrokeshire

– St David's Cathedral, The Close –

The twelfth-century cathedral was built on the site of a sixth-century monastery founded by St David, the patron saint of Wales. It took some time to build, the original tower falling down and the building then being damaged by an earthquake. But it soon become a place of pilgrimage, two visits to St David's being counted the equivalent of one to Rome. William the Conqueror was among those who came here to pray.

Thomas Tomkins, one of England's leading musicians at the end of the sixteenth century, was born here in 1572. His father, also Thomas, had moved from Cornwall to Wales in order to become a vicar choral at St David's, and later organist. The family then moved to Gloucester and it is thought young Thomas went to London to become a chorister of the Chapel Royal and to study with William Byrd. While there he almost certainly got to know Thomas Morley who included one of Tomkins' madrigals in *The Triumphs of Oriana*. By 1596 Tomkins had taken up the post of choral instructor and organist at Worcester Cathedral.

As well as madrigals, Tomkins wrote anthems, keyboard works, consort music and liturgical music. Three of Thomas's brothers were musicians and the family is said to have produced more musicians than any other in Britain.

The St David's choir was the first cathedral choir in Britain to use a combination of girls and men.

197. WHITLAND, Carmarthenshire

– Cilhawl, North Road, Whitland –

This was the birthplace in 1934 of the composer William Mathias. His father taught history at the local grammar school, which Mathias attended; his mother was a keen amateur musician who taught piano and organ. Mathias was an infant prodigy, starting to play the piano by the age of three and composing when he was five. Some of the pieces he wrote while a student at Whitland Grammar School are still played today. He won an open competition to study composition at the Royal Academy.

SCOTLAND

CAITHNESS

SUTHERLAND

ROSS-SHIRE AND
CROMARTY-SHIRE

214

MORAY

200

NAIRNSHIRE

BANFFSHIRE

208

ABERDEENSHIRE

198

INVERNESS-SHIRE

KINCARDINE-
SHIRE

210

ANGUS

215

PERTHSHIRE

202

ARGYLL

204 211

CLACKMANNAN-
SHIRE

KINROSS-
SHIRE

FIFE

212

201

DUNBARTON-
SHIRE

216

STIRLINGSHIRE

217

209

207

EAST
LOTHIAN

206

WIGTON-
SHIRE

203

205

RENFREWSHIRE

213

BERWICKSHIRE

MIDLOTHIAN

218

BUTE

LANARKSHIRE

PEEBLES-
SHIRE

199

AYRSHIRE

SELKIRK-
SHIRE

ROXBURGHSHIRE

DUMFRIESSHIRE

WIGTOWN-
SHIRE

KIRKCUDBRIGHT-
SHIRE

NORTHERN
IRELAND

0   10   20   30   40   50 miles

Music hasn't always been classified into neat little boxes, the way we tend to treat it today. There was always crossover long before particular genres or styles became fashionable, especially in Scotland. In the Baroque period, 1600–1750, Scottish music was very much a mixture of classical European with traditional styles. It was only later that a clear distinction arose between the concert tradition and folk.

The men who wrote the early crossover music were people like William Marshall, Niel Gow and his son Nathaniel, James Oswald, Simon Fraser and Robert Macintosh. Not all of them were professional musicians. Marshall, for example, was a multi-tasking butler who worked for the Duke of Gordon and just happened to be a superb fiddler. More than two hundred of his compositions have survived, having, in his lifetime, been printed and sold in cities throughout Britain. Listen to his music today and the first surprise is that he wrote not for solo fiddle but for the fiddle accompanied by a violoncello or a harpsichord. Sometimes he wrote violin duets. It may sound Scottish, being almost exclusively written for dancing reels and other Scottish dances, but the instruments used give the music a classically Baroque sound.

Dance, from the time of the Renaissance luters and viol players, was to have a considerable influence on Scottish music, as did the 1707 Act of Union. Many Scottish musicians, foreseeing the loss of their folk culture that legally joining the Kingdoms of England and Scotland might engender, decided it must be collected and protected before it was too late. At the same time, Scottish songs became fashionable in London's theatres and drawing-rooms, with English composers rushing to fill the market.

Many of Scotland's monarchs have been excellent musicians. On his wedding night, James IV apparently entertained his bride by playing the lute and clavichord!

198. ABERDEEN

– Craigie Loanings, Aberdeen –

A small memorial garden commemorates one of Aberdeen's most famous musicians, the soprano Mary Garden. A granite stone contains the inscription: 'This garden was planted in memory of Mary Garden, the famous opera singer, who lived near here at Belgrave Terrace'. There is also a bench.

From the north of Scotland to the glittering lights of Paris: Mary Garden's life was a story of extremes and contradictions encompassing great success and wealth, but also poverty and criticism. She was born in Aberdeen at 35 Charlotte Street in February 1874, the daughter of a clerk at a local iron works. As the family grew, they moved to larger premises at 41 Dee Street (a commemorative yellow plaque notes this), then in 1883 emigrated to the United States where her father eventually got a job in Chicago selling bicycles and motor cars. Garden was heard by a local singing teacher who got her a job as a nanny for David Mayer, a Chicago department store owner, so she could pay to have singing lessons. Her voice was considered so outstanding that Mayer agreed to send her to Paris in 1896, but when rumours reached him she was leading a life of leisure rather than concentrating on her singing and had allegedly given birth to an illegitimate child, he ceased all funding and Garden ended up on the streets, penniless. She was rescued by the American soprano Sybil Sanderson who arranged to provide her with food, shelter, and a piano. In April 1900, Garden made her stage debut when at the end of Act 1 she took over the title role in Charpentier's *Louise* at the Opéra-Comique. Two years later Debussy chose her to create the role of Mélisande in *Pelléas et Mélisande,* as much it seems for her mysterious Aberdonian accent as for her singing. Returning to America, she both scandalised and riveted audiences in Richard Strauss's *Salome,* in which she kissed the severed head of John the Baptist lustfully and seduced the menfolk of America with her Dance of the Seven Veils (for which she wore a tantalising pink body-stocking). She became a household name in America, giving her name to face powder, make-up, hotel suites, and even the highway leading to Mount Rushmore. In the early 1920s Garden served as a controversial director of the Chicago Opera Association, the first woman to both direct and sing leading operatic roles. After retiring from the stage in 1934, she worked as a talent scout for Metro-Goldwyn-Mayer, then returned to live in Aberdeen, renting a flat at 28 Belgrave Terrace. She died on 3 January 1967 in a mental home at Inverurie, suffering from dementia.

199. ALLOWAY, Ayrshire

– Burns Cottage, Alloway –

The birthplace of Robert Burns (1759–96), Scotland's greatest and most well-known poet. He was born in the single-room cottage built by his father. The museum behind contains original Burns letters, songs and other relics. When he was six, the family moved to Mount Oliphant Farm (1.5 miles to the south) where Burns became an efficient ploughman. He was educated locally at Alloway School and then at the Grammar School in Ayr. As well as writing poems, Burns was also a musician and his first poems were almost entirely song lyrics. From 1787 until 1792, he produced some 370 with the lyrics set to existing tunes. Burns died at his home in Dumfries in 1796 and is buried in St Michael's Churchyard.

200. BELLIE, Fochabers, Moray

– Bellie Parish Churchyard –

William Marshall, one of the major composers of Scottish fiddle music, is buried here. Marshall wasn't a professional musician. Born in 1748 in the village of Fochabers, he entered the Duke of Gordon's service when he was twelve, eventually becoming the Duke's butler, a post he held for thirty years. In his spare time he was also a clockmaker, an excellent shot, dancer, trout fisherman and trainer of hawks. In the evening, after dinner, he would entertain the Duke's guests by playing his fiddle. He is credited with more than 250 compositions (many named after the guests), not just for fiddle but also for the cello, harp and harpsichord. Robert Burns described him as 'the first composer of Strathspeys of the age'. Marshall died in 1833. There is a portrait of him by John Moir in the Scottish National Portrait Gallery. Gordon Castle, where he spent so much of his life, has been demolished.

201. **BRIDGE OF ALLAN, Stirlingshire**

~ Keir House, Bridge of Allan ~

Keir House, three miles north of Bridge of Allan on the road to Dunblane, was the ancestral home of the Stirling family. The family no longer live there, the house having been sold by the brother of David Stirling, founder of the SAS, to an Arab consortium. Chopin stayed here at the beginning of October 1848 when on his Scottish tour with Jane Stirling. He was astonished to find himself in the middle of a huge house party. Jane Stirling had been born in nearby Kippenross House, not far from Dunblane in 1804. Both her parents had died when she was young and she was brought up by her much older, widowed sister, Mrs Katherine Erskine. They spent much of their time travelling in Europe and had met Chopin in Paris.

202. **DUNKELD, Tayside**

~ Little Dunkeld Graveyard ~

The fiddler Niel Gow, the most famous Scottish fiddler of the eigteenth century, is buried here. The ravages of the weather almost destroyed his headstone so the original was moved to the Chapterhouse of Dunkeld Cathedral and a new headstone carved for his grave. Gow was born in Inver in 1727 and was intended for the weaving trade but showed such skill with the fiddle that he was given lessons. Taking part in a fiddle competition being judged by the blind musician John McCraw, he was awarded first prize. McCraw commented that he would recognise Gow's style immediately out of a hundred players. The Duke of Atholl became his patron and it was for the Duke he wrote much of his dance music, some of which is still played today.

203. EDINBURGH

– 22 Braid Crescent, Edinburgh –

This is the house in which the Scottish composer Learmont Drysdale died. He was only forty-three and considered to be the great hope in establishing a Scottish school of composers. He is now almost entirely forgotten. Born in Edinburgh on 3 October 1866, he began studies to become an architect but switched to music. He became assistant organist at St George's Parish Church and Greenside Parish Church where the choir performed some of his early compositions. In 1887 he moved to London to become assistant organist at All Saints Church, Notting Hill, and a student at the Royal Academy where his talent was soon recognized. However, a public row with the Academy's head, Alexander McKenzie, ironically a leading Scottish composer himself, over mistakes in the score of the piece the principal was conducting, led to Drysdale being thrown out. In 1904 he returned to Scotland to teach composition in Glasgow, and then, because he felt teaching was getting in the way of his own composition, he moved back to Edinburgh. Not long after, his mother contracted pneumonia and died. Drysdale also caught it and died on 18 June 1909. Among the pieces he wrote were the *Tam O'Shanter* overture, the orchestral ballad *The Spirit of the Glen* and the opera *The Red Spider*.

– Calder House –

Chopin stayed here with Jane Stirling's brother-in-law, Lord Torphichen, on his 1848 tour of Scotland. After Chopin's death, Jane Stirling started a small museum here in his memory but it did not last long. The house is situated 10 miles west of Edinburgh and is a private home not open to the public.

– Canongate Kirk –

David Rizzio, private secretary to Mary Queen of Scots, is buried here; there is a small plaque to him on the wall above an unmarked grave. He was murdered in nearby Holyrood Palace in the queen's upper room and in front of her on 9 March 1566. Rizzio, who came from Turin, was the son of a musician and was himself a singer of some standing. He has been attributed with starting the Scottish folk-song movement but that is now considered inaccurate.

Also buried in the graveyard are the German cellist and composer Johann Schetky (1737–1824) and composer and bassoonist John Frederick Lampe (1703–51). Schetky had arrived in Scotland in 1772 to become the principal cellist of the new Edinburgh Music Society Orchestra and became a great friend of Robert Burns.

– St Cecilia's Hall, Niddry Street, Cowgate –

The oldest purpose-built concert hall in Scotland. It was opened in 1763 to house the Edinburgh Musical Society, a group of keen amateur musicians who met regularly in hired rooms to play. They also promoted concerts with international artists. For a time the hall played an important role in the musical life of Edinburgh and Scotland but mounting debts brought the Musical Society's tenure to an end and in 1798 they sold the building. It went through various owners and changes of use including being a church, a Masonic Lodge and a dance hall, until the University of Edinburgh bought it in 1959 for its expanding music faculty and to house the Russell Collection of Early Keyboard Instruments donated by Raymond Russell (1922-64), an English antiquarian and collector of early keyboard instruments.

The hall as it is today is largely reconstruction. In the lobby hangs a portrait of John Reid (1721-1807), the army general and amateur flute player who bequeathed a large part of his fortune to the university to finance the teaching of music and establish a Chair of Music. This led eventually to the building of the Reid Concert Hall in Bristo Place. The Reid Music Library is acknowledged as one of Britain's leading music libraries. The first Reid Professor of Music was the composer John Thomson. Born in Sprouston in 1805, Thomson met Mendelssohn during Mendelssohn's 1829 visit to Scotland, and the two became friends. Mendelssohn was particularly taken with Thomson's piano trio and Fanny said of him that she liked him best of all the Britons they knew. Among Thomson's compositions were a flute concerto, flute quartet, glees, concert arias and three operas. He was one of the first people to issue programme notes for his audiences. Thomson died in 1841 at the age of only 35.

In the Newman Gallery (named after Sidney Newman, then Reid Professor of Music) hangs a portrait of Thomas Erskine, Earl of Kelly (1753-81), one of Scotland's leading composers, now almost totally forgotten. He introduced the Mannheim symphonic style to Britain, and was a keen socialiser: his fondness for drinking liquor led to the saying 'his ruddy countenance would ripen cucumbers'.

204. GASK, Perthshire

– Gask House, Gask –

Caroline Oliphant (1766–1845), who wrote the words for many well-known Scottish ballads and collected Scottish folk tunes was born in the Auld Gask House which had been burnt down as a punishment for the Oliphant family's support of Bonnie Prince Charlie in 1745 and then rebuilt. She died here on 26 October 1845 and is buried in the private chapel. Caroline became Lady Nairne when her husband, Major William Nairne, was raised to the peerage in 1824. Her father was a Jacobite and many of the songs she wrote to the traditional tunes she collected reflect her sympathies: *Will ye no' come back again* was written for the exiled Prince Charles Edward Stuart. Other works include *The Auld Hoose* and *The Rowan Tree*. Because song writing was not considered a suitable occupation for a person of her social standing, she adopted the pseudonym Mrs Bogan of Bogan. She didn't even tell her husband about her secret vice. After his death, she travelled extensively in Europe for the benefit of a sick son who needed a more clement climate and died in 1837. After her own death much of Oliphant's verse was published by her sister in *Lays of Strathearn*. There is a granite memorial to her in the grounds of Gask House.

205. GIFFORD, East Lothian

~ Yester House, Yester, Gifford ~

In 1970 the Italian-American composer Gian Carlo Menotti, a New York resident, decided to try and find a European base. He began by looking in France but then, during a visit to Scotland, came across the village of Gifford and fell in love with it. Looking for a property to buy, he discovered Yester House, built at the beginning of the eighteenth century by Robert Adam among others for the first Marquess of Tweedsdale. The house wasn't for sale but that didn't stop Menotti making an offer. After two years, the owners finally gave in and Yester changed hands to become a retreat, a place to which Menotti could escape and compose. He also planned to convert the stables into a music school concentrating on opera and to hold festivals there. Opera was Menotti's passion. He had written two by the time he was thirteen, and *Amahl and the Night Visitors*, for which he is probably best-known, was one of the most performed operas of the last century. Menotti died in Monte Carlo on 1 February 2007, the evening before a new production of *The Medium*, staged by his adopted son Francis, was due to open. He was 93 and was buried in the churchyard of Yester Kirk while his friend the Duke of Hamilton did acrobatic manoeuvres in his plane overhead. Menotti lived at Yester for more than thirty years. He was known locally as Mr McNotty.

206. GLASGOW, Strathclyde

24 Briar Road was the home of Sir Hugh S Roberton, founder and conductor of the world-famous Glasgow Orpheus Choir. Roberton (the S stands for Stevenson) was born in 1874 at 2 Hallcroft Place, Tradeston, where his father was an undertaker. At the age of seventeen, he joined the family business. A self-taught musician, he had very strong ideas about how choirs should be trained and run, and in 1901 formed the Toynbee Musical Association to put his ideas into practice. Five years later this became the Glasgow Orpheus Choir which quickly became one of the most distinctive choirs on radio (or the wireless as it was then) with a world-wide reputation. It was for the choir that Roberton wrote his best-known piece, *All In the April Evening*. In 1951, he was forced to give up the choir because of ill-health. The choir members responded by voting to disband: no Roberton, no choir. Knighted in 1931, he died in 1952.

The Glasgow Art Gallery and Museum, Kelvingrove, Glasgow, contains a fine collection of almost four hundred instruments including the Glen Collection assembled by the Edinburgh instrument makers of that name, starting with Thomas McBain Glen (1804–73). This was one of the earliest collections of musical instruments to be made. The Farmer collection was amassed by musicologist Henry George Farmer (1882–1965), a member of the Royal Artillery band before he became music director of various theatres in London and then in Glasgow. His collection includes some ethnic pieces. The collection also houses the

Kelvingrove Organ built in 1901 and since restored. Concerts and recitals are given on this instrument.

– Johnstone Castle, Tower Place (off Tower Road), – Johnstone, Renfrewshire

The wife of Ludovic Houston, fifth Laird of Johnstone Castle, was Anne, another of Jane Stirling's sisters, who had also been one of Chopin's pupils in Paris. Chopin stayed here for three weeks in September 1848 and although not well gave a recital in nearby Glasgow on 27 September. 'I am unwell, depressed, and people weary me with their excessive attentions,' he wrote home. 'I can't breathe, I can't work. I feel alone, alone, alone, though I'm surrounded by people.' It is thought that Jane Stirling proposed to Chopin during this stay. Whether that is true or not, the relationship never went any further. During World War Two, the grounds of the castle were used for a prisoner-of-war camp. It is still possible, according to locals, to hear the sounds of a piano drifting out of the woods where a Polish airman died.

Only the sixteenth-century tower of the castle survives – and that is now in the middle of a housing estate built for the Glasgow overspill. The rest of the castle was demolished in 1960. There is a plaque on a fence near the tower, recording Chopin's stay.

9 Newton Terrace, Glasgow, was the birthplace of the German composer and virtuoso pianist Eugene d'Albert, who died from choking after his wife hit him during supper. He was born on 10 April 1864. His parents were Anglo-Italian, his German-born father being a distinguished musician and dancer who worked in London theatres. D'Albert, best known for his opera *Tiefland*, was a brilliant pianist and while at the Royal Academy, where he studied with Arthur Sullivan and John Stainer, made a piano reduction of Sullivan's oratorio *The Martyr of Antioch*. He is also credited with writing the overture to *Patience* while Sullivan's student. A scholarship took him to Germany to study with Liszt and he never came back to live, renouncing his British citizenship. As well as being a brilliant performer, d'Albert was an important teacher who wrote some twenty-one operas, a symphony, fifty songs and four volumes of piano works. He also married six times, likening his marriages to Beethoven symphonies: he would, he said, keep getting married until he got up to number nine 'with chorus'! It was number six who took exception to a remark he made about number two, hit him and brought about his death in Riga in 1932.

207. HADDINGTON, East Lothian

– Lennoxlove House, Haddington –

Owned by the Duke of Hamilton, the house contains a Pleyel piano reputedly played at Hamilton Palace by Chopin on his 1848 Scottish tour. Chopin stayed with the Duke and Duchess (Susan Beckford) at Hamilton Palace on the banks of the Clyde. The Palace was pulled down in 1927 and the site now contains a superstore, a fitness centre and municipal sports facilities. All that remains of the Palace is the family mausoleum.
www.lennoxlove.com

208. HUNTLY, Aberdeenshire

– Wallakirk, Glass, Huntly –

The churchyard contains the grave of Sir Frederick Bridge, composer, conductor and organist. Born in Oldbury, Worcestershire, in 1844, Bridge became organist at Rochester Cathedral, then Manchester, before moving to Westminster Abbey, where he was deputy then organist from 1875 until 1919. He wrote a considerable body of church music including cantatas, hymns and large-scale choral works. He also provided music for such state occasions as Queen Victoria's Jubilee and the Coronation of King Edward VII. He conducted the Coronation. Bridge became professor of music at London University where he was extremely popular and was, according to his colleagues, inspirational. A keen huntsman, Bridge leased Cairnborrow Lodge in Huntly as a bolt-hole for when he could get away from London. He died in London in 1924 and is buried in Walla Kirk graveyard where there is a memorial stone to him and to his daughter who married John Stainer's son.

209. INCHCOLM

King Alexander I of Scotland was shipwrecked on Inchcolm, an island in the Firth of Forth, and after prayers to St Columba to save his life were answered, built an Augustinian Priory on the island. This is where the Inchcolm Antiphoner manuscript, a very important source of mediaeval Scottish songs, comes from. It dates from around 1300.

210. MORAR, Highland

– Morar Hotel, Morar –

Arnold Bax, Master of the King's Music, discovered this Highland village, one of the locations for the film *Local Hero*, in 1928 and returned regularly every winter from 1930 until 1940 to work here undisturbed. He stayed in what was then called The Station Hotel, invariably in Room 9, where he completed his *Third Symphony* and did the bulk of work on the next four, as well as writing two concertos. He found the local beaches and views across the sea to the isles of Eigg and Rhum inspiring. He invariably took with him Mary Gleaves, the mistress of whom not even Harriet Cohen was aware. According to a romantic but not necessarily totally accurate account, the hotel was dingy and unheated and Bax was forced to work wearing a heavy overcoat. There is a plaque in the hotel recalling Bax's patronage.

211. PERTH, Perthshire

– The Fair Maid of Perth's house, Curfew Row, North Perth –

This was the house which Sir Walter Scott used as his setting for the home of Catherine Glover in his novel *The Fair Maid of Perth*, later turned into an opera by Bizet. The house, the oldest surviving home in Perth, has parts which are genuinely medieval. In 1629 it was bought by the Glover Incorporation and their motto – Grace and Peace – can be seen carved over the door. It was, however, much restored in 1893–4 and subsequently. It is now a craft shop.

212. PITTENWEEM, Fife

– Kellie Castle, Pittenweem –

Thomas Erskine, the sixth Earl of Kelly, an important figure in Scottish musical life, was born here in 1732. His family were Jacobites and his schooling was interrupted by the 1745 rebellion. Kelly's first involvement with orchestral music appears to have been when he joined the Edinburgh Musical Society at the age of 17. Like all young gentlemen of the time, he embarked on the Grand Tour, studying composition and violin with Johann Stamitz, the Czech composer who helped establish the Mannheim School. He became a versatile composer skilled at writing for orchestras with an output that included overtures, symphonies and chamber works. He was one of the composers invited to contribute to one of the major events of the age, Lord Stanley's Fête Champetre, held near Epsom in 1774. Kelly was also a member of The Temple of Apollo, a secret society of composers in London. Sadly most of his compositions have been lost. Charles Burney wrote of him that 'there was no part of theoretical or practical music, in which he was not equally versed with the greatest professors of his time'. Kellie Castle, 3 miles from Pittenweem, is now owned by the Scottish National Trust.

www.nts.org.uk

213. ROSLIN, Midlothian

– Rosslyn Chapel –

This fifteenth-century building became known world-wide as a result of Dan Brown's bestselling book *The Da Vinci*

Code, the final scenes being set here. Rosslyn Chapel was founded in 1446 by Sir William St Clair and the present building was only the choir of what was intended to be a much larger construction with a central tower. The Chapel's connection to music is slightly less tenuous than its supposed link with the Knights Templar. The lute seems to have reached Scotland during the Crusades and on one wall are engravings of lute players, or luters as they were called in Scotland. One of them is wearing a turban, reminding us that during the Middle Ages, Scotland attracted many overseas musicians. Among the many intricate carvings in the chapel are a series of 213 cubes and boxes with patterns on. There have been many attempts to decipher these patterns, one of the most recent being by the Edinburgh composer Stuart Mitchell, whose father, Thomas, has spent twenty years trying to crack the code. They claim that the patterns are a form of musical notation and have produced *The Rosslyn Motet* to prove their theories.

www.rosslynchapel.org.uk

214. SKIBO, Sutherland

– Skibo Castle, Dornoch –

The castle qualifies for an entry not because it is where Madonna married Guy Ritchie but because the castle was bought and rebuilt by Andrew Carnegie, the steel magnate who gave his name to New York's premier concert venue, Carnegie Hall. Carnegie was born in a weaver's cottage in Dunfermline in 1835. When the family fell on hard times, they moved to the United States where Carnegie began work as a telegraph boy. In a real rags-to-riches story, he built up a steel business that turned him into the richest man in the world. But he gave away most of his money to good causes. As well as building Carnegie Hall, he financed the construction of some 7,000 organs. On retiring, he bought Skibo Castle in 1898 for £85,000 and spent £2 million turning it into the grandest of grand houses. Having become interested in golf, he also had a course built in the garden. The house is now a very exclusive members' country club, not open to the general public. There is a statue of Carnegie in Dunfermline's Pittencrief Park, a park he created, and the Andrew Carnegie Birthplace Museum, created by his widow, is still in Moodie Street.

215. STAFFA, the Hebrides

A visit to Fingal's Cave on the Isle of Staffa in 1829 provided the inspiration for Felix Mendelssohn's Hebrides Overture. Mendelssohn's parents had insisted the twenty-year-old composer and conductor travel abroad to broaden his outlook and so, after a successful concert trip to London in the spring of 1829, at which he conducted his *First Symphony*, Mendelssohn travelled to Scotland in July. His first experience of the bagpipes he found excruciating but Edinburgh, the ruined chapel of Holyrood where Mary Queen of Scots had been crowned, and the highland scenery, gave him ideas for writing a Scottish symphony (not completed until thirteen years later in 1842 and dedicated to Queen Victoria). It was the stormy crossing to see the basaltic rock columns of Fingal's Cave on 7 August which may have had most passengers (including probably the composer) rushing for the side of the ship, but also apparently gave him the musical phrase which in 1832 he was to turn into one of his most popular pieces, known universally after the place that inspired it, as *Fingal's Cave*. Apparently he wrote down the phrase the day before heading for Staffa, but why let the truth stand in the way of a good story?

216. STIRLING

– Stirling Castle –

This is where King Alexander I founded the Scottish Chapel Royal in 1110. The present building dates from the reign of James VI who rebuilt it for the christening of his son in 1594. Mary Queen of Scots was crowned here and the choir moved with her when she went to the palace of Holyrood, taking up residence in Holyrood Abbey (now a ruin following an attack made by Henry VIII in a fit of pique because the Scots had rejected his plan to marry off Mary to his son Prince Edward). The choir still exists today with a duty of providing singers whenever the sovereign is in residence at Balmoral.

It was in Stirling Castle that a fascinating discovery was made in 2009. During restoration of the sixteenth-century royal bedchamber, a carved ceiling rose was discovered containing mysterious markings. These have since been confirmed to be the oldest example of musical notation so far found in Scotland. The sequence of Os and Is on the rose are, according to early music specialist Barnaby Brown, a form of notation for court harpists.

217. WEMYSS CASTLE, Fife

Wemyss Castle, on the Firth of Forth between East and West Wemyss, is the home of the Wemyss family and it was here in the seventeenth century that thirteen-year-old Lady Margaret Wemyss began to write in a book her favourite pieces of lute music. This musical scrapbook, known as the Wemyss Lute Book and now in the National Library of Scotland, is one of the most important sources of seventeenth century Scottish lute and harp music. Lady Margaret, who lived in the old part of the Castle, was eighteen when she died. The castle is not open to the public but the grounds are by appointment. www.wemysscastlegardens.com

218. WESTRUTHER, Berwickshire

In the ruined seventeenth-century kirk at Westruther are buried members of the Spottiswoode family including Alicia Anne Spottiswoode, known also by her married name as Lady John Scott. Lady John Scott had been born in 1810 in Spottiswoode House (which was demolished in 1938). She was an antiquarian (she used to rush around digging up cairns) and songwriter best known for her setting of the William Douglas poem *Annie Laurie*. This song became a great favourite with troops in the Crimean War. At Rundiesford, on a back road to Raecleugh, is the 'popping' stone where she and her husband first plighted their troth. Outspoken and eccentric, Lady John Scott died on 12 March 1900 and was buried in a snow storm.

NORTHERN
IRELAND AND
EIRE

In the middle of the eighteenth century, Dublin was one of the music capitals of Europe. The second largest city in the British Empire, it was a major trading port with a huge garrison, and a musical life that attracted composers and performers from all over Europe. As it is located approximately 300 miles from London, they often stayed for weeks, if not months. One of these visitors was Handel who was so delighted with the response to his music that he decided to give the first performance of *Messiah* in the city. Thomas Arne, together with his wife the singer Cecilia Young, paid the Irish capital several visits, while the eminent Italian composer and violinist Francesco Geminiani – who had studied with Corelli and Scarlatti – moved to Dublin to teach. The operatic composer Tommaso Giordani made Dublin his home, as did violinist Matthew Dubourg, who was taught by Geminiani and led the orchestra for the first performance of Messiah. The German music teacher and composer Johann Logier, who introduced class piano lessons to the United States, and the tenor Antonio Sapio (English, despite the name) are two more figures who flourished amid Dublin's music scene of the time.

The English family of musicians, the Roseingraves, became organists of Christ Church and St Patrick's Cathedrals, while the violinist and composer William Rooke was born in Dublin, as was John Field, one of the most important and influential composers of the period. And not only were composers and performers flocking to the city, for it also supported an entire industry associated with the production and maintenance of a growing cultural phenomenon: Dublin as a musical melting pot.

From instrument manufacturers and music publishers to musical societies such as the Hibernian Catch Club and Academy of Music, Ireland has a rich and surprising history as the backdrop to and participant in numerous notable musical events.

In 1795, the Lord Lieutenant of Ireland, who had the power to confer a knighthood, decided to knight William Parsons, George III's Master of Musick. Parsons thus became the first English musician to be given a knighthood, 'more' it was said, 'on the score of his merits than the merits of his scores.'

219. ARMAGH, Armagh

– 11 Vicar's Hill, Armagh –

The composer Charles Wood, known in particular for his church music, was born here on 15 June 1866. His father was a tenor in the choir of St Patrick's Cathedral, Armagh, and Wood, too, became a chorister, attending the church school from 1872 until 1883 when he left for London as one of the first intake into the new Royal College of Music. There he studied composition with another Irish composer, Charles Villiers Stanford. Wood went on to become Professor of Music at Cambridge University. He wrote over 250 sacred works as well as many hymn tunes, songs, music for plays and chamber works, and his church music is still sung by choirs around the world. Every summer in Armagh there is a festival of his music.

220. BELFAST, Antrim

– Shimna, Deramore Park, Belfast –

This was birthplace of composer Howard Ferguson on 21 October 1908. He was the fifth child of the managing director of the Ulster Bank and soon showed a talent for music. The distinguished piano teacher Harold Samuel, who heard him when adjudicating a piano competition in Belfast, persuaded his parents to send him to London to study at the Royal College, where he became friends with fellow-student Gerald Finzi. His early works were well-received. During the war, he was seconded from the RAF to help Myra Hess put on her morale-boosting concerts at the National Gallery. After composing the choral work *The Dream of the Rood* in 1958, Ferguson announced he had said all he wanted to say musically and was stopping composition to become a musicologist. He never went back on his decision even though many people regarded him, on an output of only twenty works, as the most distinguished composer Northern Ireland has ever produced. He died in Cambridge in 1999.

– Richmond Lodge, Holywood Road, Belfast –

Twenty-one-year-old Arthur Sullivan spent a holiday here during the summer of 1863 with his friend Robert Dunville. He got his initial ideas for the *Irish Symphony in E Flat* while on the visit. They were driving back from Holywood 'through the wind and rain on an open jaunting car' when, according to Sullivan, the whole of the first movement came into his head together with 'scraps' for the other movements.

221. CORK, County Cork

– St Finbarr's Cemetery, Cork –

The composer Arnold Bax is buried here. He was on holiday at Glen House, Ballyvolane, the home of his friend Aloys Fleischmann, when he died suddenly on 3 October 1953 just short of his seventieth birthday. Fleischmann was a pianist, composer and conductor, who ran the choir in Cork's Catholic Cathedral. Bax and he had been friends for twenty-four years and it was through Fleischmann that Bax met many Irish musicians and become involved in Irish music-making.

– Old Head of Kinsale, Cork –

Not much to see perhaps except for the sea, but O'Brien Butler (1870–1915), who composed *Muirgheis*, the first opera in Gaelic, was on board the *Lusitania* when it was sunk off Old Head of Kinsale by a German submarine on 7 May 1915.

222. DANGAN, Co Meath

– Dangan Castle –

Five kilometers north of Summerhill, Dangan Castle was the home of the Wellesley family. Indeed, the Duke of Wellington may well have been born here; he certainly spent much of his childhood at the castle. The Duke's father, Garrett Wellesley, Earl of Mornington, was born here in 1735. As a nine-year-old he learnt the violin and being prodigiously gifted, within a year could, it was said, play anything put in front of him. At fourteen, he began to study the harpsichord and organ. At that time Dublin was a centre of musical excellence and among the Italian musicians who had settled in the city was composer and violinist Franceso Geminiani. He first came to Ireland in 1733 and died in Dublin on17 September 1762, his death hastened, it was claimed, by the shock of a servant stealing one of his manuscripts. Wellesley asked Geminiani and Thomas Roseingrave, organist of both Christ Church and St Patrick's cathedrals, to teach him but both are alleged to have told the Earl there was nothing they could teach him. Wellesley was noted in particular for his glees (*Come, fairest Nymph* and *Here in cool grot* being among his best). Wellesley's music was much enjoyed by King George III, and he went on to become the first Professor of Music at Trinity College. Dangan Castle has been in ruins for many years.

223. DUBLIN

– 10 Balfe Street, Dublin 2 –

Michael Balfe, composer of the opera *The Bohemian Girl*, was born in 1808 in a house on this site when it was called Pitt Street. The street name was changed in his honour in 1917. The original house no longer exists. Balfe, who was a child prodigy and made his debut as a violinist aged nine, lived here until he was ten, then moved to 2 Hamilton's Row where he wrote his first important song, *The Lover's Mistake*.

– Christ Church Cathedral, Christ Church Place, Dublin 8 –

Thomas Bateson (c1570–1630), the first music graduate from Trinity College, joined the cathedral choir in 1609, later becoming organist and Master of the Choristers. He wrote some church music, but Bateson's fame today rests on his two volumes of madrigals. Although his grave has been lost, it is thought he was buried in the cathedral.

Another madrigalist who became organist here was John Farmer. Born in about 1570 somewhere in England, he managed to acquire the Earl of Oxford as a patron. In 1595 he was appointed organist and choirmaster at Christ Church, and also organist of St Patrick's Cathedral. It became the custom for the two cathedrals to have their organist and choirmaster in common. Farmer composed such madrigals as *Fair Nymph*, *I Heard One Telling* and *Fair Phyllis I Saw*.

Little is known about the background of Daniel Roseingrave who became organist and choirmaster in 1698. He was born in about 1655 and may well have been Irish. He may also have been taught by Purcell and Blow since he became a chorister of the Chapel Royal. Certainly he became organist at Gloucester Cathedral, Winchester Cathedral and Salisbury Cathedral before moving to Dublin. He retained the position at St Patrick's until his death in 1727, having given his son Ralph the post in Christ Church, possibly because of failing health. Daniel was noted for his propensity to fly off the handle. In Gloucester he had been admonished for violent behavior, while in Dublin he came to the notice of the authorities for fighting in a tavern. His worst misdemeanor, however, was to cut off the ear of a colleague with his sword, during a service. The cathedral authorities promptly banned the wearing of swords during services. He was buried in St Bride's Church (which no longer exists). His son Ralph succeeded him at both Christ Church and St Patrick's.

Richard Woodward (1743–77), whose father was a member of both cathedral choirs, became organist and then master of choristers at both, by the age of twenty-two. He is buried in the cathedral where there is a memorial tablet.

Sir John Stevenson (1761–1833), one of Ireland's major classical composers, was born in Crane Lane off Dame Street, Dublin. He was the son of a Scottish coachbuilder and became a choirboy in Christ Church when he was six. He became a Vicar Choral at St Patrick's in 1783 and at Christ Church in 1800. He was also appointed the first organist and musical director of the new Chapel Royal built in Dublin Castle. He wrote prolifically for the church, with some twenty-six anthems, eight services, numbers of chants and even an oratorio. He wrote operas, glees, catches and even symphonies but is best remembered today for his glees and songs, especially his settings of Thomas Moore's poems, the best-known of which is probably 'The Last Rose of Summer'. Stevenson was knighted in 1902. He died in Headfort House, Kells, Co Meath, the home of his daughter The Marchioness of Headfort. There is a memorial to him in the Musicians' Corner of Christ Church by Irish sculptor Thomas Kirk, consisting of a bust and a choirboy. There should have been two choirboys but Kirk had such trouble getting the money he was owed, he removed the second one.

~ Fishamble Street, Dublin 8 ~

The doorway of the engineering works Kennan and Sons is all that remains of Neale's Musick Hall where George Frideric Handel directed the world premiere of his oratorio *Messiah*, on 13 April 1742. Handel had arrived in Dublin the previous November at the invitation of the Duke of Devonshire, Lord Lieutenant of Ireland. He planned to stage a series of concerts over the winter months and return to London in the spring. In fact he stayed for nine months, until mid-August, renting a house in Abbey Street. Handel gave six concerts from Christmas until mid-February and all were wildly received, so he decided to stage a second series beginning on 17 February. Included in the series was a benefit concert on 12 April, for prisoners' charities and two local hospitals, at which he announced he would perform the Grand Oratorio he had completed just before leaving London. Handel also planned to play some concertos on the organ as well. So great was the demand for tickets that the opening night had to be put back a day and in order to squeeze in an extra hundred people, ladies were asked not to wear hoops and gentlemen not to wear swords. The performance, given by the joint choirs of Christ Church and St Patrick's, began at mid-day. The reception was tumultuous, so much so that Handel had to arrange a second performance. Once he had completed his appearances in the city, Handel didn't go home but stayed on for an extra two months, enjoying the local hospitality. He is said to have spent many evenings at Clontarf Castle and to have visited Cork.

– Golden Lane, Dublin 8 –

Composer and pianist John Field was born in Golden Lane in July 1782, and baptised in nearby St Werburgh's Church. The house no longer exists but there is a plaque marking where it stood. Soon after Field's birth, the family moved to Camden Street. Field's father Robert, a member of a musical family, was a violinist in a Dublin theatre. He had become a Protestant because it made life easier than being a Catholic. Field, who created the Nocturne (a single movement work for piano), was a precociously talented pianist who became the pioneer of romantic piano playing. His first teachers were his father and his grandfather, and they were strict. Field is supposed to have run away from home as a young child to avoid a beating for not getting a piece right. At the age of nine he was apprenticed to Tommaso Giordani, the Italian composer who was then living in Dublin, and it was Giordani who sponsored Field's first public appearances in the Rotunda Assembly Rooms in Rutland Square. In 1793, the Field family moved to Bath and then to London where Field was apprenticed to Clementi and really began his career as a performer and composer. He wrote seven piano concertos, the first being performed before he was 17, and eighteen Nocturnes which were to have a profound influence on Chopin. In 1821 Field moved to Moscow where he taught Glinka. He never returned to Dublin, dying in Moscow on 23 January 1837. He is buried in the Vedensky Cemetery.

– 2 Herbert Street, Dublin 8 –

The birthplace, in 1852, of Charles Villiers Stanford, Ireland's most prolific composer and a major influence on

British music of the nineteenth century. Both his father and mother were keen amateur musicians and Stanford was brought up with music in the house. His first composition to be performed was a march written for *Puss in Boots*, the 1860 pantomime at the Theatre Royal. As well as learning instruments, he studied composition with Sir Robert Stewart. Stanford left Dublin to continue his studies in London when he was ten, then went to Cambridge. He was not only a prolific composer – ten operas, seven symphonies, thirty-three oratorios and cantatas, three piano concertos, eight string quartets, songs and an impressive body of chamber music – but he was extremely popular. One of his symphonies was chosen to open the new concert hall in Berlin.

– St Patrick's Cathedral, St Patrick's Close, Dublin 8 –

This is the cathedral of which the great satirist Jonathan Swift was Dean and, like Christ Church Cathedral, has a long musical history. In 1727, when his father died, Ralph Roseingrave, in addition to continuing his duties at Christ Church, officially took over as organist and choirmaster of St Patrick's. He died in 1747 and is buried here as is his brother Thomas, who was buried in the same grave. Thomas Roseingrave was born in Winchester and brought up in Dublin. The cathedral gave him a grant to go to Italy where he met and became an admirer of Domenico Scarlatti. He helped introduce Scarlatti's music to Britain by publishing a book of his harpsichord sonatas and he staged one of the first Scarlatti operas seen in London. He became organist of St George's Hanover Square, Handel's church, where he was noted for his sight-reading and his improvisations. His music did not win universal approval however: 'His style of both playing and composing was very harsh and disgusting,' according to one member of the congregation. Thomas retired from St George's as a result of mental instability, something from which his father may well have suffered. He died in the seaside town of Dun Laoghaire in 1766.

There is a stained glass window in the south aisle in memory of Sir John Stevenson.

224. GLENCOLUMBKILLE, DONEGAL

– Roarty's Hotel –

The English composer and Master of the King's Music, Sir Arnold Bax stayed here every summer from 1904 until the 1930s. He wrote that on his deathbed he liked to think his final glimpse of this life would be the view from his window on the upper floor at Glencolumbkille, 'of the still, brooding, dove-grey mystery of the Atlantic at twilight.' It was here that he composed much of the Fourth Symphony.

225. HILLSBOROUGH, CO DOWN

– St Malachy Parish Church –

The composer and conductor Sir Hamilton Harty was born in Main Street, Hillsborough, on 4 December 1879. His father was the organist at St Malachy's and Harty spent his childhood in the Organist's House, Ballynahinch Street. His father became his first teacher. He was a receptive pupil who, at the age of 12, became organist of Magheragall Church, four miles north of the town. He held that position for almost two years before moving to St Barnabas' Church and then to Christ Church, Bray, Co Wicklow. In 1901 he moved to London to become the organist of All Saints, Norfolk Square, but only lasted a week following a row with the vicar. Instead he became very well-known as an accompanist, appearing with such artists as John McCormack and Fritz Kreisler. Harty moved naturally into conducting and for thirteen years was conductor of the Hallé. He also composed, several of his works being specifically Irish including Irish songs, an Irish symphony and his last major work, the tone poem *The Children of Lir* for which he got inspiration on a walk from Portballintrae to Runkerry in 1936. Harty died in 1941 in Hove following a brain tumour. His ashes are buried in the churchyard of St Malachy in Hillsborough, marked by a bird bath.

226. KENMARE, CO KERRY

– The Lansdowne Arms Hotel, Kenmare –

The English composer E(rnest) J(ohn) Moeran, known to his friends as Jack, spent a lot of his time in Kenmare. He was born in 1894 in a vicarage in Isleworth but was brought up mostly in Norfolk where his clergyman father held several livings. Not long after he had become a student at the Royal College of Music in London, at the age of nineteen, World War One started. Moeran immediately enlisted, became a dispatch rider and was sent to France where he received a bullet in the head. After the war, he became an avid folk-song collector and also, thanks to three boozy years spent sharing a house in Kent with Peter Warlock, an alcoholic. Fascinated by his Irish roots (his father, although raised in England, had been born in Dublin) he frequently visited Kenmare, drawing inspiration from the surrounding countryside. He stayed in The Lodge, an annex for long-term residents of The Lansdowne Arms Hotel. His rooms in The Lodge (now demolished) contained a piano and it was here he completed his first symphony and wrote much of his violin concerto. He also spent the last six months of his life in Kenmare. His stormy marriage to the cellist Peers Coetmore was effectively over, he was ill and couldn't concentrate, and he was worried about being certified insane. On 1 December 1950, during a spell of bad weather, he was seen to fall from Kenmare pier into the water. By the time his body was recovered, he was dead. Was it suicide? The local coroner ruled he had died from a cerebral hemorrhage following a massive heart attack but the doubts remain. He is buried in the local cemetery.

227. LIMERICK, CO LIMERICK

– St Mary's Cathedral, Limerick –

The father of composer and virtuoso pianist George Alexander Osborne was the organist and choirmaster of the cathedral. He also taught the harpsichord and is reputed to have written some 300 piano pieces. It was from him that Osborne, who was born in Limerick in 1806, received his initial tuition. Osborne almost certainly sang in the cathedral choir, and his first choice for a career was to become a priest. A phenomenal pianist, he was sent to Paris to continue his studies and there met a newly arrived Polish pianist whom he befriended and with whom he became good friends: Chopin. Asked by his father to go to Brussels to comfort a sick aunt, he became involved in the 1830 Belgian revolution on the side of the royalists, was captured and imprisoned. The following year, he returned to Paris where he spent the next fourteen years. He took part in Chopin's Paris debut when six pianists, including himself and Chopin, played six grand pianos in a specially written polonaise. He also got to know Berlioz (helping him out by playing his compositions on the piano, something Berlioz couldn't manage himself), Cherubini, Liszt and Rossini, and taught Charles Hallé who couldn't afford Liszt's fees. This was the time when pianos in the home were becoming fashionable and people were desperate for sheet music to play. Osborne provided it for them. In 1844, he moved to London, where he was in big demand as a soloist, eventually being offered a teaching post at the Royal Academy. He died at his home at 5 Ulster Terrace, Regent's Park, on 17 November 1893.

228. MONKSTOWN, DUBLIN

– Meadowcroft, The Hill, Monkstown –

Malcolm Arnold lived here from 1972 until 1977 during a particularly turbulent time in his private life which saw his second marriage to Isobel break up and him attempt suicide. However, he loved Ireland and was fascinated by

Irish music. To this period belong the second clarinet concerto, the *Song of Freedom*, the *Fantasy on a theme of John Field* and the violent *Seventh Symphony*, a portrait of his family. There are Irish elements in all of these: 'All my music,' Arnold once said, 'is biographical.' His heavy drinking and increasingly erratic behaviour brought an end to his second marriage. Arnold left Ireland in 1977 and spent some time in psychiatric hospitals being treated for alcoholism and depression. He was given a year to live, but lasted another twenty and even began to compose again.

229. WATERFORD, CO WATERFORD

– 7 Colebeck Street, Waterford City –

William Vincent Wallace, adventurer, composer, bigamist and one of Waterford's greatest sons (after whom the city's new Millennium Plaza has been named), was born here on 11 March 1812. His father was a regimental bandmaster who encouraged his son to take up several instruments including the violin, piano, organ and clarinet. He was sufficiently talented to be playing the violin in a Dublin theatre orchestra and even leading it while still in his mid-teens. At the age of eighteen he was appointed organist at Thurles Catholic Cathedral and became head of music at the local Ursuline Convent. There he fell in love with one of his pupils, Isabella Kelly. Her father agreed to their marriage provided Wallace took the middle name of Vincent and converted to Catholicism, both of which he was quite happy to do. Throughout his life Wallace suffered from a lung complaint and it was on doctor's orders that he, Isabella and their young son emigrated to Australia in 1835, the idea being he would become a sheep farmer. A bandmaster uncle had emigrated there already. When the Wallaces arrived, with sister Elisabeth, a singer, and brother Wellington, a flautist, they immediately began giving family concerts. Wallace also opened Australia's first music school. With his marriage starting to fall apart and being heavily in debt, he took off travelling. He joined a whaling fleet, just escaped being eaten by cannibals, was mauled by a tiger, survived a shipboard explosion and survived an earthquake; and that was just for starters. It's hard to know how many of Wallace's escapades actually happened the way he told them, but he certainly visited New Zealand, Fiji, India, Chile, Peru and Argentina, before conducting an Italian opera in Mexico and touring the United States. In the major cities of each country he visited, he gave at least one recital, thus making him the first classical musician to do a world tour. In 1845 he was back in Britain for the premiere at Drury Lane of *Maritana*, his first opera and the work with which he really made his name internationally. The opera ran in London for fifty consecutive performances and was later staged at Covent Garden, in Vienna, Paris and Australia. He displayed a real ability to write tunes in a dramatic context. Wallace went on to write a further five operas as well as many songs and piano pieces. He became an American citizen and entered into a bigamous marriage with an American pianist. His final years were spent in dire poverty in southern France, suffering from ill health including incipient blindness. Among the eminent musicians who visited him there was Rossini. He died in France in 1865, his body being brought back for burial in London's Kensal Green Cemetery.

GLOSSARY

Anthem a short vocal composition used in Anglican church services.

Bardic name a pseudonym adopted by poets and musicians in Wales, Cornwall and Brittany, especially when taking part in an eisteddfod (a singing competition).

Canon a voice or instrument states a melody which is then picked up by a second part and in turn picked up by a third and so on, before the previous person has finished, resulting in overlapping.

Cantata an extended choral work usually accompanied by an orchestra and designed to tell a story. It may or may not have soloists. The word literally means 'a thing to sing'.

Canticle either a hymn with biblical words other than from the Psalms or, in the concert hall, a piece with a religious or quasi-religious text.

Castrato an adult male with the voice of a soprano or contralto brought about by undergoing an operation before the voice breaks at the onset of puberty.

Catch a type of sung round, with tricky and amusing lyrics, very often of a bawdy nature. Purcell was a master of this sort of piece.

Chant usually used to describe music sung in church unaccompanied and according to tradition; it is also used to describe a way of singing Psalms.

Chorale a metrical (that is, composed in poetic meter) hymn tune. The most famous is probably the chorale used by Bach in his cantata *Wachet Auf!* (*Sleepers, Wake*).

Console organs have one or more keyboards, a number of stops to control the flow of wind through the pipes, and a footboard containing pedals played with the feet. These, all together, are known as the console.

Continuo also known as a figured bass. This was the bass part, played on a keyboard or other instrument that could produce chords and so provide the harmony.

Extemporise to improvise.

Falsetto singing or speech by an adult male in a voice much higher than normal. This is how counter-tenors and some pop singers produce their sound.

Fancy a term used in the sixteenth and seventeenth centuries for a fantasy, that is a piece that allows the composer to abandon rigid rules and let his imagination take over.

Fugue a composition in which all the lines or voices (vocal or instrumental) enter successively and in imitation of each other.

Galliard a lively dance in triple time.

Glee a simple and short part-song in several sections for male voices. Very popular in Britain between 1650 and 1830.

Introit a piece sung at Mass while the celebrant recites the preparatory prayers.

Madrigal a secular, unaccompanied vocal setting for two or more independent voice parts.

Masque an elaborate stage entertainment very popular in England in the seventeenth century. It involved poetry, dancing, scenery, costumes and both instrumental and vocal music.

Master of the King's/Queen's Musick the musician in charge of all the monarch's music with the exception of the services provided by the Chapel Royal. The first Master of Musick, Nicholas Lanier, was appointed in 1626 by King Charles I. In return for the title and a salary, the holder was also expected to write music for royal occasions such as birthdays. It became a post similar to that of the Poet Laureate, more honorary than functional. It was Elgar who dropped the archaic spelling of Music.

Motet in medieval times, a motet was a choral composition based on a given set of words and melody. This melody could be taken from a secular song. Later it came to mean the Roman Catholic equivalent of the Anglican anthem.

Nocturne a short single movement piece for the piano.

Oratorio a work for solo singers, chorus and orchestra, traditionally taking its text from biblical stories or from religious texts.

Pavan a slow, stately dance in duple time often performed immediately before a galliard and sometimes employing the same theme

Polonaise a stately Polish dance, moderately fast, in three-quarter time.

Prelude originally an introductory piece before a fugue, it became, in the hands of Chopin, a short, single-movement piano piece.

Round a vocal perpetual canon in which voices enter in turn to sing a melody either at the octave or at the same pitch, for example *London's Burning*.

Serial music developed mostly by Schoenberg, this involves the composer putting twelve notes into an order which uses each note only once. This becomes the tone row or series on which the composition is based and can be used backwards, upside down or in any other combination.

Sonata originally used to describe any work in which an instrument was accompanied by a continuo instrument of some kind, from the classical period onwards it has been used to mean a work in three or four movements for solo instruments accompanied by a piano.

Spinet a wing-shaped keyboard instrument similar to a harpsichord but smaller.

Suite an instrumental piece in several movements.

Tone Poem a piece for orchestra which is symphonic in size but about something non-musical. The term was coined by Liszt.

Viol a string instrument played with a bow which was superseded by the violin family.

SUGGESTED LISTENING

ENGLAND

Gerald Finzi Clarinet concerto

Benjamin Britten The Sea Interludes from *Peter Grimes*

Thomas Linley the Younger Music for *The Tempest*

Roger Quilter 'O Mistress Mine'

Rosalind Ellicott Piano Trio No. 2 in D Minor

Muzio Clementi Piano Sonata in D Major

Richard Davy 'O Domine caeli terraeque creator'

William Alwyn *Lyra Angelica*, concerto for harp

Elizabeth Maconchy Clarinet concerto

John Taverner *The Western Wynde Mass*

Frederic Curzon 'The Boulavardier'

Frederick Delius Florida Suite for orchestra

Edward Elgar The Violin concerto

George Butterworth 'Bredon Hill'

Frank Bridge Cello Sonata

Havergal Brian Symphony No. 1 *The Gothic*

George Kirbye 'With Angel's Face and Brightness'

Roberto Gerhard Concerto for orchestra
Orlando Gibbons 'The Silver Swan'
Gustav Holst *The Planets* ('Jupiter')
Thomas Weelkes 'As Vesta was from Latmos hill ascending'
John Wilbye 'Sweet Hony Sucking Bees'
Kaikhosru Shapurji Sorabji Three Pastiches for piano
Samuel Coleridge Taylor *Hiawatha's Wedding Feast*
Cecil Armstrong Gibbs *Odysseus*
Henry Lawes 'A dialogue on a kiss'
Ralph Vaughan Williams Fantasia on a Theme of
  Thomas Tallis
Claude Debussy *La Mer*
Eric Coates The Three Elizabeths
Samuel Sebastian Wesley 'Thou wilt keep him in
  perfect peace'
Thomas Attwood Walmisley Evening Service in D minor
John Goss 'The Lord is my Shepherd'
Lord Berners *The Triumph of Neptune* ballet suite
Ethel Smyth Mass in D
William Shield *Rosina*
Ivor Gurney 'In Flanders'
John Dunstaple 'Quam pulchra es'
Hubert Parry *Blest Pair of Sirens*
William Byrd Mass for 4 voices
EJ Moeran Symphony in G
Richard Strauss *Symphonia Domestica*
Edwin Lemare Andantino in D Flat Op. 83
Rutland Boughton Concerto for oboe and orchestra
John Jenkins Suite in A minor for viola da gamba
  and ensemble
James Oswald Serenata No 4

Michael Tippett Concerto for Double String Orchestra
Granville Bantock *Hebridian Symphony*
Herbert Howells *Hymnus Paradisi*
Thomas Tomkins 'A sad Pavan for these Distracted Times'
Charles Avison any of his twelve Concerti Grossi
Edmund Rubbra Symphony No. 7
Malcolm Arnold *Four Cornish Dances*
William Crotch Concerto for organ and orchestra No. 2
   in A
William Walton *Spitfire Prelude and Fugue*
Henry Walford Davies 'God Be in my Head'
John Sheppard 'Media Vita'
John Stainer 'God so loved the world' from *The
   Crucifixion*
Charles Wilfrid Orr *A Cotswold Hill Tune*
Andrezj Panufnik *Sinfonia Sacra*
Gordon Jacob Mini concerto for clarinet
Haydn Wood Fantasy concerto for Orchestra
George Dyson 'Four Songs for Sailors'

WALES
William Mathias Sinfonietta
Grace Williams *Fantasia on Welsh Nursery Tunes*
Brinley Richards Evening (Nocturne)
Gabriel Fauré Nocturne No. 7
Geoffrey Bush Overture *Yorick*
Peter Warlock *The Capriol Suite*
Joseph Parry *Myfanwy*
Felix Mendelssohn Three piano Fantasies or Caprices,
   Op. 16

SCOTLAND
William Marshall 'Mrs McPherson of Gibton'
Neil Gow 'Neil Gow's Lament for his second wife'
John Thomson Bagatelle
Eugene d'Albert *Esther Overture*
Frederick Bridge 'The Goslings'
Thomas Erskine Overture in C

IRELAND
Charles Wood 'Oh Thou the Central Orb'
Howard Ferguson Partita for Two Pianos
Arthur Sullivan *The Irish Symphony*
Michael Balfe Cello sonata in A Flat Major
John Farmer 'Fair Phyllis I Saw Sitting All Alone'
Sir John Stevenson 'The Last Rose of Summer'
John Field any of the Nocturnes
Charles Villiers Stanford Irish Rhapsody No 6
Hamilton Harty *An Irish Symphony*
George Osborne Trio No 3 in G Major
William Vincent Wallace Aria 'Scenes that are Brightest'
    from *Maritana*
Thomas Roseingrave Sonata No. 2 in D

A WORD ABOUT CLASSIC FM

Classic FM is the UK's only 100% classical music radio station. Since we began broadcasting in September 1992, the station has brought classical music to millions of people across the UK. If you've yet to discover for yourself the delights of being able to listen to classical music 24 hours a day, you can find Classic FM on 10-102 FM, on Digital Radio, online at www.classicfm.com, on Sky channel 0106, on FreeSat channel 721 and on Virgin Media channel 922.

Among Classic FM's many CD releases is a range exclusively available from HMV. The Classic FM Full Works series provides top quality recordings of many of the most popular classical works, played in full by world famous musicians. Priced at just £5.99, these CDs are perfect for both the dedicated collector and for those who are just discovering classical music. You can find out more at www.classicfm.com/fullworks.

Classic FM works particularly closely with five orchestras around the UK, with the aim of encouraging new listeners to enjoy the power and passion of hearing a live orchestra playing in a concert hall. Check the station's website to find out if the Royal Scottish National Orchestra, Northern Sinfonia, the Royal Liverpool Philharmonic Orchestra, the Philharmonic Orchestra or the London Symphony Orchestra are performing near you.

INDEX